The Great Taste of Virginia Seafood

A Cookbook and Guide to Virginia Waters

Written and
Edited by
Mary Reid Barrow
with Robyn Browder

Interior art by
Connie Johnson

THE
**DONNING
COMPANY**
Publishers

This book is publishers by special arrangement with the Public Relations Institute, Inc., and the Virginia Marine Products Commission.

FIRST EDITION, AUGUST 1984
SECOND EDITION, DECEMBER 1985

Library of Congress Cataloging-in-Publication Data

The Great Taste of Virginia Seafood.

1. Cookery (Seafood) 2. Cookery, American—Virginia.
3. Fishes—Virginia. 4. Shellfish—Virginia.
I. Barrow, Mary Reid. II. Browder, Robyn.
TX747.G78   1984   641.6'92'09755   84-13559
ISBN 0-89865-323-1

Printed in the United States of America

Cover and interior photography copyright © 1984 by the Public Relations Institute, Inc.

Material by Mary Reid Barrow copyright © 1984 by Mary Reid Barrow.

Illustrations by Connie Johnson, Art Adventures

Book design by Brenda Miller, Art Adventures

This book is dedicated to those who handle Virginia's seafood with care —

To those on the water who harvest it;

To those in the business who process, wholesale and retail it;

To those in state government who protect and promote it;

To those in Virginia who cherish it.

Table of Contents

Acknowledgements

Robyn Browder and I are especially grateful to members of the Virginia Marine Products Commission whose enthusiasm and support for this book are the reasons for its publication.

We also extend special thanks to the superlative Virginia chefs whose recipes from "The Great Taste of Virginia Seafood" (see introduction) give this book a true gourmet flavor. Equal thanks go to all the fine cooks across the state who entered their own creative efforts in the Virginia Seafood Month recipe contest and to the food editors at newspapers across the state who assisted with the contest. The combination of recipes made this book a unique adventure into the world of Virginia seafood.

Some of the material in the following articles I wrote for **Metro Magazine** were reprinted or adapted for use in this book by permission, **Commonwealth Magazine, Inc.:** "The Oyster," September, 1978, "Our Incredible Edible Finny Friends from Beneath the Deep Blue Sea," May, 1979, and "Seafood Smorgasbord," October, 1980. My appreciation goes to **Commonwealth's** editor Susan Spence for this permission.

Robyn and I also thank our typist, Lynda Newcomb, who performed miracles with our edited recipes.

A number of leaflets on various species produced by the Virginia Institute of Marine Science provided valuable information for the book as did the following publications: **Seafood Products Resource Guide,** published by the Sea Grant Program at Virginia Polytechnic Institute and State University, and **Seafood Adventures from the Gulf and South Atlantic,** produced by Gulf and South Atlantic Fisheries Development Foundation, Inc.

—Mary Reid Barrow

PREFACE

This year I have proclaimed September the third annual Virginia Seafood Month to formally recognize the cultural and economic significance of the Virginia Seafood Industry. The harvest of seafood began in Virginia when the first settlers arrived in 1607 and continues today across our Tidewater. The industry has grown to what is now a $422 million a year business that puts us in the top four of the nation's seafood producing states.

The waters of Virginia are blessed with a natural bounty of seafood— oysters, blue crabs, clams, scallops, blue fish, flounder, sea trout, bass, spot, and croaker, to name only a few.

This bounty provides a way of life for countless number of Virginians, from our own rugged watermen and harvesters to those who process and supply seafood to restaurants and retail stores across the nation and who, in turn, make it possible for all of us to feast on the delights of our own native seafood.

Virginia Seafood Month provides an opportunity for us to celebrate this, our oldest and most cherished tradition. The publication of **The Great Taste of Virginia Seafood** will not only offer Virginians an opportunity to celebrate their seafood every month of the year in a myriad of delicious recipes but also will spread the word to seafood lovers everywhere. The eating of Virginia seafood is one of the greatest pleasures known. Don't miss out on it.

Charles S. Robb

Charles S. Robb, Governor
The Commonwealth of Virginia

August, 1984

INTRODUCTION . . .

The Advent of a Virginia Seafood Cookbook
with Notes on Its Use

This cookbook is a celebration of the great role that seafood plays in the life of Virginia. As the nation's fourth largest producer of seafood, the Commonwealth and its citizens reap great benefits from their sea harvest—from revenue generated, from employment opportunities, and from support industries.

In 1982 a record amount of finfish and shellfish were harvested in Virginia, bringing a dockside value of $68.8 million. Much of Virginia's seafood is shipped to cities throughout the United States and overseas. For instance, Virginia provides more fresh-shucked oysters than any other state and approximately one-third of the nation's blue crab harvest.

To formally recognize the cultural and economic significance of Virginia's seafood industry, the Virginia Marine Products Commission annually sponsors Virginia Seafood Month in September. Two major events take place. One, billed as "The Great Taste of Virginia Seafood," for which this book is named, is a seafood tasting at which the Governor is the guest of honor. The Governor's Tasting features a sampling of native Virginia seafood prepared by great Virginia chefs. The other event is the Virginia Seafood Month recipe contest which brings in favorite fish and shellfish recipes from fine cooks across the state.

These two culinary events and the resulting recipes from both 1982 and 1983 have created the framework for this cookbook, a tangible tribute to Virginia seafood.

Notes on the use of this cookbook: Throughout the book, you will find a fish symbol on some recipes. One fish denotes a recipe that won first, second, or third prize or honorable mention in a Virginia Seafood Month recipe contest. Two fish denotes a recipe that was used by a Virginia chef at the Governor's seafood tasting.

Minor changes in titles, terminology, and ingredients have been made in some cases to make the recipes consistent. In addition, some recipes have been moved to different categories for balance.

Virginia on the Half Shell
Hors D'oeuvres and Appetizers

Clam Pastries

YIELD: about 3 dozen

Pastry for 2 9-inch pies
1 cup chopped fresh mushrooms
2 tablespoons butter
1 tablespoon vegetable oil
2 6-1/2-ounce cans minced clams,
    drained

1 8-ounce package cream cheese,
    cheese, cut up
2/3 cup chopped green onion
    with tops
1/2 teaspoon dry mustard
1 teaspoon Worchestershire sauce
1/4 teaspoon garlic powder
1/4 cup evaporated milk

Preheat oven to 350°. Cut pastry into 3-inch squares. Cook and stir mushrooms in butter and oil in skillet until tender. Stir in all ingredients except evaporated milk. Stir until cheese melts. Spoon 1 tablespoon clam mixture into center of each pastry square. Bring opposite sides together. Pinch edges and ends to seal. Place on ungreased cookie sheet. Brush with evaporated milk and bake until golden, 20 to 30 minutes.

Marilyn C. Fall
Virginia Beach, Virginia

Clam Pizza Spread

YIELD: about 4 cups

1 8-ounce package cream cheese,
    at room temperature
1 jar cocktail sauce
1 cup Virginia clams, cooked
    and minced

1 cup shredded mozzarella cheese
1/4 cup chopped bell pepper
1/4 cup chopped green onion
1/4 cup chopped celery
1/4 cup chopped olives

Spread the cream cheese on a 9- or 10-inch serving dish, preferably one with a slight rim. Spread the cocktail sauce over the cream cheese. Drain the clams very well between paper towels until all moisture is removed. Then, sprinkle the clams and the mozzarella cheese over the cocktail sauce. Combine the bell pepper, green onion, celery, and olives and sprinkle over the clams and cheese. Press down slightly to combine all the ingredients. Refrigerate. Remove from the refrigerator before serving in time for the cream cheese to soften slightly. Serve with crackers.

Mrs. T.J. Westbury, Jr.
Charlottesville, Virginia

Clam-Stuffed Mushrooms

YIELD: 10 to 12 servings

1 4 1/2-ounce can minced clams,
   drained
4 tablespoons melted butter

1/4 cup Italian bread crumbs
1/4 cup shredded mozzarella
   cheese
1 pound large mushroom caps

Preheat oven to 350°. Mix by hand the drained clams, butter, crumbs, and cheese. Stuff 1 tablespoon mixture into each mushroom cap and bake for 15 minutes.

Sharon E. Hwalek
Virginia Beach, Virginia

Cheese Puffs with Crab

YIELD: 3 dozen

1/2 pound crab meat
1 8-ounce package cream cheese
1 ripe avocado
1 lemon
1 cup water

1/2 cup (1 stick) butter
1 teaspoon salt
1/8 teaspoon pepper
1 cup flour
4 eggs
1 cup shredded sharp
   Cheddar cheese

Preheat oven at 425°. Combine water, butter, salt, and pepper and heat until mixture is boiling. Add flour all at once and cook and stir until mixture forms a ball. Remove from heat and add eggs one at a time, beating well after each addition. Stir in cheese. Lightly grease a cookie sheet and place small spoonfuls of dough on pan. Bake 12 to 18 minutes, until puffed and golden brown. Let cool away from drafts. Split open, but do not cut all the way through.

Cut brick of cream cheese into 36 cubes. Cut avocado in chunks and sprinkle with lemon to prevent discoloration. On each puff place cube of cheese, then a lump of crab meat, and then a chunk of avocado. Close puff.

Nancy Jo Leachman
Charlottesville, Virginia

Photo - Seafood Brochettes

Scallops lend themselves to outdoor cookery on a grill because they thread so easily on a skewer. For a gourmet touch to skewered scallops, see Seafood Brochettes (page 49), a recipe prepared by Chef David Jordan of the Virginia Museum in Richmond, Virginia, for the 1983 Governor's Tasting.

Chesapeake Crab Puffs

David Jordan, Chef at the Virginia Museum in Richmond, Virginia, offered this recipe for Virginia Crab Puffs for the 1983 Governor's Tasting. Wonderful as an entrée, the crab puffs also can be served as hors d'oeuvres.

YIELD: 6 servings

1 stalk celery, diced fine
1 small onion, diced fine
1 to 2 tablespoons butter
1 6-by-10-inch sheet puff pastry

1 tablespoon Dijon-type mustard
1 pound blue crab meat, picked
Salt and pepper to taste
1 egg, beaten
1 tablespoon water

Preheat oven to 350°. Saute' the celery and onion in butter until tender. Remove from heat. Roll out pastry dough and, using a pastry brush, spread thinly with mustard. Cut into 3-inch square pieces. Mix celery and onion with crab meat. Place crab mixture (approximately 1 ounce) on puff pastry. Pull sides of pastry up equally and twist the top to seal. (If not sealed properly, they will open during baking.) Beat egg and water together to make egg wash. Brush pastry with egg wash. Bake 10 minutes until golden brown. May be served as is or with numerous sauces (cocktail, Mornay, cheese, etc.)

Chef David Jordan

🦪 🦪 🦪 🦪 🦪 🦪 🦪

In 1770 when a colonist applied for a patent on the land around Cape Henry in what is now Seashore State Park in Virginia Beach, the local citizens became alarmed. They petitioned the Governor's Council in Williamsburg asking that Cape Henry and its vicinity be preserved as common land. The petition explained that a "Common Fishery hath been carried on by many of the Inhabitants of said County."

The petition requested that no patent be granted to anyone for the land, that it remain instead a "Common for the benefit of the Inhabitants of this Colony in General for carrying on a Fishery and for such other publick Uses as the same premises shall be found convenient."

The petition was granted and the land remained in the public domain until 1790 when two acres were deeded by Virginia to the United States for the construction of a lighthouse. The deed stipulated, however that citizens shall not be banned "from the privileges they now enjoy of hauling their seines and fishing on the shores of said land. . . ."

Today the land so cherished by early fishermen still remains a "Common for the benefit of the Inhabitants of Virginia," in the form of Seashore State Park.

Crab Balls

YIELD: about 2 dozen

1 pound Virginia crab meat
1 egg
1 tablespoon chopped onion
1 tablespoon parsley
1-1/2 teaspoon Worcestershire
    sauce
1/2 teaspoon dry mustard
1/2 teaspoon coarse ground
    pepper

1 slice bread (grated)
1 dash tabasco sauce
1/2 teaspoon lemon
1/4 cup mayonnaise
1 dash garlic salt
3/4 teaspoon Old Bay seafood
    seasoning
1 cup pancake mix
3/4 cup half and half cream
1 egg
1 tablespoon vegetable oil

Mix all ingredients together except pancake mix, cream, egg, and oil; roll in cocktail-size balls. Put on waxed paper covered cookie sheet and chill. Meanwhile, mix together pancake mix, half and half, egg, and oil. Pour over crab balls and roll in batter with spoon. Deep fry in hot oil till golden brown.
    NOTE: These can be made in advance and reheated in moderate oven.

Sue Lunsford
Woodbridge, Virginia

Crab Cheese Paté

YIELD: 2-1/2 cups

1/2 pound crab meat
1 tablespoon lemon juice
1 tablespoon grated onion
1 tablespoon prepared
    horseradish

1/4 teaspoon pepper
1 8-ounce package cream cheese,
    at room temperature
1/4 cup chopped pecans
2 tablespoons snipped parsley

Flake crab meat in bowl. Add lemon juice, onion, horseradish, pepper, and cream cheese. Blend thoroughly. Stir in pecans and chill until firm. Shape into fish shape on board or serving plate. Garnish with snipped parsley. Serve with crisp crackers.

Dorothy L. Mangels
Madison, Virginia

Crabby Cheese Puffs

YIELD: 60

4 ounces blue crab meat
1/2 cup shredded Swiss cheese
1 small onion, finely chopped
1 egg
1 teaspoon dry mustard

2 teaspoons lemon juice
1 teaspoon Worcestershire sauce
1 teaspoon salt
1 teaspoon paprika
1 tablespoon parsley
2 cups biscuit mix
1/4 cup water

Toss crab, Swiss cheese, and onion together to mix thoroughly. Add egg to crab mixture and mix well. Add next six ingredients and mix. Add biscuit mix and water. Stir until well moistened. Form dough into small balls (if mixture sticks to hands, lightly oil palms of hands). Deep fry at 425° until golden brown, drain well and serve.

NOTE: These may be prepared well in advance and reheated on a cookie sheet for 15 minutes at 350°.

Lee Ann Shaw
Richmond, Virginia

🐚🐚🐚🐚🐚🐚

Clams: Money from the Sea

Unlike many of its bivalve relatives, the clam's scientific name, *Mercenaria mercenaria*, reflects man's use of clams rather than their physical features. "Mercenaria" comes from the Latin word for "wages" and was probably chosen as a descriptive word for the clam because the American Indians used clam shells as "wampum" or money. Because the clam shell has a lovely purple streak on the inside, it was considered more valuable than money made of other plainer shells.

More commonly known as the "quahog," the clam received this name from the settlers who were attempting to pronounce the Indian's name for their source of wampum.

The smallest of clams are called "littlenecks." This name refers to the siphon the clam extends up through the sand to take in plankton-rich seawater which is its food source. The siphon of all quahog clams is short compared to the much longer siphon of the New England soft-shell clam, hence the name "littleneck."

Though little of siphon, the hard clam is big of flavor. It is available all year long for eating in a variety of ways, from raw to steamed to chopped in chowders and fritters.

Crab Crustades

YIELD: about 100

CASINGS
6 loaves very fresh regular-sliced Pepperidge Farm bread, or other similar coarse grained bread
1/2 cup (1 stick) butter, at room temperature

FILLING
12 ounces crab meat, flaked, cartilage removed

6 tablespoons finely chopped shallots or green onions, including some green tops
1 cup finely chopped fresh mushrooms
2 tablespoons chopped parsley
1 teaspoon lemon juice
4 tablespoons flour
2 cups half and half cream
1 teaspoon salt
Dash cayenne
4 tablespoons grated Parmesan cheese

Preheat oven to 400°. Cut bread into circles. Grease miniature muffin tins well and press bread circles into tins. Brush tops with a little butter. Bake 10 minutes.

Sauté crab, onion, mushrooms and parsley. Add flour, salt, cayenne, and lemon juice. Stir in half and half and cook until thickened. Fill casings with filling (about 1 teaspoon in each). Bake in preheated 350° oven for ten minutes. Freeze on cookie sheets and then bag for storage. Reheat at 400° for ten minutes.

NOTE: Filling may also be frozen for future use.

Priscilla B. Cady
Fairfax, Virginia

Crab Delight

YIELD: 10 to 12 servings

7-1/2 ounces lump crab meat
1/2 cup mayonnaise

1 cup grated Cheddar cheese
1/4 cup diced celery
3 tablespoons chili sauce
2 tablespoons pickle relish

Preheat oven to 325°. Mix ingredients thoroughly and place in oven-proof dish. Bake mixture until heated throughout, about 15 minutes. Serve in chafing dish with your favorite crackers.

NOTE: A microwave may be used to preheat ingredients. Use high setting for 5 minutes.

Mrs. E. Charles Hanbury
Richmond, Virginia

Crab Dip Cromer

YIELD: 12 to 15 servings

1 6-ounce roll garlic cheese

1 10-ounce can shrimp soup
1 pound backfin crab meat
1 dash Worcestershire sauce

In top of double boiler, melt cheese and soup. Add Worcestershire sauce and crab meat. Serve in chafing dish on small patty shells or Ritz crackers.

NOTE: This makes a delicious casserole. Just add some bread crumbs on top of casserole and bake at 325° till bubbly and brown.

Dolly F. Cromer
Midlothian, Virginia

Crab Dip Killmon

YIELD: 2 cups

1 pound Virginia blue crab meat
1 8-ounce package cream cheese,
    at room temperature
1/3 cup mayonnaise
1 teaspoon prepared mustard

1 teaspoon horseradish
1-1/2 tablespoons dried minced
    onion
1/2 teaspoon salt
1 tablespoon dried chopped
    parsley
1/4 teaspoon garlic powder

Combine ingredients, mixing gently. Serve with party crackers or potato chips.

Margaret G. Killmon
Annandale, Virginia

Crab Dip Wankmiller

YIELD: about 4 cups

1 pound blue crab meat
2 tablespoons milk
1 teaspoon horseradish
2 dashes pepper

4 tablespoons minced onion
2 8-ounce packages cream cheese,
   at room temperature
1/2 teaspoon salt
1 cup slivered almonds

Preheat oven to 375°. Combine ingredients except for the almonds. Bake uncovered in a casserole for 15 to 20 minutes. Before serving, sprinkle slivered almonds on top. Serve hot with crackers.

Joan Wankmiller
Silver Spring, Maryland

Crab Meat Bacon Rolls

YIELD: 2 dozen

1/2 cup tomato juice
1 egg, well beaten
1 cup dry bread crumbs
1/4 teaspoon salt

1/4 teaspoon pepper
1/2 teaspoon chopped parsley
1/2 teaspoon chopped celery
   leaves
1 cup Virginia blue crab meat
12 slices bacon, halved

Mix tomato juice and egg; add crumbs, seasonings, and crab meat. Roll into fingerlengths; wrap each roll with 1/2 slice bacon. Fasten with toothpick. Broil, turning frequently, until bacon is crisp and evenly browned.

Margaret G. Killmon
Annandale, Virginia

Crab Meat Balls

YIELD: 2 dozen

1/2 cup tomato juice
1 egg, well-beaten
1 cup dry bread crumbs
Dash salt and pepper

1/2 teaspoon chopped parsley
1/2 teaspoon chopped celery
   leaves
1/2 pound crab meat, flaked
1 egg, slightly beaten
3/4 cup fine, dry bread crumbs

Mix tomato juice and egg. Add 1 cup crumbs, seasonings, parsley, celery leaves, and crab meat. Mix thoroughly; roll into balls. Dip in egg, then in fine, dry bread crumbs. Fry in deep fat (until golden). Serve on cocktail picks.
    NOTE: These may be frozen ahead.

Betty R. Pennington
Lynchburg, Virginia

Crab Meat Dip

YIELD: 15 to 20 servings

3 8-ounce packages cream cheese,
   at room temperature
1/2 cup mayonnaise
1/4 cup dry white wine

2 tablespoons Dijon-type mustard
1-1/2 teaspoon powdered sugar
1/2 teaspoon onion powder
2 garlic cloves, minced
1 pound flaked crab meat
1/4 cup minced fresh parsley

Combine cream cheese, mayonnaise, wine, mustard, sugar, onion powder, and garlic. Fold in crab meat and heat until warm. Transfer to chafing dish or fondue pot. Sprinkle with parsley. Serve with crackers.

Liz Becker
Virginia Beach, Virginia

Crab Meat Mousse

YIELD: 12 servings

2 8-ounce packages cream cheese
1 10-ounce can cream of
    mushroom soup
3 tablespoons of gelatin

1/4 cup water
1 cup finely chopped celery
1 cup finely chopped onions
1 cup mayonnaise
1 pound lump crab meat
1/2 teaspoon curry

Mix cream cheese and soup in a sauce pan over low heat until well blended. Soften gelatin in water and add to soup mixture. Then add remaining ingredients. Mix all the ingredients together and place in a greased mold. Refrigerate until firm. Turn out of mold and serve with crackers.

Betty L. Hamel
Onancock, Virginia

Crab Meat Wontons

YIELD: about 4 dozen

1/2 pound Virginia crab meat,
    ready to eat
8 ounces cream cheese, at room
    temperature
1 8-ounce can water chestnuts,
    drained and chopped

1/2 teaspoon garlic powder
1/4 cup chopped green onion
1/4 teaspoon Worcestershire sauce
Salt and pepper to taste
About 4 dozen wonton wrappers
Oil for frying

Combine all ingredients, except wonton wrappers and oil for frying. Put 1 rounded teaspoon of crab meat mixture in the center of wonton skin. Fold over skin diagonally to make a triangle. Crimp edges together and seal with water if necessary. Heat oil to hot (375°). Fry wontons a few at a time until golden brown on both sides. Drain on paper towels and serve immediately.

Ann K. Kahan
Stuart, Virginia

Crab-Stuffed Mushrooms

YIELD: 15 to 20

1 pound mushrooms
4 ounces blue crab meat
10 saltine crackers, crumbled
2 tablespoons chopped onion
1 egg
1/2 teaspoon horseradish

1/2 teaspoon Worcestershire sauce
1 teaspoon salt
1/4 teaspoon pepper
1/2 teaspoon paprika
1 teaspoon dry mustard
Dash tabasco sauce
1 tablespoon vegetable oil

Preheat oven to 350°. Wash mushrooms and remove stems, placing mushroom caps upside down on a cookie sheet. Thoroughly mix remaining ingredients. Place small amount of crab mixture on each mushroom, packing securely with fingers. Bake for 15 minutes and serve.

NOTE: These may be prepared well ahead of time and stored in refrigerator unbaked. Bake immediately before serving.

Lee Ann Shaw
Richmond, Virginia

Crab Puffs

YIELD: 4 dozen

8 ounces crab meat
1/2 cup (1 stick) butter or
    margarine

1 8-ounce jar soft Cheddar cheese
2 tablespoons mayonnaise
6 English muffins, split

Combine crab, butter, cheese, and mayonnaise. Blend well. Spread on muffins and cut into 4 pieces. Freeze. When ready to use, take out of freezer, and immediately broil for 10 minutes or more.

NOTE: Be sure to freeze before cooking. This cuts down on soggy bottom.

Sharon Harrell
Suffolk, Virginia

Crispy Crabites

YIELD: 4 dozen

2 tablespoons grated onion
4 tablespoons melted butter or
    margarine
1/4 cup flour
1 cup milk
1 egg yolk, beaten
1/2 teaspoon Worcestershire sauce

1/4 teaspoon salt
Dash pepper
1/4 teaspoon garlic powder
2 tablespoons finely chopped
    parsley
1/4 teaspoon celery seed
1 pound crab meat
3/4 cup fine cracker or dry bread
    crumbs

Cook onion in butter until golden; blend in flour. Gradually add milk and cook until thickened, stirring constantly. Combine egg yolk and seasonings and add to sauce, stirring. Carefully add crab meat. Blend into a paste and cool. With a teaspoon, shape mixture into balls, roll in crumbs, and fry in hot deep fat (375°) until golden. Drain on toweling. Serve hot or cold.

Marilyn C. Fall
Virginia Beach, Virginia

Deviled Crab Cakes

YIELD: 8 to 10 servings

1 pound blue crab meat, flaked
4 tablespoons mayonnaise
1 teaspoon mustard
1 medium onion, grated

1 teaspoon Worcestershire sauce
Dash tabasco sauce
Salt and pepper to taste
1 egg, slightly beaten
Cracker crumbs as needed

Mix all ingredients except egg and crumbs; refrigerate for two or three hours. Form into very small cakes or balls; dip in slightly beaten egg and roll in cracker crumbs. Fry in hot fat until brown.

Maxine R. Harrison
Salem, Virginia

Dot's Crab-Stuffed Mushrooms

YIELD: 30 appetizers

1/2 cup chopped celery
1/2 cup chopped bell pepper
4 tablespoons melted butter
4 ounces herb stuffing
1 pound crab meat, preferably
    back fin

1 10-ounce can cream of
    mushroom soup
1/2 cup sour cream
1/4 cup mayonnaise or salad
    dressing
2 tablespoons pickle relish
2 teaspoons Worcestershire sauce
30 medium sized mushrooms

Preheat oven to 350°. Sauté celery and pepper in butter until transparent. Stir in herb stuffing and mix well. Set aside. Separate crab lumps with fork and add soup, sour cream, mayonnaise, relish, and Worcestershire sauce and mix well. Add to stuffing mixture and mix well. Remove stems from mushrooms and scoop out some of the center and save for another recipe. Stuff with crab mixture. Bake for 20 to 30 minutes or until the mushrooms are done.

Kathryn G. Westbury
Charlottesville, Virginia

Hot Crab Dip

YIELD: about 5 cups

3 cups Virginia blue crab meat
2 8-ounce packages cream cheese,
    at room temperature

1/2 cup mayonnaise
1/2 teaspoon onion juice
1 teaspoon Worcestershire sauce

Heat all ingredients in pan over low flame or in double boiler. Stir to mix well. Serve in chafing dish (preferably over water). Keep warm. Serve with crackers for dipping.

Margaret G. Killmon
Annandale, Virginia

Hot Crab Meat Casserole

YIELD: 4 to 6 servings

1 8-ounce package cream cheese
1 tablespoon milk
2 teaspoons Worcestershire sauce
1 teaspoon tabasco sauce
1 teaspoon horseradish sauce
1/2 teaspoon seafood seasoning

1 teaspoon lemon juice
1/2 pound crab meat
4 tablespoons finely chopped
  onions
2 tablespoons finely chopped
  bell pepper
4 tablespoons chopped nuts

Preheat oven to 350°. Combine first 5 ingredients; add the next 5 ingredients and mix. Pour in 8-to-9-inch baking dish. Top with nuts. Bake for 15 to 20 minutes. Serve in a fondue or chafing dish with crackers.

Sharon Harrell
Suffolk, Virginia

Hot Crab Pie

YIELD: 10 to 12 servings

1 pound backfin crab meat

1-1/2 cups mayonnaise
3 ounces capers
Sharp Cheddar cheese as needed

Preheat oven to 350°. Mix first three ingredients together. Put in greased pie plate. Grate cheese on top to cover. Refrigerate until time to use. Heat until cheese melts and mixture is hot through. Serve with crackers.

Jeannette G. Heath
Lovingston, Virginia

Naval Academy Crab Spread

YIELD: 15 to 20 servings

2 pounds crab meat
3 8-ounce packages cream cheese,
    at room temperature
3 teaspoons horseradish
3 teaspoons dry mustard

3 teaspoons Worcestershire sauce
1-1/2 cups grated onion
Salt and pepper to taste
3 tablespoons cream
1/4 cup sherry
Shaved almonds (optional)

Preheat oven to 350°. Mix all ingredients except almonds; put into greased 2-quart baking dish; top with almonds. Bake for 20 minutes. Serve with crackers.
    NOTE: Recipe may be halved.

Betty Ann DiMare
Virginia Beach, Virginia

Nita Chase's Crab Meat Spread

YIELD: 8 to 10 servings

1 pound crab meat
1/2 cup (1 stick) butter, at room
    temperature
2 hot hard-boiled egg yolks
2 tablespoons flour, browned

1-1/2 teaspoon dry mustard
1 teaspoon ground red pepper
1 teaspoon black pepper
2 level teaspoons salt
1 cup milk
1 raw egg yolk
1 tablespoon minced onion

Preheat oven to 350°. Mix all ingredients together. Add crab meat and bake 20 minutes. Serve in a chafing dish with assorted crackers or toast points.

Ramona B. Stenzhorn
Virginia Beach, Virginia

Tangy Crab Spread

YIELD: 2 cups

1 cup Virginia blue crab meat
3 ounces cream cheese, at room
    temperature

1/4 cup mayonnaise
2 tablespoons minced onion
1 tablespoon ketchup
1/2 cup sour cream

Blend all ingredients. Serve with favorite crackers.

Margaret G. Killmon
Annandale, Virginia

Smithfield-Backfin Crab Rollup with Old Bay Sauce

Two Virginia favorites, crab meat and ham, provide the essential ingredients in this recipe, furnished by Bill Pearce of Pearce's Parties, Richmond, Virginia for the 1983 Governor's Tasting.

YIELD: 6 servings

2 teaspoons Dijon-type mustard
1/2 teaspoon Old Bay seasoning
1 teaspoon paprika
6 eggs, beaten
1 pound backfin crab meat
    (loosely picked to remove
    shells)

1/2 pound Smithfield ham, sliced
    1/8 inch thick

SAUCE
1/4 cup chablis wine
1/4 cup sour cream
1 tablespoon Old Bay seasoning
Juice and peel of 1 lemon

Preheat oven to 325°. Blend mustard, Old Bay, paprika, and eggs together. Fold in crab meat. Form mixture into 5-by-1-inch cylinders. Place on greased cookie sheet and bake until firm, about 20 minutes. Wrap ham around crab meat cylinders and fasten with tooth picks every 1/2 inch. Cut between tooth picks. Make sauce by blending all ingredients in blender until smooth. Serve cold as dip for rollups.

Chef Bill Pearce

Tidewater's Deviled Crab

YIELD: 10 to 12 servings

1-1/2 slices white bread without
    crust, cubed
3/4 cup mayonnaise
1-1/2 teaspoon baking powder
1 egg, beaten
2 tablespoons melted butter
Red pepper or tabasco sauce to
    taste

2 tablespoons vinegar
1 tablespoon Worcestershire sauce
1 teaspoon bottled onion juice or
    2 teaspoons fresh onion juice
1 teaspoon prepared mustard
1/4 teaspoon Old Bay seafood
    seasoning
1 pound regular or backfin
    crab meat

Preheat oven to 350°. Mix first six ingredients until fluffy and well blended.
Add all of the seasonings. Gently fold in crab meat without breaking it up.
Lightly spoon all of the mixture into a greased 1-quart Pyrex dish. Sprinkle
with paprika and bake for 35 to 40 minutes. Serve with crackers.

    NOTE: For entrée, grease 6 to 8 crab shaped Pyrex or aluminum
ramekins and lightly place the crab mixture into the shells. Sprinkle with
paprika and bake at 350° for about 20 minutes.

Peggy Freeman
Chesapeake, Virginia

    George Washington ran his own fishery on the Potomac River for many years.
He wrote of the river being "well stocked with various kinds of fish at all seasons of
the year and in the spring with shad, herrings, bass, carp, perch, sturgeon, etc., in
great abundance. The borders of the estate (Mount Vernon) are washed by more
than ten miles of tidewater, the whole shore, in fact, is one entire fishery."

Virginia Crab Puffs Trader

YIELD: 4 servings

10 saltine crackers, crushed fine
5 tablespoons mayonnaise
1 egg, beaten
1/2 teaspoon prepared mustard
3 tablespoons melted butter
2 tablespoons fresh lemon juice
1/2 teaspoon Old Bay seafood
    seasoning

1 teaspoon baking powder
1 pound regular crab meat

BATTER
1 cup flour
3/4 cup water
3/4 teaspoon seasoning salt
1/2 teaspoon red pepper
1 egg, separated

Mix all the ingredients through baking powder. Beat with fork until fluffy and well blended. Fold in crab meat, leaving the meat in chunks. Make into small round crab balls and dip each one into the batter, made by combining flour, water, salt, pepper, and egg yolk. Beat until smooth. Fold in stiffly beaten egg white. Deep fry crab balls in vegetable oil until golden brown. Drain on paper towels. Serve hot.

Elizabeth Trader
Chesapeake, Virginia

Chafing Dish Oysters

YIELD: 20 to 25 servings

24 ounces oysters
4 tablespoons butter
1 8-ounce package cream cheese,
    at room temperature
1/2 cup plus 2 tablespoons dry
    white wine
3 tablespoons chopped green
    onions

1/2 teaspoon paprika
1/2 teaspoon anchovy paste
1/4 teaspoon cayenne pepper
1/4 teaspoon salt
5 to 6 drops tabasco
Chopped parsley
Toast or miniature shells

Place undrained oysters in a sauce pan; cook over moderate heat about two minutes or until edges begin to curl. Drain and set aside.

Combine butter and cream cheese in a medium pan. Place over low heat, stirring until melted. Add wine and blend with a whisk until smooth. Stir in green onions and seasonings, except parsley. Bring to a boil over high heat, stirring constantly. Gently fold in oysters. Garnish with parsley. Serve from chafing dish on toast or shells.

Mary Ann Muse
Richmond, Virginia

Golden Oyster Flags

YIELD: 3 dozen

1 medium garlic clove, minced
4 tablespoons butter
1 teaspoon vegetable oil
1/2 cup chopped green onion
1/2 pound fresh spinach, cooked, squeezed dry, and chopped
1/2 cup wheat germ

1 8-ounce container fresh oysters, drained and chopped
3 tablespoons dry vermouth
2 teaspoons lemon juice
1/4 teaspoon oregano
1/4 cup grated Swiss cheese
1/2 pound filo dough
1/2 cup (1 stick) melted butter

Sauté garlic in butter and oil. Remove garlic and cook onions until tender. Combine remainder of ingredients.

Preheat oven to 425°. Cut filo into 2-by-10-inch strips for each "flag." Brush 2 strips lightly with butter. Put one rounded teaspoonful of oyster mixture in the corner of one strip. Fold the corner over the mixture to form a triangle. Continue to fold in uniform triangles until the oyster mixture is completely wrapped with the first strip. Lay the triangle in the corner of the second strip of filo and repeat. Arrange "flags" well apart on an ungreased baking sheet. Bake for 12 to 15 minutes, or until golden brown. Serve warm.

NOTE: The prepared triangles may be frozen before baking or stored in refrigerator (covered) for 24 hours before baking.

Marilyn C. Fall
Virginia Beach, Virginia

Golden Oyster Triangles

YIELD: varies

Preheat oven to 450°. Roll out flaky pastry. Cut into 2-1/2-inch squares. Place a prime Virginia oyster in the center of each square. Add 1/2 teaspoon butter and a shake each of salt and pepper. Moisten edges and fold into triangles, crimping together with tines of a fork. Brush with milk and bake for 12 to 15 minutes or until golden.

NOTE: Frozen pie crust pastry may also be used.

Maxine Foster
Lexington, Virginia

Oyster Angels

YIELD: 2 dozen appetizers

2 dozen shucked oysters
8 slices bacon, cut in thirds

2 tablespoons chopped parsley
1/2 teaspoon salt
Paprika to taste
Pepper to taste

Drain oysters; place an oyster on each piece of bacon. Sprinkle with parsley and seasonings. Wrap bacon around oyster and secure with a toothpick. Place "angels" on broiler rack and broil about 4 inches from source of heat for 8 to 10 minutes. Turn carefully. Broil 4 to 5 minutes longer or until bacon is crisp and oysters begin to curl at the edges.

Evelyn Simpson
Lynchburg, Virginia

Savory Creamed Oysters

YIELD: about 8 servings

6 tablespoons butter
6 tablespoons flour
1 cup light cream
1/2 cup finely diced green pepper
1/4 cup minced parsley
1/4 cup diced pimento

1 cup grated Cheddar cheese
1/2 cup grated Parmesan cheese
1 tablespoon prepared horseradish
1 teaspoon Worcestershire sauce
1 teaspoon rosemary
1 teaspoon salt
1/8 teaspoon black pepper
1 quart oysters

Combine all ingredients except oysters in order given and cook over medium heat until sauce thickens. (Sauce will be quite thick.) Combine with oysters and their liquor, heating in double boiler until oysters begin to curl. Serve in patty shells or on toast points.

NOTE: Sauce may be made day before, adding oysters and heating just before serving.

Janice W. Smith
Onancock, Virginia

Smoked Oysters
Florentine en Croute

This recipe was developed especially in 1982 for "The Great Taste of Virginia Seafood" by Michael Sigler and Ronald Rosenbaum of the Omni International Hotel, Norfolk, Virginia.

YIELD: about 15 servings

Croissant or puff pastry dough
30 smoked select oysters
30 fresh spinach leaves, blanched

HORSERADISH BUTTER
1 pound sweet butter, at room temperature
1/2 cup horseradish
1/2 cup sliced green onion tops
1 teaspoon white pepper
Juice of 2 lemons

Preheat oven to 400°. Roll out dough to 1/8-inch thickness. Cut dough into triangles with sides 2 inches long. Wrap each oyster and 1/2 teaspoon Horseradish Butter in spinach leaf. Place slightly below center of triangle. Roll up and bend corners down. Bake for 10 minutes.

Chef Michael Sigler
Chef Ronald Rosenbaum

❀ ❀ ❀ ❀ ❀ ❀ ❀

Oyster Crab: The Gourmet's Oyster Pearl

Not much bigger than a pearl, this roundish pinkish crab lives in a commensal relationship with the oyster. The female crab meets up with her male counterpart only when he slips in her shell for a brief mating.

Highly esteemed by many gourmets, and a favorite of George Washington, this little crab can be eaten deep-fried or sautéed if enough are available. Show offs let the little crab crawl to the back of their mouths before swallowing them alive. Experts say they taste better that way. Tasting a little like celery, the oyster crab can serve as a palate cleanser between oysters.

Tootsie's Oyster Fritters

Every year, thousands flock to Urbanna, Virginia's Oyster Festival held the last weekend in October, to feast on oysters harvested by local watermen and prepared in every imaginable fashion by community residents. This crisp oyster fritter is the festival's contribution to the great taste of Virginia's seafood.

YIELD: 16 fritters

3/4 cup flour
1/4 cup cornmeal
1 teaspoon baking powder
1/4 teaspoon salt
1/4 teaspoon paprika

1/4 teaspoon celery seed
1 egg
1 tablespoon sour cream
1/4 cup milk
1/2 pint oysters, drained and
    chopped

Sift into a bowl flour, cornmeal, baking powder, salt, paprika, and celery seed. Slightly beat egg with 1 tablespoon sour cream and add to mixture. Stir in milk and oysters. Drop the fritters, a few at a time, by tablespoon into hot deep fat. Fry until golden brown. Place on paper towel with slotted spoon. Drain and sprinkle with salt to taste.

Urbanna Oyster Festival Cookbook
Courtesy Urbanna Chamber of Commerce

Easy Scallop Roll-Ups

YIELD: 6 to 10 servings

1 pound scallops

1/2 cup lemon juice
1 pound bacon strips, cut in half

Preheat oven to 425°. In mixing bowl, toss scallops and lemon juice until well coated. Wrap 1/2 bacon strip around a scallop. Secure with toothpick. Repeat with remaining bacon and scallops. Place on a broiling pan that has been coated with non-stick spray. Bake for about 30 minutes, turning once during baking time, until bacon is fully cooked. Serve with favorite seafood cocktail sauce.

Shirley Jean Lewis
Charlottesville, Virginia

Cookie's Mock Crab (Blue Fish) Balls

YIELD: 12 to 16 servings

1 pound blue fish or striped bass
1 teaspoon Old Bay seafood
    seasoning

8 ounces cream cheese, at room
    temperature
1 6-ounce bottle sweet red
    cocktail sauce

Broil fish until it becomes white and you can flake it into large pieces. Mix all ingredients together thoroughly. Form into a ball and cover with plastic wrap. Chill at least 2 hours. Serve with crackers.

Eileen "Cookie" Gross
Silver Spring, Maryland

Sherried Crab and Shrimp

YIELD: 8 dozen

1 pound fresh mushrooms, sliced
3/4 cup melted butter or
    margarine
1/2 cup plus 1 tablespoon flour
1 tablespoon salt
1/2 teaspoon pepper
4-1/2 cups milk
1-1/2 cups shredded Cheddar
    cheese

2 tablespoons Worcestershire
    sauce
6 to 8 drops tabasco sauce
2 pounds crab meat
1 pound medium shrimp, cooked,
    peeled, and deveined
3/4 cup sherry
8 dozen 1-inch pastry shells,
    baked

Preheat oven to 350°. Sauté mushrooms in butter until tender; remove from pan with a slotted spoon and set aside. Reserve drippings. Add flour, salt, and pepper to reserved drippings; place over medium heat and blend until smooth. Add milk gradually; cook until smooth and thickened, stirring constantly. Add cheese, Worcestershire sauce, and tabasco; cook and stir until cheese melts. Stir crab, shrimp, sautéed mushrooms, and sherry into cheese sauce. Spoon into a greased 3-quart baking dish. Bake for 30 minutes. Serve in pastry shells.

Alice M. Alexander
Hampton, Virginia

Chesapeake Clams

YIELD: 3 servings

6 clams, scrubbed in shell
6 thick slices of French or Italian
    bread

SAUCE
4 tablespoons olive oil
2 garlic cloves
1 28-ounce can tomatoes
1 tablespoon oregano

Preheat oven to 350°. Place bread in a large pan and clams in shell on top of the bread. To make sauce, sauté garlic cloves in oil for five minutes. Add tomatoes and oregano. Simmer 15 minutes. Pour sauce over clams and bake about 20 minutes or until clams open up. Be patient as it sometimes takes a while.

Shirley Booker
Charlottesville, Virginia

Clams Casino Cottrill

YIELD: 1 dozen

12 Virginia Littleneck clams
1/4 cup spaghetti sauce

1/4 medium onion, minced
Bacon bits as needed
Lemon slices (optional)

Steam clams. Remove top shell. Preheat oven to 350°. Put a teaspoon of spaghetti sauce on top of each clam. Top with minced onion and bacon bits. Bake three to five minutes. Serve hot.

Jean Cottrill
Bladensburg, Maryland

Clams Casino Karageorge

This recipe for Clams Casino was furnished by Pete Karageorge of La Maison du Gourmet in Roanoke, Virginia for the 1982 Governor's Tasting. (Ingredients will vary, depending on the number of servings.)

Chopped bacon
Butter
Garlic
Chopped onions
Chopped pimento

White pepper
Salt
Worcestershire sauce
Bay leaves
Clams

Preheat oven to 425° and sauté chopped bacon, and then add butter and clarify. Add a little garlic, a few onions (just enough for taste), pimentos, and white pepper. Add a little salt, little Worcestershire, and bay leaves. Stir well. Take out bay leaves, pour mixture over clam on the half shell, and bake for about 15 minutes.

Chef Pete Karageorge

Clams Casino Rutledge

YIELD: 2 dozen

24 clams (1-1/2- to 2-inch
    diameter)
1/2 cup grated Parmesan cheese
1 cup dry bread crumbs
3 tablespoons minced parsley

1-1/2 tablespoons minced onion
3/4 teaspoon oregano
1/2 teaspoon garlic salt
1 teaspoon crushed red pepper
Olive oil or vegetable oil as needed
3 slices bacon
Paprika to taste

Scrub clams and steam open. Remove clams and chop into small pieces. Save one half of each shell. Preheat oven to 350°. Divide chopped clams among 24 halves of shells. Mix all other ingredients together except paprika and bacon, using enough oil to moisten. Pack mixed crumbs in clam shell on top of chopped clams, about 1 tablespoon per shell. Place a small square of bacon on top of each prepared shell. Bake until bacon is almost crisp. Remove from oven and dash with paprika. Serve hot.

NOTE: These clams can be frozen and warmed in radar range for TV snack.

Dorothy F. Rutledge
Lynchburg, Virginia

Clams Casino Vick

YIELD: 3 to 4 dozen

3 to 4 dozen clams
3 slices bacon, chopped
1 small onion, chopped
1 small stalk celery, chopped

1-1/2 teaspoon lemon juice
1 teaspoon salt
1/8 teaspoon pepper
6 to 8 drops Worcestershire sauce
4 drops tabasco sauce (optional)

Heat clams in small amount of water just until they start to open. Cool a few minutes and remove top shell. Arrange shells with clams in a shallow pan. Preheat oven to 400°. Fry bacon until partially cooked. Add onion and celery and cook until tender. Add lemon juice and seasoning. Pour mixture over clams and bake for 10 to 15 minutes.

Doris Vick
Chesapeake, Virginia

Clams on Toast

YIELD: 2 servings

12 fresh clams in shell
1/4 cup minced parsley
1/4 cup minced leeks or chives

1/4 cup olive oil
1 tablespoon salt
1 teaspoon pepper
Toast cubes

Wash clam shells well. Using a large skillet, sauté parsley and leek or chives in oil with salt and pepper. When delicately crisp, add clams in shells. Simmer 5 minutes, or until shells open and liquor is expelled. Remove shells, and cook another 5 minutes. Serve over crostini (cubed toast) in soup bowls.

Marie Vita
Lexington, Virginia

Deviled Clams

YIELD: 12 servings

12 fresh clams, juice reserved
1 small onion
1 medium green pepper

8 or 9 slices white bread
3 slices bacon
1 teaspoon salt
1/2 teaspoon pepper

Preheat oven to 350°. Wash shells. Grind first five ingredients. Add last two ingredients and mix well. If mixture is too dry add clam juice. Oil shells and fill with mixture. Set in shallow pan of water. Bake for 45 minutes. If it is not brown at the end of the 45 minutes on the outside, place under the broiler for a few seconds until browned.

Virginia C. Wiesen
Fincastle, Virginia

Hot Crab Open Face Sandwich

YIELD: 6 servings

1/2 pound fresh crab meat
1/4 cup mayonnaise
3 ounces cream cheese
1 egg yolk

1 teaspoon finely chopped onions
1/4 teaspoon mustard
Salt to taste
3 English muffins, split and
    toasted
2 tablespoons butter

Mix crab and mayonnaise. In a separate bowl, beat cheese, egg, onion, mustard, and salt. Spread muffins with butter, then crab meat mixture, and then cream cheese mixture. Broil 5 to 6 inches from broiler for 2 to 3 minutes, or until brown.

Patricia Reeder
Barboursville, Virginia

Chesapeake Baked Oysters

YIELD: 8 servings

1/4 cup finely chopped green
  pepper
1/4 cup finely chopped
  mushrooms
1/4 cup finely chopped pimento

1/4 cup finely chopped shallots
4 tablespoons butter
1 tablespoon white wine
8 oysters on half shell
8 2-1/2-inch strips sliced bacon,
  half cooked

Preheat oven to 475°. Sauté green peppers, mushrooms, pimento, and shallots in butter until tender. Add white wine and sauté over low heat for one minute longer. Place a teaspoon of vegetable mixture on top of each oyster and cover with a strip of bacon. Place oyster in a pan of rock salt and bake about 15 minutes. Garnish with a lemon section and parsley.

Charlotte M. Crews
Lynchburg, Virginia

Oysters a là Raymond

Raymond Greeno of the Skilligalee Restaurant in Richmond, Virginia, furnished this oyster specialty for the 1982 Governor's Tasting.

YIELD: 4 servings

Ice cream salt as needed
1 dozen oysters on half-shell
1 bunch shallots, chopped
1 tablespoon butter
1 tablespoon flour
1/2 cup chicken broth

1/2 cup chopped, cooked shrimp
1/3 cup chopped mushrooms
1 egg yolk
1/3 cup white wine
Salt and pepper to taste
1 cup bread crumbs
1 tablespoon paprika
1/2 cup grated Parmesan cheese

Preheat oven to 350°. Place ice cream salt in 9-inch pie plate or cake pan (about 1/2 full). Place oysters on half shell on salt. Bake oysters until partially done, about 6 to 8 minutes.

Fry shallots in butter until browned. Add flour and heat until browned. Add chicken broth, shrimp, and mushrooms. Beat egg yolk and wine with wire whisk and slowly add to sauce. Beat rapidly and then season to taste with salt and pepper. Simmer for 10 to 15 minutes, stirring constantly. Pour sauce over each oyster and cover with bread crumbs and a mixture of paprika and grated cheese. Place in oven to brown, about 12 minutes.

Chef Raymond Greeno

Oysters Bingo

Oysters Bingo was prepared by Joseph L. Hoggard of the Ships Cabin Seafood Restaurant in Norfolk for the 1982 Governor's Tasting.

YIELD: 2 servings

1 cup flour
Salt and pepper to taste
6 fresh oysters
2 tablespoons butter

1 tablespoon white wine
1 tablespoon oyster juice
1 tablespoon lemon juice
1 tablespoon shallots
6 oyster shells, cleaned

Combine flour with salt and pepper. Lightly coat oysters in flour. Sauté in butter until golden brown. Remove from pan. To make sauce, remove pan from heat and add the wine, oyster juice, lemon juice, and shallots to the butter in the pan. Place each oyster in a shell and pour sauce over it. Serve hot.

Chef Joseph L. Hoggard

Oysters Rockefeller

YIELD: 6 servings

3 dozen oysters in the shell
2 cups chopped, cooked spinach
1/4 cup diced onion
2 bay leaves
1 tablespoon parsley flakes

1/2 teaspoon celery salt
1/2 teaspoon salt
6 drops tabasco sauce
6 tablespoons melted butter
1/2 cup dry bread crumbs
Grated cheese (optional)

Preheat oven to 400°. Shuck and drain oysters. Place oysters on deep half of shells and arrange shells in single layer on a shallow baking pan. Combine spinach and onion with seasonings and sauté mixture in butter for about 5 minutes. Remove from heat and toss in bread crumbs. Spread mixture evenly over oysters; sprinkle cheese on top if desired. Bake for 10 to 15 minutes or until brown and bubbly.

Virginia Marine Products Commission

Oysters Rockwell

Oysters on the half shell form the centerpiece for this recipe developed by Samih Husein of the Lynnhaven Fish House of Virginia Beach, Virginia for the 1983 Governor's Tasting.

YIELD: 2 servings

12 fresh oysters on the half shell
Rock salt as needed

STUFFING
1/4 pound bacon
2 medium onions, sliced
2 medium green peppers, sliced
1/2 cup white wine
4 tablespoons toasted almonds, sliced

1 bay leaf
Dash salt and pepper

SAUCE
4 tablespoons butter
1 cup flour
1-1/2 cup milk, scalded
6 slices yellow American cheese, halved
12 sprigs parsley

Preheat oven to 350°. Place oysters on bed of rock salt on oblong baking sheet. Set aside. Fry bacon until crisp. Remove from pan and chop. Sauté onions and peppers in bacon drippings over medium-low heat until tender. Add wine, almonds, bay leaf, salt, and pepper. Set aside. Melt butter and carefully blend in flour, stirring over medium-low heat until golden. Slowly add scalded milk and stir over medium-low heat until thick and creamy. Fold in onions and peppers in wine, removing bay leaf. Place mixture over oysters filling shell to brim, and place half a slice of cheese on top of each. Bake until cheese melts. Garnish with parsley and serve.

Chef Samih Husein

🐚 🐚 🐚 🐚 🐚 🐚

Captain John Smith wrote in his diary of a great school of fish, "lying so thicke wih their heads above water." He tried to catch them with a cooking pot he had on hand but the pot did not work. "We found it a bad instrument to catch fish with," he wrote.

Gwynn's Island Broiled Scallops

YIELD: 6 to 12 servings

2 pounds fresh scallops
**1 cup (2 sticks) butter or
  margarine**

1/4 teaspoon tabasco sauce
Juice of one lemon
1 garlic clove, minced
Seasoned salt to taste

Preheat oven to broil. Place scallops on baking dish or cookie sheet. In sauce pan, melt butter; add tabasco sauce and garlic. Drizzle butter-tabasco-garlic mixture on scallops. Sprinkle scallops with seasoned salt. Broil scallops no more than 5 minutes on each side. If scallops are small, do not broil more than 3 minutes on each side. Serve with any reserved butter-tabasco-garlic sauce.

Rebecca Novak
Huddleston, Virginia

Sautéed Scallops Simplistique

YIELD: 6 servings

1 pound scallops

2 tablespoons butter
Garlic salt to taste

Rinse scallops with cold water. Cut large scallops in half crosswise. Sauté scallops in butter and garlic salt for 5 to 6 minutes.

Raymond J. Hanlein
Annandale, Virginia

41

Scallop Ceviche

YIELD: 4 servings

1/2 pound bay scallops
Juice and sliced peel of 2 limes
3 tablespoons olive oil
2 tablespoons chopped green
   onion

1 tablespoon chopped green
   pepper
Salt and freshly ground pepper
   to taste
Artichoke hearts as needed

Combine scallops, lime juice, peel, olive oil, green onion, green pepper, salt, and freshly ground pepper. Marinate for 6 hours. Discard lime peel and serve on artichoke hearts.

Marilyn C. Fall
Virginia Beach, Virginia

🐚🐚🐚🐚🐚🐚

Scallop: Mobile Bivalve

The scallop has several namesakes. Because of the fluted edge on its shell, the word "scallop" has come to be a descriptive one, such as the scalloped hem of a bedspread. A dish such as scalloped potatoes derived its name from the ancient practice of using large scallop shells as dishes.

The scallop swims backward and can't see where it is going even though it has fifty green eyes, ringed with blue, around the outer edge of its mantle. Scientists say the eyes are closer to vertebrate eyes than any other eyes found in bivalves.

Though a backwards swimmer, the scallop is the most mobile of all bivalves. It moves through the water by opening and closing its two shells and squirting water through an opening in its mantle.

The strong muscle which opens and closes the shell is what is eaten by the consumer as a "scallop." The muscle is usually cleaned from the shell while the fishermen are still at sea, then iced and brought to market.

Whether it is the large, meaty sea scallop, harvested in deep water, or the small, sweet bay scallop, found in shallow eel grass beds, this shellfish lends itself to a variety of preparations and is a tasty complement to other forms of seafood.

Scallops Villeroi

This recipe for Scallops was furnished for the 1982 Governor's Tasting by Debora Pianka of the Chamberlin Hotel in Hampton, Virginia.

YIELD: 12 servings

VILLEROI SAUCE
1-1/2 ounces chopped onion
1 ounce chopped celery
4 tablespoons melted butter
1/4 cup flour
4 cups white stock (chicken or
    white veal)
1/2 cup finely chopped, fresh
    mushrooms
1/2 ounce smoked ham, chopped

3 ounces light cream
1 egg yolk
1 teaspoon fresh lemon juice
2 tablespoons cooked, drained,
    finely chopped spinach
Pinch saffron
5 pounds sea scallops

BATTER
3 whole eggs
2 drops vegetable oil
Salt and pepper to taste

Sauté onion, celery, and melted butter until onions are clear. Add flour, stir, and cook without browning flour. Add stock. Stir and then add mushrooms and ham. Simmer for 1 to 1-1/2 hours, stirring occasionally. Strain and set liquid aside. (You can keep vegetables and ham and use them in omelets, scrambled eggs, etc.)

Blend egg yolk and cream, and then add sauce slowly, stirring constantly. Heat to almost boiling; add lemon juice and spinach. Simmer for 1/2 hour. Strain and stir until completely cooled. Cover tightly with waxed paper and refrigerate to prevent lumps.

Boil water with a pinch of saffron and them blanch scallops for approximately 2 minutes. Then chill scallops and coat with cold villeroi sauce.

Beat batter ingredients. Coat already dipped scallops and then roll in bread crumbs. Heat approximately 2 inches of vegetable oil in skillet or deep fryer (you can use a drop of water as a test for how hot it is), and then fry scallops until golden brown. Drain and then serve.

Chef Debora Pianka

Ceviche Scallops

John Durham of the nationally acclaimed C&O in Charlottesville, Virginia, offered this recipe for the 1983 Governor's Tasting.

YIELD: 4 servings

1 pound scallops
Lime juice
Orange juice

1/4 to 1/2 cup finely chopped green pepper
1/4 to 1/2 cup finely chopped onion
Salt and pepper to taste

Place scallops in a bowl. Cover completely with marinade made with 4 parts lime juice to 1 part orange juice. Quantity of marinade needed will differ depending on size of bowl used. Refrigerate overnight. Add green pepper, onions, salt, and pepper to mixture several hours before serving.

Chef John Durham

Succulent Scallop Mini-Crêpes

YIELD: 4 to 6 servings

4 tablespoons butter
2 tablespoons grated onion
1 tablespoon slivered green pepper

4 tablespoons flour
1/4 teaspoon dry mustard
2 cups milk
2 cups scallops, cooked
12 4-inch crêpes

Preheat oven to 350°. Cook first three ingredients till soft. Blend in flour and mustard. Add milk. Cook till thick. Add scallops. Fill crêpes with equal portions of scallop mixture. Bake in greased casserole dish for 20 minutes.

Helen Keeler
Martinsville, Virginia

Crab-Oysters Charles

YIELD: 4 servings

1 pound lump crab meat
1 cup fresh bread crumbs
   (no crust)
1/2 medium green pepper
1 pimento, finely chopped
1 egg

3/4 cup mayonnaise
Dash tabasco sauce
1 teaspoon salt
Dash white pepper
1/2 teaspoon dry mustard
1 teaspoon chives
1 dozen oysters in half shell

Preheat oven to 350°. Mix all ingredients except oysters to make crab filling. Top oysters in half shell with 1-1/2 to 2 inches of crab filling. Bake for 15 minutes.

Scott B. Robertson
Newport News, Virginia

Paté of Eel and Pike

The combination of smoked and fresh eel makes a satisfyingly unusual paté, as demonstrated by Pierre Monet of the Colonial Williamsburg Foundation, Williamsburg, Virginia. It was served at the 1983 Governor's Tasting.

YIELD: 8 servings

1 tablespoon butter
1 shallot, chopped
2 egg whites
2 tablespoons heavy cream
2 ounces fresh bread crumbs
5 ounces pike filets

Salt and pepper to taste
1/2 cup heavy cream, whipped
3/4 ounce chopped dill
Dash nutmeg
1 pound fresh eel, boned
8 ounces smoked eel, boned and
   skinned

Preheat oven to 180°. Grease a 2-cup mold and then line bottom and sides with aluminum foil. Melt the butter and add the shallot; cook slowly. Cool. Mix the egg white and cream together, and add bread crumbs. Cut the pike into strips and put through the food processor twice, using the metal chopping blade. Fold in whipped cream, chopped dill, and nutmeg. Place fresh eel in mold; carefully cover the bottom and line the sides of the mold. Spread approximately 2/3 of the pike mixture on top of the fresh eel which is lining the bottom of the mold. Cut smoked eel into small strips and place in center of the pike mixture. Use the remaining pike mixture to top the smoked eel. Cook in bain marie for 40 minutes.

Chef Pierre Monet

Paté of Virginia Sea Scallops and Sea Bass

Peter Stogbuchner of Henry Africa in Alexandria, Virginia, combined the complimentary flavors of shellfish and finfish in this paté for the 1983 Governor's Tasting.

YIELD: 16 servings

Lemon juice as needed
8 ounces fresh spinach leaves
Salt and white pepper to taste
4 ounces carrot strips, blanched
**2 pounds unsweetened pastry
     dough**
**1 pound fresh sea bass filets,
     slightly flattened**
2 pounds fresh sea scallops

12 ounces light cream
2 egg yolks
1 to 2 teaspoons water

FISH STOCK GELATIN
1 pound fish bones
2 quarts water
Salt to taste
2 ounces dry white wine
1-1/2 ounces gelatin
4 egg whites

Into a small sauce pan, add fresh lemon juice to the depth of 1/2 inch. Blanch spinach in the lemon juice; add salt and pepper. Drain and cool. Blanch carrots in water. Drain and cool. Roll out pastry to the size of the paté's mold. Refrigerate. Using approximately 1/2 of the sea bass filets, line the paté mold and refrigerate. Prepare scallops by grinding them twice through the fine blade of a grinder or in a food processor, using the metal chopping blade. Chill for 1/2 hour.

Preheat oven to 310°. After chilling, add cream, salt, and pepper to the scallops and mix well enough to have a binding consistency. Remove paté mold of sea bass filets from refrigerator. Spread a two-inch layer of the scallop mixture on top of the filets. Add a layer of the carrots and then another layer of scallops. Follow with a layer of spinach and again another layer of scallops. Continue with the layers until you reach the top of the paté mold. Cover the layered mixture with the remaining sea bass filets. Remove pastry from refrigerator and place on top of the mold, sealing edges. Cut a 1/2-inch diameter round from the center of the pastry. Beat egg yolks with water and brush top of pastry. Bake "au bain marie" for 50 minutes. To make fish stock gelatin, place water and fish bones in sauce pan and bring to boil. Turn down heat and add wine and salt. Allow stock to simmer for about an hour, skimming the scum as it forms on the surface. Strain twice through cheese cloth. Stir in gelatin; mix until dissolved. Cool mixture until tepid. Whip egg whites and fold into tepid stock. Allow to set. When paté is cool, place gelatin fish stock in the cavity that has been cut in the pastry. Allow to set firm. Serve in slices cut 1/2-inch thick.

Chef Peter Stogbuchner

Seafood Brochettes

Chef David Jordan of the Virginia Museum in Richmond, Virginia, stated that when using Virginia's fine seafood, he prefers to keep the preparation simple, thereby enhancing the freshness, quality, and nutrients. This recipe, served at the 1983 Governor's Tasting, is simple to prepare, and will serve as an hors d'oeuvres or entree, depending on the portions.

YIELD: 10 to 12 servings

2 pounds flounder filets
2 pounds bay or ocean scallops

1 pound bacon
Dry sherry as needed
Juice of fresh lemon
Salt and pepper to taste

Cut the flounder filets into 1- to 2-inch pieces. Wash and drain scallops. Begin threading skewer: bacon, scallop, bacon, flounder, etc. Proceed to desired size, making sure the bacon intertwines each seafood piece. Marinate in sherry. Chill for several hours. Before cooking add juice of fresh lemon and a dash of salt and pepper. Broil under medium heat until bacon is well done. Do not overcook.

Chef David Jordan

"As for fish, both of fresh and salt water, of shellfish and others, no country can boast of more variety, greater plenty, or of better in their several kinds," wrote Robert Beverley in *The History and Present State of Virginia*, first published in 1705.

Photo - Virginia Sea Scallops and Sea Bass

This delicious Pate of Virginia Sea Scallops and Sea Bass was created by Peter Stogbuchner of Henry Africa in Alexandria, Virginia, for the 1983 Governor's Tasting. (See page 46.)

Virginia in a Stew
Soups and Chowders

Clam Chowder

YIELD:

5 strips bacon,
   diced in 1/4-inch strips
1 medium onion, diced
4 cups diced potatoes

1-1/2 cups of water
Juice of clams
2 6-ounce cans minced clams
2 13-ounce cans evaporated milk
1/2 cup (1 stick) butter

Fry bacon and onion together; remove bacon and put aside. Add potatoes, water, and juice of clams to bacon grease; cook over medium heat until potatoes are done. Add clams, milk, bacon, and butter. Simmer for 30 minutes.

Ethel Payne
Forest, Virginia

Clear Clam Soup with Mushrooms

YIELD: 6 servings

7 cups cold water, divided
12 sprigs fresh, young spinach
   leaves (stripped from stems)
1 tablespoon kelp seasoning

1 teaspoon salt, divided
12 small fresh clams (scrubbed
   under cold running water)
6 small white fresh mushrooms
1 tablespoon soy sauce
6 thin slices lime or lemon

In small sauce pan, combine 1 cup cold water, spinach leaves, and 1/2 teaspoon salt. Bring to a boil quickly. Boil one minute. Drain and set leaves aside. In 2 quart sauce pan, put 6 cups cold water, kelp seasoning, 1/2 teaspoon salt, and clams. Bring to boil quickly over high heat. Boil for about 2 minutes, or until clams open. Skim off any scum while boiling. Stir in soy (or mushroom) sauce. Boil 30 seconds. Remove from heat. In each of 6 bowls, place 2 clams in the shells. Garnish with 2 sprigs of spinach, one mushroom, and a slice of lime (or lemon). Gently pour into each bowl an equal amount of hot broth. (Avoid disturbing the decorative arrangement). Serve immediately.

Dorothy C. Kirby
Richmond, Virginia

Gingered Virginia Clams with Spinach Soup

YIELD: 6 servings

1 tablespoon fresh ginger,
  cut into thin strips
1 garlic clove, minced
1 small onion, sliced
1 tablespoon vegetable oil
1 teaspoon salt

1/2 teaspoon sweet paprika
4 cups water
1 pound clams, thoroughly cleaned
1/4 pound fresh spinach leaves
1/2 cup finely sliced green onion
  leaves, for garnish

Sauté ginger, garlic, and onions in oil. Season with salt and paprika. Add water and bring to a brisk boil. Add clams to the boiling mixture and cook about three minutes or until the shells are half-opened. Add the spinach leaves; cover pot. Cook until the leaves are tender but still crunchy. Remove immediately from heat. Let stand for a few minutes. Garnish with finely sliced green onion leaves. Serve hot.

Mercedes Aurora B. Tira-Andrei
Falls Church, Virginia

New England Clam Chowder

YIELD: 3 servings

12 medium clams
5 slices bacon, diced small
1 medium onion, diced small

6 medium potatoes, diced small
1 10-ounce can tomato soup
Salt and pepper as desired
Tabasco to taste

Clean clams. Cover with water and boil till shells open. Remove clams from shells and dice clams and save broth. Cook diced clams 10 minutes. In skillet, fry bacon until slightly brown. Add diced onions and brown. Boil diced potatoes until soft. Save broth. Add clams, broth, potatoes, onions, and tomato soup. Cook 10 minutes and add salt, pepper, and tabasco as desired.

William A. Goodreau
Auburn, California

Rich and Southern New England Clam Chowder

YIELD: 6 servings

2 dozen clams
2 cups diced raw potatoes
1/2 cup chopped onion
2 cups milk
1/2 cup (1 stick) butter, divided

2 tablespoons flour
1/2 pint light cream
1 1/2 ounces cream sherry
1 teaspoon salt
1 teaspoon celery salt
Dash white pepper

Shuck clams, saving juice. Mince clams. Add enough water to clam liquid to make 1 cup. To this liquid add potatoes and onions. Bring to a light boil, and then add milk. Cover ingredients and simmer for 1/2 hour or until potatoes are tender. Melt 1/2 stick butter, stir in flour, and then slowly add cream stirring constantly until mixture thickens slightly. Add cream, sherry, salt, celery salt, and white pepper. Then add the clams, vegetables, and broth. Simmer 5 minutes. Serve hot. Prior to serving, float 1 teaspoon of butter on top of each bowl.

Raymond J. Hanlein
Annandale, Virginia

Virginia Clam Chowder

YIELD: 6 to 8 servings

4 medium potatoes, peeled and
diced
1 large or 2 small onions, thinly
sliced
4 slices bacon, cut up
1 1/2 dozen hard-shelled clams
with liquid, cut up

1 quart milk
3 tablespoons flour
Salt and pepper to taste
2 tablespoons Worcestershire
sauce
2 tablespoons butter or margarine
Paprika for garnish

In large sauce pan, cover potatoes, onion, and bacon with water; cook until potatoes are done but not mushy. Add cut up clams and liquid, cook 7 minutes. Add milk and heat; do not boil. Combine flour with enough water to make a smooth paste; add salt, pepper, and Worcestershire sauce. Heat 5 minutes. Add butter or margarine and garnish with paprika. Serve in warm bowls.

Maxine R. Harrison
Salem, Virginia

Virginia Clam Corn Chowder

YIELD: 6 servings

1 quart whole fresh shucked clams
   OR 2 7-ounce cans minced clams
Water as needed
3 slices bacon, chopped
1 cup chopped onion
2 cups diced raw potatoes
1 1/2 cups drained whole-kernel
      corn

3 cups milk
2 tablespoons flour
1 tablespoon butter or margarine
1 teaspoon celery salt
1 teaspoon salt
Dash pepper
1/2 cup coarse cracker crumbs
   (optional)

Chop whole clams or drain canned clams. Reserve liquor. Pour clam liquor into measuring cup and add water as needed to fill to 1 cup level. In a large pot, fry bacon until crisp; add onion and cook until tender. Add potatoes, clam liquor, and water. Cover; simmer gently until potatoes are tender. Add corn and milk. Blend flour and butter or margarine and stir into soup. Cook slowly until mixture thickens slightly, stirring constantly. Add seasoning and clams; simmer 5 minutes. Top with cracker crumbs. Serve hot.

Virginia Seafood Products Commission

🐚🐚🐚🐚🐚🐚

Nuisance: No More

Blow toads (or blow fish) and sharks are not the average angler's prize catch. The adventurous fisherman, however, has found these nuisance fish to be good eating when properly prepared.

The blow toad often is called "chicken of the sea" because the only edible part of the fish, a drumstick-shaped filet on either side of the tail, not only looks but also tastes like chicken. Sometimes also called "sea squab," the blow toad as a meal can offer more pleasure to the fisherman than he is able to get out of tickling the ugly creature's belly and watching him blow up like a balloom.

Though shark meat is not a favorite Virginia seafood, it does have its fans and fishing for sharks has become a popular recreational pastime. Shark, however, has long been a favorite food fish in Europe where it is served both as an elegant hors d'oeuvre and as the inexpensive fish with chips. Though the meat may have an ammonia smell when fresh, the smell will disappear with cooking. A tomato-flavored sauce compliments shark meat which also is good in steaks cooked over the grill and seasoned with lemon juice.

Photo - Virginia Clam Corn Chowder

Seafood chowders are among the most satisfying of meals, especially on a chilly fall or winter evening. Soups and chowders, ranging from Virginia Clam and Corn Chowder to Virginia Manhattan Spot Chowder, can be found on pages 51 to 86.

Blue Crab Bisque

YIELD: 4 servings

4 tablespoons butter
1/4 cup minced onion
2 tablespoons flour
1/4 teaspoon cayenne pepper
1 teaspoon finely chopped parsley

1/4 teaspoon mace
1/4 teaspoon nutmeg
1/2 teaspoon salt
3 cups milk
3 ounces dry sherry
2 cups light cream
1 pound backfin crab meat

Melt butter in 3-quart pan and sauté onion until clear. Add flour, mixing well, and cook until bubbly. Add all seasonings and stir well. Gradually add milk, using a whisk to ensure smoothness. Cook until thickened. Add sherry and cream. Continue to cook (about 5 minutes), but don't boil. Gently fold in crab meat and heat through. This soup is best made ahead, refrigerated, and then heated to serve.

NOTE: All the cooking may be done in the microwave oven using the appropriate container (e.g. 3-quart Corning Ware casserole). Be sure to watch the cooking process at each step, i.e. set timer for 2 to 3 minutes in order to stir and avoid boiling.

Elizabeth C. Holtzclaw
Arlington, Virginia

Cape Henry Crab Bisque

YIELD: 6 servings

1 1/2 pounds ripe tomatoes (5 to 6)
1 tablespoon chopped onion
1/2 bay leaf
1 teaspoon salt
4 tablespoons butter
1/4 cup flour

3 cups milk
Pepper to taste
1 cup crab meat
1 cup corn
1/4 teaspoon Old Bay seafood
seasoning
1/4 teaspoon celery salt

Core and chop tomatoes. Add onion, bay leaf, and salt. Simmer for 15 minutes or until soft. Cool and put through food mill or sieve. There should be about 2 cups of purée.

Melt butter; add flour and stir until well blended. Add milk and stir over heat until sauce is thick. Season with salt and pepper. Add tomato purée, crab meat, and corn. Stir in Old Bay seasoning and celery salt. Heat gently and serve.

Ellen Michel
Virginia Beach, Virginia

Crab Bisque

YIELD: 6 to 8 servings

1 10-ounce can cream of musroom
  soup
1 10-ounce can cream of asparagus
  soup
1 soup can of half and half cream

2 tablespoons cherry
6 ounces Virginia crab meat
1/2 teaspoon Old Bay seafood
  seasoning
Whipped cream or sour cream
  as needed
Fresh parsley, chopped

In blender add soups, cream, and sherry. Blend until smooth. Pour into sauce pan. Fold in crab meat. Add seafood seasoning. Heat until hot but don't boil. Serve hot topped with a dollop of cream (whipped or sour) and garnish with chopped parsley.

Charlene Stenger
Hampton, Virginia

Crab Broccoli

YIELD: 8 to 10 servings

2 10-ounce packages frozen
  chopped broccoli
2 cups chicken broth
1 quart half and half cream
1/2 cup (1 stick) butter
1 1/2 to 2 cups crab meat

1 tablespoon soy sauce
1 tablespoon Old Bay seafood
  seasoning
1/2 teaspoon dry mustard
Salt, white pepper, and chives to
  taste
Cornstarch as needed

Cook broccoli, reserving liquid when finished. Add water until there is 2 cups liquid. Then add chicken broth, cream, and butter. Simmer for 10 minutes. Add the rest of the ingredients and simmer for another 10 to 15 minutes. Add cornstarch last to thicken.

Suzan R. Brooks
Virginia Beach, Virginia

Crab Chowder

YIELD: 6 servings

1/2 cup chopped onion
1/2 cup chopped celery
4 tablespoons butter or margarine
3 cups milk
1 10-ounce can potato soup
1 cup cubed cooked potato

1/2 pound crab meat
1 8-ounce can cream-style corn
2 tablespoons chopped pimento
1/4 teaspoon salt
1/4 teaspoon crushed dried thyme
1 bay leaf
1/4 cup dry sherry
1/4 cup snipped parsley

In large sauce pan cook onion and celery in butter until tender. Add remaining ingredients except sherry and parsley. Cook till heated through, stirring often, about 15 minutes. Stir in sherry. Heat 2 minutes more. Remove bay leaf. Garnish with parsley.

Marilyn C. Fall
Virginia Beach, Virginia

Crab Meat Egg-Drop Soup

YIELD: 6 servings

2 14-1/2-ounce cans chicken broth
1 tablespoon cornstarch
2 tablespoons water
1 tablespoon soy sauce
1/4 cup chopped green onion
    (tops included)

1/2 pound asparagus, cut into
    bite-sized pieces
    (OR 1 10-ounce package
    frozen asparagus)
1 large egg, beaten lightly
8 ounces Virginia crab meat

Heat broth over medium flame. Dissolve cornstarch in 2 tablespoons of water and add to broth. Stir until mixture comes to a boil and thickens slightly. Add soy sauce and green onion. Add asparagus and when mixture reaches the boiling point again, add beaten egg, letting it drip into the mixture in a slow and steady stream. Add crab meat to soup; stir, reheat, and serve immediately.

NOTE: This terrific soup can be easily doubled for a crowd.

Elizabeth S. Courtney
Woolwine, Virginia

Crab Soup Parks

YIELD: 4 to 6 servings

1 small onion, finely chopped
2 celery ribs, finely chopped
4 tablespoons melted butter
4 cups milk
1/2 cup heavy cream

Salt and pepper to taste
4 tablespoons Worcestershire
  sauce
4 tablespoons flour
2 tablespoons water
1/2 to 1 pound backfin crab meat
4 tablespoons sherry

Sauté onion and celery in butter. Combine milk, cream, salt, pepper, and Worcestershire and heat. Add onion and celery. Blend together flour and water and gradually add to milk mixture. Add crab meat and sherry. Heat and serve.

NOTE: For a thicker soup add more crab meat.

Richard B. Parks, Jr.
Newport News, Virginia

Crab Soup Sawyer

YIELD: 8 to 10 servings

1 medium onion
1 stalk celery
2 tablespoons butter
2 tablespoons flour
2 cups milk
1 1/4 teaspoon salt

1/2 teaspoon pepper
1/2 teaspoon mace
1 tablespoon lemon juice
2 medium potatoes, boiled and
  mashed
4 cups half and half cream (or
  milk)
1 pound crab meat

In blender, blend onion and celery. Melt butter and sauté onion and celery for 5 minutes. Stir in flour, milk, and seasonings. Bring to boil over low heat. Mix in lemon juice. Gradually stir in mashed potatoes, half and half and crab meat. Cook over low heat until almost boiling, stirring often to prevent sticking.

NOTE: If a thinner soup is desired, add more milk.

Katherine S. Sawyer
Norfolk, Virginia

Crab Soup Snead

YIELD: 4 to 6 servings

2 tablespoons butter, no substitute
2 tablespoons flour

1/2 teaspoon salt
2 cups half and half cream
2 cups crab meat

Mix butter, flour, and salt together in sauce pan, until blended well. Then add cream and crab meat. **Do not boil**, but heat thoroughly. Serve warm.

Linda W. Snead
Maidens, Virginia

Cream of Crab Soup

YIELD: 4 to 6 servings

4 tablespoons butter, divided
1 medium onion, chopped
1 stalk celery, chopped,
 including leaves
1 large carrot, chopped
1 to 1-1/2 pounds crab meat
 (preferably backfin), picked
3 egg yolks

White pepper to taste
1/4 teaspoon paprika
1/4 teaspoon cayenne
1 tablespoon Worcestershire sauce
2 cups milk
2 cups half and half cream
1 tablespoon dried parsley
2 cups diced, cooked potatoes
 (optional)

In a small, heavy French oven (or large sauce pan), melt 2 tablespoons butter and sauté onion, celery, and carrots until tender. Add crab meat and cook, stirring frequently about 5 minutes. Slowly add milk and cream, stirring constantly. Beat eggs lightly and mix in pepper, paprika, cayenne, and Worcestershire. Reduce heat to very low and slowly stir egg mixture into crab meat. At this point, if using potatoes, add them to mixture. Add parsley and cook slowly, stirring often 15 to 20 minutes or until hot and thickened. Add remaining butter just before serving.

Deborah E. Buchanan
Charlottesville, Virginia

Curried Crab Meat Soup

YIELD: 7 to 14 servings

1 tablespoon chopped chives
2 tablespoons butter
2 teaspoons curry powder

2 tablespoons flour
3 cups milk
2 cups crab meat
1/4 cup sherry
2 cups light cream

Sauté chives in butter for 1 minute. Add curry powder and flour and cook until well blended. Add milk and cook until thickened. Heat crab meat in sherry; add cream and bring to a boil. Add this mixture to the curry mixture and simmer to combine flavors. Chill. Serve very cold or hot with ham biscuits.

John Gregory
Lively, Virginia

"Her" Crab Soup

YIELD: 6 servings

4 tablespoons butter or margarine
4 tablespoons flour
1 teaspoon salt
1/8 teaspoon black pepper

1 teaspoon Old Bay seafood
  seasoning
3 cups milk
1 teaspoon grated onion
1/2 pound fresh crab meat
2 teaspoons chopped parsley

Melt butter over medium heat. Blend in flour, salt, pepper, and Old Bay seasoning. Stir to make a paste. Remove from heat and gradually add milk and grated onion. Bring to a boil and boil 1 minute. Add crab meat and heat one minute. Serve with chopped parsley.

Mary K. Howard
Annandale, Virginia

Linda's She-Crab Soup

YIELD: 6 to 10 servings

1/2 cup (1 stick) butter
2/3 cup flour
4 chicken bouillon cubes
1 quart half and half cream

1/2 onion, chopped
Dash salt
White pepper to taste
1 teaspoon tabasco sauce
1-1/2 pounds crab meat

In small pan melt butter and stir in 2/3 cup flour to make a roux. Stir till thick and set aside. In large pot, dissolve bouillon in very little water. Pour in half and half; add chopped onion, salt, pepper, and tabasco sauce. Heat until almost boiling, and then add butter and flour mixture. Stir well. Add crab meat and cook till thickened. Soup may be thinned out with milk. This recipe makes a thick soup.

Linda Cantor
Glen Allen, Virginia

She-Crab Soup

YIELD: about 2 quarts

2 10-ounce cans cream of celery
  soup, undiluted
3 cups milk
1 cup half and half cream
1/2 cup (1 stick) butter or
  margarine
2 hard-boiled eggs, chopped

1/2 teaspoon Old Bay seafood
  seasoning
1/2 teaspoon Worcestershire sauce
1/4 teaspoon garlic salt
1/4 teaspoon white pepper
1 1/2 cups crab meat, drained and
  flaked
1/4 cup dry sherry

Combine first 9 ingredients in a large Dutch oven; bring to a boil. Add crab meat and cook over medium heat, stirring occasionally, until thoroughly heated. Stir in sherry.

Ann Q. Holderfield
Portsmouth, Virginia

Wachapreague Crab Chowder

YIELD: 2 quarts

1 cup finely chopped celery
1 medium onion, finely chopped
1/4 cup finely chopped green
    pepper
4 tablespoons butter or margarine

4 cups whole milk
2 cups half and half cream
1 teaspoon salt
2 teaspoons sugar
1/4 teaspoon cayenne pepper
1 pound crab meat

In large pot or Dutch oven, over low heat, sauté celery, onion, and green pepper in butter until tender. Add milk, cream, salt, sugar, and pepper. Stir occasionally until hot. Add flaked crab meat. Heat thoroughly. If desired, sprinkle with parsley to serve.

Cathey Sandidge Bell
Wachapreague, Virginia

Dad's Oyster Stew

YIELD: 3 to 4 servings

1 pint Chincoteague oysters (about
    20), shucked, in their own juice
1 quart plus 1 pint milk

3 tablespoons celery seed
2 tablespoons mustard seed
Big dash red pepper
1 tablespoon whole cloves
4 tablespoons butter

Place oysters, juice, and seasonings in sauce pan; boil gently until edges of oysters curl, about three minutes. Add milk and seasonings and bring stew to boiling point but do not boil; add butter.

To serve, remove oysters one at a time to serving bowls. Pour broth over oysters through a strainer.

Thomas G. Allen
Fairfax, Virginia

Photo - "Pearls of Wisdom"

A select oyster doesn't mean it is better than a standard oyster, just bigger. For other "Pearls of Oyster Wisdom," see page 248.

Chesapeake Oyster Chowder

YIELD: 6 servings

1 large bunch fresh broccoli (10 to 12 ounces), some reserved for garnish
1 1/2 cups sliced potatoes
1-medium-large onion, chopped
2 garlic cloves, minced
1/2 teaspoon curry powder
1 cup heavy cream
2 14-1/2-ounce cans chicken broth
1 pint oysters, shucked with liquor reserved
Salt and pepper to taste

Simmer broccoli, potatoes, onions, garlic, salt, pepper, and curry powder in the chicken broth 40 minutes or until potatoes are tender. Purée broccoli and potatoes in a food processor or blender and return to broth. Add cream to broccoli and broth mixture; add oysters and their liquor. Bring soup to a simmer and continue to cook 3 to 4 minutes or until edges of oysters curl. Take care not to overcook the oysters. Taste to correct seasoning. Serve immediately. Garnish each serving with reserved broccoli.

Ann K. Kahan
Stuart, Virginia

🐚 🐚 🐚 🐚 🐚 🐚

"Each Wednesday & Saturday, we dine of Fish all the Summer, always plenty of Rock, Perch & Crabs of often Sheeps-Head and Trout!" This excerpt is from the *Journal & Letters of Phillip Vickers Fithian, 1773-1774: A Plantation Tutor of the Old Dominion*, published in 1943.

Mr. Red's Oyster Stew

YIELD: 4 to 6 servings

1 pint small oysters, shucked and
  liquor reserved
1 tablespoon celery, finely chopped
1 green onion, minced
1 tablespoon Old Bay seafood
  seasoning

1 teaspoon salt
1/2 teaspoon coarse pepper
1 quart half and half cream
4 tablespoons creamery butter
1/4 teaspoon tabasco
1 teaspoon Worcestershire sauce
Cayenne pepper to taste

Combine in 2-quart sauce pan oysters in own liquor, celery, onion, Old Bay seasoning, salt, and coarse pepper. Bring mixture to boil over medium heat and simmer 3 to 4 minutes, stirring frequently. Remove mixture from heat. Add cream to mixture and bring to fast boil over medium-high heat, stirring continuously. Remove stew from heat as soon as mixture comes to fast boil. Blend in creamery butter, tabasco, and Worcestershire sauce. Sprinkle lightly with pepper. Serve immediately with oyster crackers or favorite soup cracker.

NOTE: Additional salt or hot sauce may be added to suit individual tastes.

C. B. Gambrell
Olney, Maryland

❦ ❦ ❦ ❦ ❦ ❦

Croaker: Chesapeake Bay Noisemaker

Among several fine attributes, the croaker has one major claim to fame: it does indeed croak. During World War II, a hydrophone network was set up across the entrance to the Chesapeake Bay to detect German submarines. The first spring the network was in operation, its speakers on the surface began to squawk incessantly. The network became useless until scientists were able to distinguish the noise as coming from croakers moving into the bay from their offshore wintering grounds!

The fish that foiled the United States government has the scientists still stumped in another way. Though they know the croaker croaks voluntarily, they don't know why. Croaking seems to increase during spawning season or when the fish is pursued or touched. The sound comes from a swim bladder which acts as a resonating chamber when the croaker vibrates its strong muscles against it.

If a croaker doesn't choose to croak, there are other ways to identify it. It has small dark spots on its upper body and a healthy set of "mutton chops," or rows of little barbs on each side of its jowl. It is often called a "hardhead" by fishermen because of its smooth, broad forehead, or "drum" because of its distinctive drum-like croak. Other nicknames includes "King Billy" and "grumbler." During the spawning season (August through November), the little fish may take on a rich golden color giving rise to the euphonic name, "golden croaker."

By any name, the mild, sweet-flavored pan fish is a favorite of both the commercial and sport fisherman.

Oysters and Spinach Soup

YIELD: 6 servings

1 quart fresh shucked oysters,
  drained and liquor reserved
1 10-ounce package frozen
  chopped spinach, thawed and
  drained dry
2 8-ounce bottles clam juice
4 tablespoons butter or margarine
1/2 cup flour
Water as needed
4 green onions, chopped
1/2 teaspoon ground nutmeg
1/2 teaspoon salt
1/2 teaspoon tabasco sauce
2 egg yolks
1 cup heavy cream

Remove any shell from oysters. Chop oysters in half and set aside. Purée spinach in blender with 1 bottle of the clam juice. Set aside. Over low heat, melt butter in stew pan; add flour, stirring until blended; then gradually add the remaining bottle of clam juice. Add enough water to the reserved oyster liquor to make 1 pint liquid. Pour into stew pan, stirring constantly until blended. Add the spinach, onion, nutmeg, salt, and tabasco sauce. Simmer about 20 minutes. In small bowl, mix together egg yolk and cream. Add 1/2 cup of the hot mixture to the egg mixture, stirring until blended. Pour the egg mixture into the soup mixture in stew pan. Add oysters and continue simmering until oysters curl at the edges, about 5 minutes cooking time. Serve in soup bowls. Place 1 lemon slice on top of each bowl of soup. Serve with crackers.

Ruth Dykes
Beltsville, Virginia

Oyster Stew

YIELD: 4 servings

4 tablespoons butter
1 pint oysters with juices
1-1/2 cups milk
1/2 cup heavy cream
2 tablespoons chopped parsley
1/2 teaspoon salt
Dash pepper

Melt butter in top of double boiler, add oysters, bring to boiling point but do not boil. Pour milk and cream over oysters. Place boiler over hot water. When oysters come to surface, add chopped parsley and seasonings. Serve.

Thomas L. Smith
South Hill, Virginia

Soupe des Huitres  (Oyster Soup)

John Durham of the C & O Restaurant in Charlottesville, Virginia, shared this simple-to-make but exotic-tasting soup at the 1983 Governor's Tasting.

YIELD: 8 servings

8 cups chicken stock
1/2 to 1 teaspoon tamari
(see note)

1/8 teaspoon freshly ground
ginger
1 pint select oysters

Combine stock, tamari, and ginger. Bring to a boil. Reduce heat to medium. Add oysters and cook until edges curl.
NOTE: Tamari is a spicy seasoning often used in curry.

Chef John Durham

Traditional Virginia Oyster Stew

YIELD: about 6 cups

1 pint Virginia oysters, shucked
and liquor reserved

1 quart milk
4 tablespoons butter or margarine
Salt and pepper to taste
Seafood seasoning to taste

Using 4-quart pan, cook oysters with liquor, over low heat until edges begin to curl. Add milk, butter, salt, and pepper. Heat slowly until hot; do not boil. For an extra zip, sprinkle seafood seasoning on each serving.

William Matthews
Hyattsville, Virginia

Savory Scallop Chowder

YIELD: 4 to 6 servings

1 pound bay scallops
3 cups half and half cream
1 cup clam juice
3 tablespoons butter

1 small onion, chopped
1 garlic clove, minced
1 tablespoon flour
1 1/2 cups finely diced potatoes
Salt and pepper to taste
Pinch nutmeg

Slice scallops, if large. Bring cream and clam juice to a simmer over low heat. In a large sauce pan, melt butter; sauté onion and garlic over low heat until softened. Stir in flour and cook 2 to 3 minutes. Slowly stir in the warmed liquids.

Bring the mixture just to the boiling point; add potatoes and simmer 10 minutes. Add scallops and seasonings to taste. Simmer 6 to 8 minutes or until potatoes and scallops are tender.

Sandra Carlin
Portsmouth, Virginia

Scallop Chowder

YIELD: 4 servings

3 small potatoes
Water as needed
Salt and pepper to taste
3 large scallops

2 tablespoons butter
2 tablespoons flour
1 cup milk
1 tablespoon cocktail sherry
1/4 teaspoon salt
Pinch pepper

Peel and chop potatoes into 1/2-inch cubes. Place in a 2-quart sauce pan with water barely covering them. Add salt and pepper. Bring to a boil and parboil for 5 minutes. Cut scallops into small, bite-size pieces. Place in cereal bowl and refrigerate until needed.

In stainless steel or enameled 2-quart sauce pan, melt butter over medium heat. Add flour gradually while stirring constantly with a wire whisk. Once well blended, slowly add milk, stirring constantly. Turn heat to low and cook, stirring constantly, until sauce begins to thicken. Place lid on pan, turn heat to warm, and set aside until next step is completed.

Drain potatoes, saving liquid. Pour liquid over scallops and let stand at room temperature for 3 minutes and then refrigerate. Add sherry, salt, and pepper to chowder. Add the potatoes and stir well. Cook over low heat until potatoes are tender, 5 to 10 minutes. When the potatoes are done, drain the scallops and add to chowder. Cook for 5 minutes.

Diane M. Capone
Hampton, Virginia

Blue Fish Chowder

YIELD: 1 quart

2 slices bacon, chopped
1 medium onion, chopped
1 pound fileted blue fish
1 cup chopped celery
2 large potatoes, peeled and diced

2-1/2 cups water
1-1/2 teaspoon salt
1/4 teaspoon pepper
3 tablespoons butter
1/4 cup flour
2 cups evaporated milk

Cook bacon until limp; add onions and sauté until bacon is crisp and onions are tender. Cut fish into bite-size pieces. Stir fish, celery, potatoes, water, salt, and pepper into sautéed mixture. Bring to boil; reduce heat and simmer covered 15 to 20 minutes or until potatoes are tender. Melt butter in heavy sauce pan over low heat; add flour and cook 1 minute stirring constantly. Gradually stir in milk; cook over medium heat stirring constantly until sauce is thickened and bubbly. Gradually stir white sauce into fish mixture; cook over medium heat, stirring constantly until chowder is thoroughly heated.

Charles R. Spacek
Portsmouth, Virginia

Virginia Croaker Chowder

YIELD: 12 servings

2 pounds Virginia croaker filets
1/4 pound fat salt pork, diced
1 medium onion, chopped
2 cups diced potatoes
2 cups water

1 quart milk
2/3 cup evaporated milk
8 soda crackers, crushed
3 tablespoons butter
2 tablespoons chopped parsley
2 teaspoons salt
1/8 teaspoon black pepper

Cut fish into bite-size chunks; sauté salt port until a delicate brown. Sauté onion under tender. Add potatoes and water and simmer until potatoes are tender. Add fish, simmer 5 minutes. Combine remaining ingredients and heat over low flame; don't boil. Add to fish mixture. Serve piping hot.

Margaret G. Killmon
Annandale, Virginia

Cream of Flounder Soup

YIELD: 4 to 6 servings

2 tablespoons butter
2 cups minced raw flounder filet

1 cup milk
1 cup heavy cream
1 teaspoon minced fresh dill
Salt and pepper to taste

Melt butter. Add flounder and cook about 7 minutes. Add milk, cream, and dill. Season with salt and pepper. Simmer for 30 minutes, stirring constantly. Top each serving with a sprig of dill.

Theresa Woodfolk
Charlottesville, Virginia

Flounder Chowder Fulgham

YIELD: 8 servings

3 pounds whole flounder
2 cups water
2 medium onions
Bacon drippings as needed
1/2 pound fresh mushrooms

3/4 cup (1-1/2 sticks) butter
7 medium potatoes
2 teaspoons salt
1/2 teaspoons white pepper
1 pint heavy cream
1/8 cup sherry
1 tablespoons sugar

Clean and filet flounder. Retain head, tail, and backbone and boil in 2 cups of water for 30 minutes. Strain and retain the broth. Dice onion and sauté slowly in bacon drippings. Dice mushrooms and sauté in one stick of butter. Dice potatoes and put into broth along with the fish and simmer together for one hour. Add mushrooms, onions, salt, and pepper. Simmer for 1/2 hour. Cool for one hour. Add cream, sherry, sugar, and remaining butter. Heat **slowly**. Do not boil!

Seaton B. Fulgham
Mechanicsville, Virginia

Flounder Chowder Smith

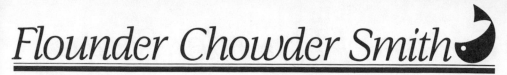

YIELD: 3 quarts

1/4 pound salt pork, cubed
6 medium-sized potatoes, diced
   (about 3 cups)
1/4 cup finely chopped onions
Salt and pepper to taste

2 cups cooked flounder, flaked
2 cups water
2 cups milk
1 tablespoon flour
1 tablespoon melted butter
Dash chopped parsley

Put pork cubes into hot skillet; sauté until light brown. Put layer of potatoes into sauce pan. Add onions on top of potatoes. Add sautéed pork cubes and juices. Salt and pepper to taste. Add layer of flaked flounder. Build layers alternately (potatoes and fish) until all ingredients are used. Add water, cover and simmer 20 minute. Add milk; add combined flour and melted butter. Stir with a fork to avoid breaking up potato cubes, until chowder boils. If desired, broken crackers, softened in a little milk may be added during last few minutes.

Thomas L. Smith
South Hill, Virginia

Spicy Flounder Stew

YIELD: 4 to 6 servings

2 pounds flounder filets
2 cups fish stock
1 cup cubed potatoes
2 large onions, diced
2 cups fresh white corn
1 cup cooked tomatoes
2 cups butterbeans

1 bell pepper, diced
2 teaspoons Old Bay seafood
   seasoning
1 tablespoon butter
1 bay leaf
1 stalk celery
Pinch oregano
1/2 teaspoon salt
Dash black or red pepper

Poach fish filets to remove skins. Place meat into stock. Add potatoes to stock and bring to a boil, reduce heat and cook for thirty minutes. Add all other ingredients and cook at a very low heat until vegetables are very tender. Adjust seasonings to taste. Resulting stew should be thick and spicy hot.

Hugh C. Rowland
Portsmouth, Virginia

Swashbuckler Flounder Stew

YIELD: 6 to 8 servings

4 medium onions, sliced
4 medium peeled potatoes, sliced
1 celery rib, chopped
2 pounds Virginia flounder
1 tablespoon salt

2 tablespoons butter
5 cups milk
1/2 cup sour cream
2 tablespoons dill pickle, grated
4 tablespoons horseradish
1 teaspoon parsley flakes

In a large sauce pan combine onions, potatoes, celery, fish, salt, and butter. Add milk. Bring to a bubbly boil, reduce heat and simmer 15 to 20 minutes. Remove from heat. Add sour cream, pickle, horseradish, and parsley. Stir to blend. Heat 5 minutes.

Nancy Sparks Morrison
Roanoke, Virginia

Virginia Flounder Chowder

YIELD: 4 servings

1 medium onion, chopped
2 stalks celery with leaves, diced
2 tablespoons butter or margarine
1 pound fresh or frozen filets of
    flounder, cut into large chunks
2 carrots sliced

1 46-ounce can tomato juice
1 cup frozen string beans
3/4 cup frozen corn kernels
1 bay leaf
1/4 teaspoon dry mustard
1/2 teaspoon ground thyme
2 medium potatoes, cubed
Salt and pepper to taste

In a Dutch oven or large heavy pot, sauté chopped onions and celery in butter until soft. Add all remaining ingredients except potatoes and cook, covered, for 25 minutes at a very low boil. Add potatoes and cook 20 minutes longer, stirring occasionally, or until potatoes are tender. Serve at once.

Ruth K. Maxwell
Norfolk, Virginia

Sea Trout Chowder with
Capers and Olives

YIELD: 4 servings

1/4 cup olive or vegetable oil
1 large onion, minced
1 garlic clove, minced
1 16-ounce can tomatoes with
    juice
3 sprigs of minced parsley
1/2 teaspoon dried thyme
1 bay leaf

1 pound trout filets, cut in 1-1/2-
    inch pieces
1/4 cup pitted small black olives
2 tablespoons drained capers
1 10-ounce can chicken broth or
    clam juice
1/2 soup can white wine
1-1/2 cups cooked, peeled, and
    cubed potatoes
Freshly ground pepper to taste

Heat oil. Add onion and sauté until softened and lightly browned, stirring. Add garlic. Cook 1 minute, stirring. Purée tomatoes and juice in blender. Add tomatoes and juice, parsley, thyme, and bay leaf. Cook mixture over moderately high heat for 15 minutes or until thickened and most of the liquid has evaporated. Add fish, black olives, capers, broth or clam juice, wine, potatoes, and pepper. Simmer over low heat for 6 to 8 minutes, or until fish flakes easily with a fork. Correct seasonings. Sprinkle servings with minced parsley and serve with slices of warm crusty French bread.

NOTE: This recipe can also be used for other fish filets.

Joan Gregory
Lively, Virginia

❀ ❀ ❀ ❀ ❀ ❀ ❀

Upon arriving at Jamestown, a colonist described the James River as "so stored with sturgeon and other sweet fish as no man's fortune has ever possessed the like."

Virginia Manhattan Spot Chowder

YIELD: about 6 servings

1 pound spot filets
1/4 cup chopped bacon (about 6
   strips)
1/2 cup chopped celery
1/2 cup chopped onions
1/4 cup ketchup

2 cups boiling water
1 tablespoon Worcestershire sauce
1 pound canned tomatoes
1/4 teaspoon each salt and pepper
1 cup diced potatoes
1/4 teaspoon thyme
1/4 teaspoon parsley
1/2 cup diced carrots

Cut fish filets into 1-inch pieces. Fry bacon till crisp. Add onions and cook till tender. Put into a large pot and add water, tomatoes, potatoes, carrots, celery, ketchup, and seasonings. Cover and simmer for 45 minutes. Add fish filets and cover and simmer for 10 minutes. Sprinkle with parsley and serve.

    NOTE: Any white meat fish such as croaker or flounder may be used.

Michael Kling
Bethesda, Maryland

❀ ❀ ❀ ❀ ❀ ❀ ❀

Blue Fish: Chesapeake Bay High Roller

Summer visitors to the beach are familiar with the blue fishes' offshore feeding frenzies which churn up the water and attract hundreds of hungry gulls. In an attempt to escape the crazy blues, small baitfish have even been known to leap upon the beach, evidently choosing the sunbathers over their greedy pursuers.

Blues literally live to eat. So insatiable are their appetites that they have been known to eat until full, regurgitate and eat again. Their mouths are full of sharp little teeth ready to capture any smaller fish that passes by, not excluding even baby blue fish.

Nicknames such as "chopper" and "snapper" reflect these voracious feeding habits. The more sedate phrase, "tailor blue" often is used when referring to smaller pan-sized blue fish.

Blue does not aptly describe the fish as its back is actually greenish in color fading down to a silvery belly.

The average size blue is generally larger than the popular tailor blues and the traditional method of preparation is fileting. Slicing away the dark meat on the larger filets will reduce the fishy flavor for those who like a milder-flavored fish.

Alexander's Virginia Bouillabaisse

"The Virginia waters are full of fish and shellfish suitable for our stew. Don't be intimidated by purists who will tell you bouillabaisse is only good in Marseille. As with many grand dishes, bouillabaisse originated as a humble fisherman's stew," said Chef Bridget Meagher. She was the chef of Alexander's in Roanoke, Virginia, when she served this bouillabaisse with a hint of citrus at the 1982 Governor's Tasting during Virginia Seafood Month.

YIELD: 8 servings

4 ounces olive oil
2 medium onions, chopped
1 stalk celery, chopped
2 large tomatoes, peeled and
    chopped
2 bay leaves
1 tablespoon fresh chopped basil
1/8 teaspoon saffron
1 tablespoon minced garlic
3 pounds mixed Virginia fish filets
    (trout, flounder, blue, croaker)
3 hard crabs, boiled and cracked
5 soft shell crabs
1 teaspoon chopped orange peel
Juice of 1 lemon

1 quart fish stock or bottled clam
    juice
1/2 pound scallops with liquid
1/2 pint oysters with liquid
2 tablespoons chopped parsley
Salt and pepper to taste
1 teaspoon Pernod (optional)
8 slices French bread, buttered
    and toasted

ROUILLE SAUCE
2 garlic cloves
1/2 teaspoon salt
1 egg
4 to 6 ounces olive oil
1/8 teaspoon saffron
1/4 teaspoon cayenne pepper

Heat oil in a heavy 7- to 10-quart pot. Add onions and celery and cook until soft. Add tomatoes, bay leaves, basil, saffron, and garlic. Cook 5 minutes. Then add firm-fleshed fish (trout and blue), hard crabs, orange peel, and lemon juice. Boil stock. Add to fish in pot, cover, and cook 7 minutes. Add tender fish (flounder, croaker), soft shell crabs; boil for 4 more minutes. Add scallops, oysters, and parsley and simmer for 3 minutes. Season with salt and pepper to taste. Add Pernod. Cover and remove from heat and allow to sit for a few minutes.

To make sauce, in a blender or processor, purée garlic with salt. Add egg and blend for 30 seconds. Slowly add olive oil, blending thoroughly. When sauce is smooth, add saffron and cayenne pepper. Transfer to sauce boat.

NOTE: Serving Recommendations — Arrange fish and seafood on heated platter. Pour broth into a tureen. Have 8 bowls and 8 plates ready. Place a slice of French bread in each bowl. Allow guests to ladle broth over French bread and eat as a soup for the first course. For second course, guests may then serve fish and shellfish on plates, seasoning with broth and the rouille.

Chef Bridget Meagher

Bountiful Bisque

YIELD: 6 servings

1 rib celery
1 green onion with top
2 cups water
1/4 teaspoon seafood seasoning
1/8 teaspoon black pepper
1/4 teaspoon salt
1/8 teaspoon cayenne pepper
3 teaspoons butter or margarine
2 cups milk

1/2 teaspoon parsley flakes OR 1 teaspoon chopped fresh parsley
1 cup flaked fish
1 cup crab meat
1 cup peeled, deveined shirmp
1/2 cup oysters
1-1/2 tablespoons instant mashed potatoes
1 cup heavy cream
4 ounces white wine

Chop celery and onion fine. Over high heat, place 2-or 2-1/2-quart sauce pan with the water, seasonings, celery, and onion. Bring to boil. Turn down to simmer. Let celery and onion cook until almost transparent, adding more hot water if necessary. Add butter or margarine. Add milk, parsley, and fish. Stir constantly. Add crab meat and shrimp. Add oysters. Add mashed potatoes to thicken. Stir well. Add cream. Stir. Add wine. Stir. Turn off completely. Stir again.

NOTE: Left over fried spot, boned and flaked, can be used, or any mild canned fish, such as bonito or other firm fish.

Lillian V. Stephenson
Norfolk, Virginia

Chesapeake Chowder

YIELD: 4 to 6 servings

1 large onion, chopped
1/2 cup chopped celery with leaves
1 large garlic clove, crushed
2 tablespoons butter or margarine
2 16-ounce cans tomatoes, cut up
1/2 cup dry white wine

1/2 cup minced parsley
Salt and pepper to taste
1/4 teaspoon chopped basil
1/4 teaspoon thyme
Tiny pinch saffron (optional)
1 pound flounder filet, cut into 1-inch chunks
12 ounces small raw shrimp, shelled and deveined

In large sauce pan sauté onion, celery, and garlic in butter until tender. Stir in tomatoes, wine, and seasonings. Cover and simmer 30 minutes. Add fish and simmer 4 minutes. Add shrimp and simmer 4 minutes. Let sit off heat, covered, for additional 5 minutes before serving.

Sandra Carlin
Portsmouth, Virginia

Sea and Shore Chowder

YIELD: 6 to 8 servings

2 medium onions, chopped
2 tablespoons vegetable oil
5 cups water
3 large potatoes, diced
2 stalks celery with leaves, diced
1 tablespoon salt
2 tablespoons chopped parsley
1/8 teaspoon savory or thyme
1 teaspoon black pepper
3 bay leaves
Dash garlic powder

3 slices bacon, fried crisp and crumbled
1-1/2 pounds flounder, cooked and flaked
1 pint clams, chopped
1 cup scallops, diced
1 cup crab meat
3 tablespoons flour
4 cups milk, at room temperature
1 17-ounce can cream-style corn
2 tablespoons oyster sauce
1 tablespoon sugar

Using a large stew pot, cook the onion in oil until translucent. Add the water, potatoes, celery, and next six ingredients. Cook over medium heat until vegetables are just tender. Remove bay leaves and stir in the bacon and seafood. Mix the flour with a bit of milk until smooth and add to pot with remaining milk. Stir in the corn, oyster sauce, and sugar. Adjust salt and seasoning to taste. Simmer for 1 hour. Do not boil. Stir gently now and then.

Anna Lea Steenburgen
Virginia Beach, Virginia

❀❀❀❀❀❀

In 1698 the General Assembly of Virginia took the first action in the New World against pollution. They found that the killing of whales within the capes destroyed quantities of fish and made the rivers "noisome and offensive." Therefore the Assembly petitioned the governor to issue a proclamation "forbidding all persons whatsoever to strike or kill any whales within the bay of Chesapeake in the limits of Virginia which we hope will prove an effectual means to prevent the many evils that arise therefrom."

Seafood Creole

YIELD: 4 to 6 servings

3/4 pound favorite seafood
   (scallops, fish, clams, shrimp,
   and/ or oysters)
1 cup chicken bouillon
2 tablespoons butter
1/4 cup chopped onion
1 garlic clove
6 olives
24 ounces canned tomatoes,
   slightly chopped
1 cup mushrooms
1/2 cup green pepper
1/2 bay leaf
1 teaspoon thyme
1 teaspoon parsley
1 teaspoon sugar
1 teaspoon salt
1/2 cup sherry or dry white wine
1/4 cup chili sauce

Using a large sauce pan, sauté seafood in butter until cooked, about 5 to 10 minutes. Combine all other ingredients and add to seafood. Cook until heated thoroughly, about 30 minutes.

Ulli Munroe
Virginia Beach, Virginia

Seafood Gumbo Martin

YIELD: 8 servings

1 cup flour
1 cup vegetable oil
1 pound crab meat
2 pounds shrimp, cleaned
1/2 pound flounder or bluefish
   filets, cut in bite-size pieces
1/2 cup (1 stick) butter
1 cup chopped onions
1/2 cup chopped celery
1/2 cup chopped green pepper
4 garlic cloves, minced
2 cups cooked, chopped okra
3 quarts water
1 tablespoon Worcestershire sauce
Salt and pepper to taste
Dash cayenne pepper
1/2 pint oysters
1 16-ounce can whole tomatoes
1/2 cup chopped green onion tops
1/2 cup parsley

Brown flour in heated oil and set aside. In a large pot, sauté in melted butter the onions, celery, green peppers, garlic, and okra for 10 minutes. Add to the vegetables the browned flour, water, Worcestershire, and seasonings. Cook on low for one hour. Add all remaining ingredients, except onion tops and parsley, and cook for another hour. Add onion tops and parsley and simmer 15 minutes. Serve in soup plate over boiled rice.

Vickie Martin
Virginia Beach, Virginia

Seafood Gumbo Spacek

YIELD: 12 servings

3/4 cup flour
1/4 to 1/3 cup bacon grease
4 tablespoons butter
1 bell pepper, finely diced
1 large onion, finely diced
1 bunch green onions, chopped
3 celery stalks, finely chopped
1/4 cup diced parsley

2 garlic cloves, finely diced
1 tomato, chopped
1-1/2 pounds shelled, deveined
   shrimp
1 pint oysters
1/2 pound crab meat
2 tablespoons salt
1 tablespoon black pepper
1/2 teaspoon red pepper
2 teaspoons file powder

Brown flour in bacon grease over low heat. Sauté in butter the bell pepper, onion, green onion, celery, parsley, garlic, and tomato. Add sauté to bacon mixture in 10-quart pot with 1/2 gallon water. Add salt, black pepper, and red pepper. Cover pot and simmer for two hours. Add 1/2 gallon water to pot and bring back to a slow boil. Add shrimp and cover for 10 minutes. Add oysters and juice. Simmer for 5 minutes. Add crab meat, turn off heat, cover, and let sit for 15 minutes. Uncover, add filé powder, and serve over rice.

Charles R. Spacek
Portsmouth, Virginia

🐚🐚🐚🐚🐚🐚

Spot: Norfolk, Virginia's Claim to Piscatorial Fame

The waters of the Chesapeake Bay off Norfolk, Virginia, are such prime spot fishing grounds that out-of-town menus often list this small, sweet fish as "Norfolk Spot." As early as the Revolutionary War, Norfolkians were enamoured with the little fish. When they chose to honor Lafayette's contribution to the war, they renamed the fish the "Lafayette Spot."

Prior to spawning season in the fall, the spot takes on a golden color much like its cousin the croaker. At that time the fish are often referred to as "Ocean View Yellow Bellies" because they congregate to feed off Ocean View, a Norfolk neighborhood on the Chesapeake Bay.

The spot's most recognizable feature is the dark shoulder spot behind the gill covers, although the male spot may also make a weak croak like its cousin. Legend has it that the spot came from the fingers of St. Peter, the renowned Biblical fisherman.

Though small, rarely over a pound in size, the spot is considered the best pan fish around. Many Tidewater Virginians salt the tiny fillets down in crocks for later eating during the winter months. Nothing, however, quite beats a spot fresh from the water and into the pan. Rolled in cornmeal and quickly fried in hot fat is the traditional way of cooking them.

Seafood Gumbo, Bayou Style

YIELD: about 1 quart

2 strips bacon, cut fine
3 large onions, cut fine
1 medium green pepper, cut fine
1 stalk celery, cut fine
3 tablespoons flour
3 fresh or 1 16-ounce can
   tomatoes

2 cups fresh or frozen okra
2 pounds peeled shrimp
1 pint oysters
1 pound crab meat
6 cups water
3 tablespoons Old Bay seasoning
Dash tabasco
1/4 teaspoon black pepper
2 tablespoons brown gravy sauce

In large, heavy skillet cook bacon over medium heat. Add onion, bell pepper, and celery. Cook until clear and soft. Add flour, stirring constantly until flour begins to turn brown. Stir in tomatoes and okra. Cook 2 minutes. Add shrimp and stir until pink. Transfer to large soup pot. Add oysters and crab; slowly stir in water 1 cup at a time. Stir in Old Bay seasoning, tabasco, and pepper. Add brown gravy sauce. Bring to slight boil and turn to low heat. Allow to simmer 3 to 5 hours. Stir occasionally. Serve over rice if desired.

Peggy N. Martin
Covesville, Virginia

Southern Seafood Chowder

YIELD: 4 to 6 servings

1 can minced clams
1 quart tomatoes
2 cups water
1 potato, peeled and cubed
2 onions, thinly sliced
1 bell pepper, chopped
1 garlic clove, minced

1 bay leaf
1/2 teaspoon salt
1/4 teaspoon basil
Dash black pepper
Dash tabasco sauce
1/2 pound okra, sliced
1/2 pound flounder, cut into bite-
   size pieces

Drain clams, reserving liquid. Combine clam liquid, tomatoes, water, potatoes, onions, pepper, garlic, bay leaf, salt, basil, pepper, tabasco, and okra. Bring to a boil, reduce heat, cover, and simmer until potatoes are done, about 30 to 45 minutes. Stir in clams and flounder and cook until flounder is done, about 8 minutes. Remove bay leaf before serving.

Kathryn G. Westbury (Mrs. T. J., Jr.)
Charlottesville, Virginia

Willoughby Spit Chowder

YIELD: 6 servings

1/2 pound bacon
1 large onion, finely chopped
1/2 cup (1 stick) butter, divided
1 pound scallops
1 pound shrimp, peeled
1 pound flounder filets
1/2 cup white wine, divided
2 tablespoons lemon juice
1 10-ounce can cream of shrimp
  soup
1 10-ounce can cream of mushroom soup

1 10-ounce can New England clam
  chowder
1 pint light cream
1/4 cup dry sherry
1 tablespoon Old Bay seafood
  seasoning
1 teaspoon white pepper
1 teaspoon dry mustard
1 pound picked crab meat
1/2 pound minced clams
1 pound sharp Cheddar cheese,
  grated

Preheat oven to 350°. Cook bacon until crisp. Crumble. Set aside. Cook onion in 1/3 stick butter until soft. Set aside. In a foil-lined roasting pan, cook scallops, shrimp, and flounder filets in 1/4 cup white wine, lemon juice, and 2/3 stick of butter for 15 minutes. In 8-quart pot combine soups, cream, 1/4 cup white wine, dry sherry, and spices. Heat over medium flame until well mixed. Add crab meat, clams, bacon, onion, and contents of roasting pan. Cook over low flame for 10 minutes. Stir often. Add grated Cheddar cheese. Stir until cheese dissolves in chowder. Cook 5 minutes at medium heat and serve.

Robert Gilson
Norfolk, Virginia

🐚 🐚 🐚 🐚 🐚 🐚

One day when Captain John Smith was on an exploring expedition near the mouth of the Rappahannock River, he set out to spear some fish with his sword. Unwittingly, he speared a stingray. The ray lashed Smith's leg with its poisonous barbed tail so viciously that he became desperately ill and directed his companions to dig his grave. Smith, however, recovered in time to "eate the fish" for dinner. The site of his disaster is commemorated forever with the name "Stingray Point."

Filet of Virginia
Salads and Side Dishes

Avocado and Crab Meat Ring

YIELD: 6 to 8 servings

3 envelopes unflavored gelatin
1-1/2 cups water
1 pound crab meat
1 large ripe avocado (3/4 pound or more)
1 cup sour cream

3 tablespoons grated onion
1 cup mayonnaise
1/4 cup thinly sliced celery
1-1/2 teaspoons salt
1/8 teaspoon pepper
1/4 cup lemon juice
Salad greens

Sprinkle gelatin over water in top of double boiler; let stand 5 minutes to soften. Place over hot water; stir until gelatin is dissolved. Refrigerate until consistency of unbeaten egg white, about 30 minutes. Flake crab. Cut avocado in half lengthwise. Remove pit and peel. Cut into chunks and press through sieve or mash to smooth consistency. Gently toss crab with avocado, sour cream, onion, mayonnaise, celery, salt, pepper, and lemon juice. Mix well. Fold into gelatin until well combined. Turn into 6-1/2-cup ring mold. Refrigerate until firm, about 3 hours.

To serve: Run spatula around edge of mold to loosen. Invert over serving platter and shake gently to release. (A warm towel held over mold will facilitate removal.) Surround with greens and other garnishes of choice.

Marilyn C. Fall
Virginia Beach, Virginia

Chesapeake Bay Crab Curry

This curried crab salad is a favorite at The Surrey House Restaurant in Surry, Virginia and was served at the 1982 Governor's Tasting.

YIELD: 6 to 8 servings

1 cup mayonnaise

1/2 cup chopped celery
1 pound backfin crab meat
2 teaspoons curry powder

Remove all shell from crab meat. Dip crab meat in lemon juice. Add celery to crab meat. Mix in mayonnaise and curry powder. Toss lightly. Chill well. Serve on a bed of fresh lettuce or stuff in ripe tomato.

Chef Elsie Evans

Crab-Avocado Salad

YIELD: 8 servings

1-1/2 cups fresh flaked Virginia
    blue crab meat
1 10-ounce package frozen English
    peas, thawed but not cooked
1 8-ounce carton sour cream

6 green onions, finely chopped
6 slices bacon, cooked and
    crumbled
1/2 teaspoon salt
1/4 teaspoon pepper
2 avocados, sliced

Combine all ingredients except avocado; gently toss. Chill thoroughly. Serve on avocado slices.

Margaret G. Killmon
Annandale, Virginia

Crab Louis

YIELD: 4 to 6 servings

1 cup mayonnaise
1/4 cup chili sauce
2 tablespoons chopped onion
3 tablespoons chopped green
    pepper

2 tablespoons lemon juice
1 tablespoon Worcestershire sauce
1/2 tablespoon tabasco sauce
1 pound crab meat

Combine mayonnaise, chili sauce, onion, green pepper, lemon juice, Worcestershire, and tabasco. Blend well. Gently toss in crab meat.

Mrs. L. V. French
Mechanicsville, Virginia

Crab Meat Salad

YIELD: 6 servings

1 pound fresh crab meat
1 medium green pepper, chopped
1/2 teaspoon celery seed
1/2 cup mayonnaise

1 tablespoon mustard
1 teaspoon seafood seasoning
1 teaspoon vinegar
1 teaspoon sugar
Dash tabasco
Granishes: parsley, tomato

Remove any shell or cartilage from crab meat. Combine all ingredients; mix well. Shape mixture in a mound on serving dish; garnish with parsley and tomato, and serve.

Martha Drummond Curry
Martha's Cooking Seafood Cookbook
Reedville, Virginia

Crab Meat Salad Villemagne

YIELD: 4 servings

2 cups finely shredded lettuce
1 pound crab meat
1 tablespoon lemon juice
1 tablespoon Worcestershire sauce
1 cup chopped celery

12 ripe olives, sliced
1 garlic clove, crushed
1 teaspoon Old Bay seafood
   seasoning
Salt and pepper to taste
1 cup mayonnaise

Shred lettuce in large bowl and add crab meat. Pour lemon juice and Worcestershire over crab meat. Add celery and olives; add garlic and Old Bay seasoning. (More or less can be added according to taste.) Add salt and pepper. Mix with mayonnaise. Serve on lettuce leaf.

Mrs. M. B. Villemagne
Richmond, Virginia

Curried Virginia Crab and Corn Salad

YIELD: 4 to 6 servings

2 cups fresh Virginia lump blue
    crab meat
2 cups yellow corn kernels,
    cooked, drained, and cooled

1/2 cup plain yogurt
1-1/2 teaspoon finely chopped
    green onion
1/2 teaspoon salt
1/2 teaspoon curry powder
Sliced kiwi fruit, optional

Combine the fresh Virginia crab meat and cooked corn in a large bowl. Set aside. In a smaller bowl mix the yogurt, onion, salt, and curry powder. Pour this dressing over the crab and corn mixture, tossing gently. Chill before serving. Serve in a flat decorative seashell and/or a bed of bib lettuce. Garnish with the sliced and peeled kiwi fruit.

Susan Kingsbury
McLean, Virginia

Fresh Crab Salad

YIELD: 4 servings

1 pound fresh crab meat
1/2 cup minced celery
1 teaspoon grated onion

1 tablespoon minced pimento
1/4 teaspoon salt
2 tablespoons lemon juice
Mayonnaise to taste

Combine crab, celery, onion, and pimento. Sprinkle with salt and lemon juice. Add mayonnaise, just enough to moisten. Mix well. Serve on bed of lettuce leaves, sprinkled with minced parsley. Serve with additional mayonnaise.

Debra S. Clark
Roanoke, Virginia

Summer Crab Salad

YIELD: 4 servings

2 ounces slivered almonds
1 cup chopped celery
1/3 cup diced green pepper
1-1/2 cup green, seedless grapes,
    halved

2 ounces coarsely grated Parmesan
    cheese
1 pound crab meat
1/8 teaspoon black pepper
1/2 cup mayonnaise

Toast almonds in oven and cool. Combine all ingredients except mayonnaise in large bowl and toss thoroughly. Add mayonnaise and continue tossing until all ingredients are moistened. Chill one hour before serving on spinach or lettuce leaves with tomato wedges.

Linda Marley Smith
Portsmouth, Virginia

Sunshine Crab Salad

YIELD: 6 servings

1 pound backfin crab meat
1/2 teaspoon salt
1/2 teaspoon lemon-pepper
    seasoning
1/2 cup finely chopped celery
1/4 cup finely chopped green
    onion
2 hard-boiled eggs, finely chopped
1/3 cup mayonnaise
1/3 cup plain yogurt

1/2 teaspoon dry mustard
1 teaspoon grated orange peel
1/4 cup finely chopped fresh
    parsley
1 2-ounce jar pimento slices,
    drained
Shredded lettuce as needed
1 ripe avocado, peeled, seeded,
    and sliced
Optional garnish:
    1 orange, seeded and sliced.
    Cut each slice in half.

Remove any cartilage or shell from crab meat. Place crab meat in a large mixing bowl. Add salt, lemon-pepper seasoning, celery, onion, and chopped egg. In small bowl, mix together: mayonnaise, yogurt, mustard, and orange peel. Add this mixture to the crab mixture. Stir gently until blended. Place salad mixture over a bed of shredded lettuce. Scatter parsley over top salad. Arrange avocado slices and pimento slices evenly spaced over salad. Garnish dish with orange slices placed attractively around salad.

Ruth Dykes
Beltsville, Maryland

Cold Scallop and Pasta Salad

YIELD: 4 to 6 servings

2 pounds tomatoes, peeled, seeded, and chopped
3/4 cup olive oil or salad oil
3 tablespoons red wine vinegar
3 garlic cloves, finely chopped
2 shallots, finely chopped
1 to 1-1/2 tablespoons finely chopped, firmly packed fresh basil

1-1/2 to 2 teaspoons finely chopped, firmly packed fresh oregano
Freshly ground black pepper to taste
1-1/2 pounds bay scallops (or ocean scallops, quartered) poached in dry white wine
1/2 pound fresh linguine

Combine all ingredients through black pepper and marinate in refrigerator several hours or overnight.

Add scallops. Cook pasta al dente; drain and quickly rinse with cold water. Add to other ingredients. Toss well. Refrigerate. Correct seasoning before serving.

Mary Reid Barrow
Virginia Beach, Virginia

🐚🐚🐚🐚🐚🐚

Coquina Clams: Beach Sparklers

Though unavailable commercially, the little multi-colored coquina clams which show up in the swash as they are uncovered by an incoming wave make a delicious clear soup. Using a colander or sieve rinse the sand from the clams as they are gathered. Use two cups of water to two quarts of clams. Boil gently for 10 minutes and strain into cups.

U.VA.'s Orange and Blue (Fish) Salad

YIELD: 4 servings

1-1/2 to 2 pounds blue fish filet
3 cups white rice, cooked
1 cup wild rice, cooked
1 cup celery, sliced or chopped
4 green onions, cleaned and cut in
    1/2-inch pieces
Grated peel of one orange
Orange slices
Salt and ground pepper

SAUCE
1 cup mayonnaise
1 cup sour cream
Juice of one orange
2 tablespoons grated orange peel

Cook the blue fish by boiling until done. Cool, remove skin, and flake meat or cut in 1-inch cubes. Toss rice, celery, green onions, and orange peel together. Season with salt and pepper; toss in blue fish. Set aside or refrigerate. Bring to room temperature before serving.

To make sauce, blend mayonnaise, sour cream, fresh orange juice, and peel.

To assemble, put rice salad on platter with lettuce leaves around edge and surround with orange slices. Sprinkle with fresh ground pepper and serve with dressing.

Barbara Wheeler
Charlottesville, Virginia

🐚🐚🐚🐚🐚🐚

The Indians had a way of catching large sturgeon when the fish migrated upriver to spawn that became a contest of athletic ability and courage. First the brave hooked the sturgeon by flinging a noose over its tail and holding fast. By grabbing on for dear life, the Indian would stay with the enraged sturgeon which would flail, dive and swim as fast as it could. He "would not let go till with swimming, wading, and diving he had tired the sturgeon and brought it ashore," wrote Robert Beverley in *The History of Present State of Virginia*, 1705.

Flounder Salad

YIELD: 6 to 8 servings

2 cups cooked, flaked flounder
1 cup chopped celery
1/2 cup chopped onions
1/2 cup chopped dill pickle

1/2 cup chopped walnuts
1/2 cup mayonnaise or salad
   dressing
1 tablespoon lemon juice
1/2 teaspoon salt

Combine fresh, celery, onions, pickle, and walnuts. Mix together mayonnaise, lemon juice, and salt. Add dressing to fish mixture. Toss lightly and chill. Serve on lettuce, with crackers, or in a wedged tomato.
   NOTE: Fish may be cooked by poaching or steaming.

Maxie S. Britt
Richmond, Virginia

Golden Flounder Salad

YIELD: 4 to 6 servings

2 tablespoons butter
1 medium onion, diced
Pinch dried oregano
Dash curry powder

2 pinches dried parsley
2 medium flounder filets
1/2 teaspoon lemon juice
1 cup chopped fresh mushroom
1/2 cup alfalfa sprouts
1 bunch fresh spinach, shredded

In sauce pan, melt butter at low setting, and sauté onion. Add oregano, curry, and parsley. Cut filets into bite-size pieces and add to mixture. Stir and turn until flounder is done and turns golden brown. Add lemon juice, chopped fresh mushrooms, and sprouts. Stir quickly for about one minute, then turn out mixture onto a bed of fresh spinach.

Sally A. Gravely
Roanoke, Virginia

Hot Seafood Salad

This seafood salad, created for the 1983 Governor's Tasting by Joseph Hoggard of the Ships Cabin in Norfolk, Virginia, provides a refreshing change from the traditional chilled versions.

YIELD: 2 servings

3 ounces lettuce, chopped
3 ounces backfin crab meat
3 ounces cooked scallops, chopped
1-1/2 ounces shredded Monterey
    Jack cheese
1 tablespoon butter

1/4 garlic clove, chopped
1 ounce white wine
1 pepperoncini pepper, chopped
1/2 stalk celery, chopped
5 broccoli flowers
2 ounces tomatoes, chopped
1 ounce onion, chopped
1 ounce mushrooms, sliced

Place chopped lettuce on a plate. Arrange crab meat and scallops on lettuce and sprinkle cheese over mixture. Heat butter and garlic in sauté pan until garlic browns; add wine and flame. Add remaining ingredients and simmer for 2 minutes. Pour over lettuce, crab meat, and cheese.

Chef Joseph Hoggard

Hot Seafood Salad Almondine

YIELD: 6 servings

2 tablespoons lemon juice
3/4 cup mayonnaise
1 teaspoon salt
2 cups finely chopped celery
4 hard-boiled eggs, chopped
1 teaspoon minced onion
3/4 cup cream of chicken soup,
    condensed

1 pound fresh backfin crab meat,
    picked
1/2 pound fresh bay scallops
1/2 cups crushed potato chips
1 cup shredded sharp Cheddar
    cheese
2/3 cup slivered almonds

Preheat oven to 375°. Mix together in medium bowl, lemon juice, mayonnaise, salt, celery, eggs, onion, and soup. Fold in crab meat and scallops. Pour into 2- to 3-quart casserole. Sprinkle over with potato chips, cheese, and almonds. Bake for 25 minutes. Serve on bed of green lettuce, garnished with tomato quarters and black olives.

Karen Anderson
Blacksburg, Virginia

Neptune's Delight Salad

YIELD: 4 servings

DRESSING
1/2 cup sour cream
1/2 cup mayonnaise
1 tablespoon seafood cocktail
    sauce

SALAD
6 ounces backfin crab meat

12 ounces frozen, tiny shrimp
    (thawed)
Boston lettuce leaves, crisped

GARNISH
2 hard-boiled eggs, quartered
    lengthwise
1 medium tomato, cut in 8 wedges

Mix dressing ingredients together and refrigerate until ready to put salad together. Toss seafood and dressing together lightly. Place on bed of lettuce leaves. Alternate wedges of egg and tomato around the salad.

Diane M. Capone
Hampton, Virginia

Seafood and Seashell Salad

YIELD: 4 servings

8 ounces cooked seashell macaroni,
    chilled
4 green onions, sliced
1/2 cup finely chopped celery
1/2 cup pitted black olives, sliced
1/2 pound shrimp, cooked and
    peeled
1/2 pound backfin crab meat
1/2 cup EACH of mayonnaise and
    sour cream

Salt and pepper to taste
4 large lettuce leaves, washed and
    dried
1 8-1/2-ounce can artichoke
    hearts, chilled
2 medium tomatoes, quartered
2 tablespoons chopped fresh
    parsley
4 wedges lemon

Mix together gently the macaroni, green onions, celery, olives, shrimp, crab, mayonnaise, sour cream, salt, and pepper. Place one lettuce leaf on each of 4 salad plates. Divide salad mixture among plates on top of leaves. Surround salad with artichoke hearts and tomato wedges. Garnish each salad with parsley and a lemon wedge.

Sandra Carlin
Portsmouth, Virginia

Shrimp and Crab Salad

YIELD: 4 to 6 servings

1 3- to 4-ounce can black olives,
    divided
1/2 pound cooked and peeled
    shrimp

3/4 cup mayonnaise
1 pound white crab meat
1 cup diced celery
1 teaspoon lemon herb seasoning
Dash garlic powder
Salt and pepper to taste

Reserve half the olives for garnish, and quarter those remaining. Mix ingredients in order given. Toss and serve on bed of lettuce. Garnish with whole black olives and tomato wedges if desired.

Virginia Garber
Richmond, Virginia

Supreme Seafood Salad

YIELD: 4 servings

1/4 cup chopped green pepper
1/4 cup chopped celery
1 2-ounce jar chopped pimento,
    drained
1 teaspoon Old Bay seafood
    seasoning

3 tablespoons lemon juice
1/2 cup mayonnaise
1/2 pound cooked, peeled shrimp
1/2 pound crab meat, drained and
    flaked
Lettuce as needed
Tomato wedges for garnish
Parsley for garnish

Stir together pepper, celery, and pimento. Combine seafood seasoning, lemon juice, and mayonnaise. Add to vegetable mixture. Gently stir in crab meat and shrimp. Place on lettuce bed and garnish with tomato wedges and parsley.

Shirley Jean Lewis
Charlottesville, Virginia

Chesapeake Style Clam Fritters

This recipe for Chesapeake Style Clam Fritters was offered for the 1983 Governor's Tasting by Bette Nohe of Hilda Crockett's Chesapeake House located on Tangier Island, Virginia.

YIELD: about 2 dozen small patties

1 quart minced clams
1 egg, beaten
2 tablespoons dehydrated minced
    onions
1 teaspoon black pepper
1/3 cup pancake mix
Vegetable oil for frying

Combine first four ingredients and mix well. Thicken the mixture with the pancake mix until the consistency is thick enough to form small-to medium-size pancakes. Using an iron skillet, heat 1/2 to 1 inch of oil over high heat. (Let it heat up well before adding patties). Place patties in oil and then turn heat down to medium. Cook until well browned on each side and drain.

Chef Bette Nohe

Clam Frittos

YIELD: about 2 dozen small patties

2 cups chopped, drained clams,
    liquid reserved
2 finely chopped medium onions
1/2 cup chopped green chilies
1-1/2 cups flour
1-1/2 teaspoons baking powder
1 egg
1/2 teaspoon minced fresh parsley
Pinch red pepper flakes
Pinch paprika
Salt to taste
Reserved clam juice
Bacon fat and corn oil for frying

Combine all ingredients except fat and oil. Use only enough clam juice to create a batter consistency. Add milk if not enough juice. Let stand for 30 minutes. Use equal parts of bacon fat and corn oil to a depth of two inches in a heavy large skillet. Heat over medium-high heat. Drop clam mixture into fat by tablespoons and fry until dark golden brown. Drain well on paper towels. Serve with lemon and tartar sauce.

Sandra Carlin
Portsmouth, Virginia

Photo - Clams and Oysters

A bushel of clams and oysters in the shell needn't be too overwhelming. "How to Bisect a Bivalve" on page 253 gives all the tricks of the shucking trade.

Clam Corn Casserole

YIELD: 6 servings

1/2 pound minced clams
Milk as needed
3 eggs, beaten
1 tablespoon minced onion

2 tablespoons chopped pimento
1/2 teaspoon salt
Dash cayenne pepper
1 cup cream-style corn
1/2 cup buttered cracker crumbs
1 tablespoon melted butter

Preheat oven to 350°. Drain liquid from clams; add enough milk to make 1 cup liquid and combine with beaten eggs. Add remaining ingredients and pour into 1-1/2-quart greased casserole. Bake for about 45 minutes.

Maxine R. Harrison
Salem, Virginia

Crab Jupiter

YIELD: 4 servings

MARINADE
3 tablespoons lemon juice
1/4 to 1/2 garlic clove, diced fine
1/4 teaspoon Old Bay seasoning

1 pound Virginia backfin crab
    meat, picked
3 to 4 tablespoons finely diced
    celery heart
2 tablespoons finely diced onion
1/2 tablespoon olive oil
2 to 3 hard-boiled eggs, diced

1/2 cup diced Swiss cheese
1 teaspoon pimento slices
Several sprigs fresh parsley
1/3 cup mayonnaise
6 ounces fettucine, cooked
Bread crumbs as needed

SAUCE
1/4 cup dry white wine
1 tablespoon melted butter or
    margarine
1 tablespoon flour

Preheat oven to 400°. Prepare the marinade by blending lemon juice, garlic, and Old Bay seasoning. Lightly mix crab meat in this marinade and refrigerate.

Sauté celery and onion in olive oil. Gently combine mayonnaise, crab meat, celery, onion, eggs, cheese, pimento, and parsley.

Place a thin layer of fettucine in a lightly greased casserole dish. Spoon the crab meat mixture over the noodles and top with a thin sprinkling of bread crumbs.

Combine sauce ingredients and drizzle over the crab mixture. Bake for 10 minutes. Garnish with cherry tomatoes, lemon slices, and tabasco sauce.

Michael S. Forbes
Troy, Virginia

Crab Meat Casserole

YIELD: 4 servings

6 ounces crab meat
1 10-ounce can cream of shrimp
  soup

2/3 cup milk
1 cup sour cream
2 cups uncooked fine egg noodles
1/3 cup shredded sharp Cheddar
  cheese

Preheat oven to 350°. Drain crab meat. Blend soup, milk, and sour cream. Stir in noodles and crab meat. Place in 10-by-6-inch greased dish; top with cheese. Bake for 35 minutes.

Mrs. L. V. French
Mechanicsville, Virginia

Crab Meat Chesapeake

YIELD: 4 servings

3 tablespoons butter (preferably
  unsalted), divided
4 whole artichoke hearts
2 tablespoons chopped green
  onions
1/2 teaspoon anchovy paste
1 cup heavy cream
1/4 cup dry white wine or
  vermouth

1/2 teaspoon freshly ground
  coriander
1/2 teaspoon basil
1/2 teaspoon cayenne pepper
1/2 teaspoon thyme
1/2 pound lump crab meat
Salt and pepper to taste
1/4 cup bread crumbs
1/4 cup grated Parmesan cheese

Melt 2 tablespoons butter and sauté artichoke hearts and green onions over moderately low heat for approximately 10 minutes or until tender. Purée artichoke hearts and onion along with the anchovy paste and 1 tablespoon of the cream. In a small sauce pan, pour the remaining of the cream. Add artichoke purée, wine, and spices. Cook over moderately low heat, stirring constantly, approximately 15 minutes until sauce has thickened. Sauté crab meat briefly in 1 tablespoon butter (2 to 3 minutes). Pour the sauce over crab meat and cook 2 to 3 minutes more over medium heat until well blended and creamy. Add salt and pepper to taste. Spoon into individual ramekins or small gratin dish. Mix bread crumbs and Parmesan cheese and sprinkle over crab meat. Broil until top is nicely browned.

Elizabeth W. Donnelly
Charlottesville, Virginia

Crab Meat Fantastic

YIELD: 10 servings

1/2 pound backfin crab meat
1/2 cup mayonnaise

1/2 avocado, chopped
2 ounces black caviar
Lemon juice to taste
Salt and pepper to taste

Pick over crab meat to remove all shell. Combine balance of the ingredients; add crab meat and mix gently. Serve in small scallop shells or ramekins.

Joan Gregory
Lively, Virginia

Crab Meat Rockefeller

YIELD: 12 servings

12 thick slices of tomato
2 10-ounce packages frozen
    chopped spinach
1 cup soft bread crumbs
3/4 cup melted butter or margarine

1/2 pound flaked fresh crab meat
6 beaten eggs
1 cup finely chopped onions
1/2 cup grated medium sharp
    cheese
1/2 teaspoon garlic salt
Tabasco to taste

Preheat oven to 350°. Place tomato slices in flat greased casserole dish. Cook and drain spinach according to package instructions. Mix soft bread crumbs in melted butter or margarine. Add spinach to bread mixture and all other ingredients. Form into patties or mounds and put on tomato slices. Bake for 12 to 15 minutes. Serve hot.

Nancy H. Aden
Midlothian, Virginia

Crab Meat Treasure

Samih Husein of Virginia Beach's Lynnhaven Fish House furnished this recipe for the 1983 Governor's Tasting.

YIELD: 4 servings

1 pound backfin crab meat
1 cup bread crumbs
4 medium eggs
2 tablespoons mayonnaise
1 tablespoon prepared mustard
1 tablespoon vegetable oil
1 teaspoon sugar
Salt and pepper to taste

STUFFING
1/4 pound backfin crab meat

2 tablespoons chopped onion
1 medium garlic clove, minced
1 pinch parsley
2 tablespoons sliced toasted almonds
Dash salt, pepper, thyme, oregano, and cumin
2 tablespoons butter
2 tablespoons grated Cheddar cheese
2 tablespoons creme de menthe

Mix crab meat, bread crumbs, eggs, mayonnaise, mustard, oil, sugar, salt, and pepper. Shape into 8 medium-thick discs, each large enough to contain and be folded around stuffing. Make stuffing by mixing the 1/4 pound of crab meat, onion, garlic, parsley, almonds, and spices. Sauté mixture in butter over medium-low heat until heated thoroughly. Add cheese and creme de menthe. Divide sautéed stuffing and place into center of each disc. After folding edges of disc over stuffing, gently mold by hand into desired shape (either oval or round). Deep fry until golden brown.

Chef Samih Husein

Festive Crab Stuffing for Chicken or Turkey

YIELD: Enough for a 10- to 16-pound bird

1 15-ounce package stuffing mix
1 package dry onion soup mix
1 medium green pepper

2 to 3 stalks celery
About 1/2 cup (1 stick) butter, at room temperature
2 to 3 cups crab meat
2 eggs
Water as needed

Combine ingredients using enough water to make mixture slightly moist.

Suzan R. Brooks
Virginia Beach, Virginia

Alexander's Oysters Suzette

This oyster dish was created by Chef Bridget Meagher for Alexander's in Roanoke, Virginia, and was served at the 1982 Governor's Tasting.

YIELD: 6 to 8 servings

1-1/2 quarts fresh oysters, well drained and patted dry with paper towels
3 tablespoons flour, divided
1 cup chopped green onions with tops
1/4 cup chopped green pepper
1/2 teaspoon cayenne pepper
12 slices lean bacon, fried crisp and chopped

6 ounces sharp Cheddar cheese, grated
3 ounces fresh Parmesan cheese, grated
2 cups French bread crumbs
4 ounces olive oil
4 ounces melted butter
2 teaspoons chopped garlic
2 teaspoons chopped parsley

Preheat oven to 400°. Grease bottom and sides of a 2-quart rectangular casserole. Sprinkle with 1 tablespoon flour. Pour oysters into casserole. Mix in green onions, green pepper, 2 tablespoons flour, and cayenne pepper. Sprinkle with chopped bacon, and then cover with a layer of the Cheddar and Parmesan cheeses. Toss bread crumbs with parsley and garlic. Mix in melted butter and olive oil. Spread the crumb mixture over casserole. Bake for 25 minutes or until topping is brown. Do not overbake.

Chef Bridget Meagher

✿ ✿ ✿ ✿ ✿ ✿

"Oysters there be in whole banks and beds, and those of the best. I have seen some thirteen inches long. The savages use to boil oysters and mussels together and with the broth they make a good spoon bread, thickened with the flour of their wheat and it is a great thrift and husbandry with them to hang the oysters upon strings . . . and dried in smoke, thereby to preserve them all the year," wrote William Strachey in 1612.

Baked Oysters Chincoteague

YIELD: 6 servings

1 pint oysters
3 slices bacon, diced
1 onion, chopped
1 stalk celery, chopped

3 tablespoons minced green
   pepper
6 tablespoons ketchup
3 tablespoons lemon juice
Tabasco sauce to taste
Salt and pepper to taste

Lightly poach oysters; drain and divide among six 3/4 cup ramekins. Preheat oven to 350°. Cook bacon, onion, celery, and green pepper over moderate heat, stirring for 5 minutes or until bacon is just cooked. Pour off bacon grease. Add ketchup, lemon juice, tabasco, salt, and pepper. Divide mixture evenly over the six ramekins of oysters. Bake for 15 minutes.

Joan Gregory
Lively, Virginia

🐚🐚🐚🐚🐚🐚

Oyster: Witness to History

The oyster created one of the first impressions of the New World for the settlers who arrived at Cape Henry in 1607. While exploring the land around the cape, the Englishmen frightened away a band of Indians who had been roasting oysters over a fire. Tasting the oysters, the settlers found them to be "large and delicate in taste."

Oysters became one of the mainstays of the colonists' diet in the early days of Jamestown. Captain John Smith recorded in his journal that he sent some of his men to live off the oyster beds in the Elizabeth River until ships arrived with a supply of food.

By the turn of the century Lynnhaven oysters from the Lynnhaven River in Virginia Beach had become nationally acclaimed. Diamond Jim Brady, the notorious gourmand, had extra large Lynnhavens shipped to him in New York with the words "For Mr. Brady," printed on the barrels. The oysters' reputation even reached across the sea to England where the king reputedly insisted upon Lynnhaven oysters on his Christmas menu. When President Taft visited Virginia Beach, he consumed so many oysters that he said, "I feel like an oyster."

Though Lynnhaven oysters are not so plentiful today, other Virginia oysters more than suffice. The James River seed beds provide approximately 80 percent of the seed oysters planted in all the Virginia rivers. Eastern Shore oysters, both seaside (salty) and soundside (less salty) are also popular and oyster aficionados swear they can tell the difference in each by the taste.

Although often plagued by disease and unfavorable environmental conditions, the oyster continues to thrive, perhaps due to its variable sex life. Most oysters start life as males and emerge as females in the spring. They continue to reverse the process, often more than once in a season usually ending up as a female once and for all.

Male or female, the oyster plays a special role in Virginia seafood cookery where they are served raw on the half shell, in stews, in casseroles, as stuffings, fried and in fritters.

Baked Oyster Spinach Stuffed Tomatoes

YIELD: 6 servings

1 10-ounce package frozen
   chopped spinach
6 large tomatoes
1/2 cup (1 stick) butter or
   margarine
3 medium celery stalks, chopped
3 green onions with tops OR 1
   medium onion, chopped

1/2 pint oysters, drained and
   chopped
1 tablespoon Worcestershire sauce
3/4 cup herb-seasoned cornbread
   stuffing
1 cup shredded Cheddar cheese
Salt to taste

Preheat oven to 350°. Cook spinach in salt water until tender (about 5 minutes). Drain and set aside. Wash tomatoes and cut across bottom at stem end and make a large opening in each tomato; scoop out pulp, turn upside down to drain. Meanwhile, sauté very lightly in the butter the celery and onions (about 5 minutes). Drain most of liquid from the oysters; chop and add to vegetables in skillet. Cook about 5 minutes more and add Worcestershire sauce, spinach, and cornbread stuffing. Lastly, stir in cheese. Sprinkle a little salt inside each tomato, fill with mixture and place in a greased 1-1/2-quart shallow baking dish and bake for 25 or 30 minutes. Serve warm.

NOTE: Refrigerate tomato pulp and use in soups, casseroles, etc.

Marie H. Webb
Roanoke, Virginia

🐚🐚🐚🐚🐚🐚🐚

Lime, manufactured from oyster shells, was an essential ingredient in the mortar which went into the construction of Virginia's first buildings. Oysters and other shellfish also were used to "pave" the first roads in Virginia. Thus it could be said that Virginia literally was built on its seafood industry.

Cajun Oyster Pie

Chef Bridget Meagher's New Orleans training is deliciously apparent in this recipe for Cajun Oyster Pie, a dish she brought to the 1983 Governor's Tasting from Alexander's in Roanoke, Virginia.

YIELD: 6 servings

Flaky or puff pastry for two 8- to
    9-inch pie crusts
5 tablespoons butter
3 tablespoons flour
1/2 bunch scallions, chopped

1 pint select oysters, with liquid
1 pound roast pork, sliced and
    shredded
Salt to taste
Cayenne pepper to taste
2 tablespoons chopped parsley

Preheat oven to 350°. Roll out 2/3 of the pastry and place into pie plate. Prick pastry. Melt butter. Add flour and cook, stirring constantly until it turns the color of peanut butter. Add scallions and cook one minute. Add 1/2 to 1 cup of the oyster liquid, using enough to thicken the sauce. Add pork and oysters. Mix until blended and thickened. Season with salt and cayenne pepper to taste. Add chopped parsley. Pour into prepared pie shell. Roll out remaining pastry and place on top of pie, crimping edges. Bake for 30 to 40 minutes or until golden brown.

Chef Bridget Meagher

Chesapeake Bay Oysters en Cocotte

YIELD: 4 servings

12 ounces oysters, drained
Liquid smoke seasoning (optional)
Sea salt to taste

Freshly ground black pepper
1 tomato, peeled, seeded, and
    diced
1 cup heavy cream
5 teaspoons sweet butter

Preheat oven to 350°. Lightly grease 4 three-inch cocottes (individual soufflé dishes). Divide the drained oysters between the 4 cocottes. Add a few drops liquid smoke seasoning to each, as desired. Divide the tomato between the 4 cocottes. Pour on 1/4 cup cream to each cocotte; season lightly with salt and 1 or 2 grinds of pepper. Top each with 1 teaspoon butter. Set the 4 cocottes in a shallow pan of water and cook until cream bubbles and edges of oysters begin to curl. Do not overcook.

Mrs. Paul H. Masselin
Richmond, Virginia

Chesapeake Oysters and Shiitake Mushrooms Served in Warm Brioche

Chef Marcel Desaulniers, of The Trellis in Williamsburg, Virginia, used all Virginia-grown and harvested products in this elegant brioche dish at the 1983 Governor's Tasting.

YIELD: 4 servings

pint heavy cream
ounces sliced Shiitake
    mushrooms

2 tablespoons white wine
1 teaspoon chopped shallots
2 cups Chesapeake oysters
Salt and pepper to taste
4 brioche (see note)

Pour heavy cream in a heavy duty sauce pot. Place pot on stove top and adjust the heat so that cream will simmer slowly. Allow cream to reduce in volume by half. Cook Shiitake mushrooms with white wine and shallots for 10 minutes; add oysters and cook only until oysters begin to curl. Add reduced cream to the oysters and Shiitake mushrooms. Season with salt and pepper. Divide the hot mixture equally into the baked and hollowed brioche.

   NOTE: Use 3 ounces of brioche dough baked in a coffee cup for each brioche.

Chef Marcel Desaulniers

Black Sea Bass: Quick Change Artists

   Well known in the gourmet community for its delicious, tender, but firm, white meat which almost falls away from the bones, the black sea bass is known for a more bizarre trait in the scientific community. These fish are protogynous hermaphrodites, scientific lingo for creatures which start life as females and transform into males at a later age.

   The transformation takes place any time between the ages of two to five years. This sex reversal creates a matriarchal society in the black sea bass community since the females dominate the more numerous younger age groups.

   On the other hand, the males dominate the grandparents' group. During spawning season, these old codgers develop a blue bump on their heads, possibly to enhance their May-December relationships.

   A black sea bass is easily identifiable even without its blue bump. Its large pouting mouth and black back and sides are unmistakable and belie the delicate meat which is often used in Oriental fish dishes.

111

Chuck Hoster's Oyster Supreme

YIELD: 2 to 4 servings

1 tablespoon garlic butter (3
    cloves to 1/2 cup butter)
4 to 6 medium fresh-shucked
    oysters (standard)

1 teaspoon fresh lemon juice
1 teaspoon white wine (optional)
1 ounce shredded Gouda or
    Fontina cheese (see note)
Bread crumbs for light topping
Rock salt for broiler pan

Coat scallop shells or shallow baking dishes with small amount of garlic butter and place oysters flat in shell. Add lemon juice, garlic butter, and white wine. Cover oysters with cheese mixture and add light topping of bread crumbs. Place filled shells in broiling pan (or pie pans) with bottom covered with rock salt. Broil at low level until cheese melts and brown lightly. Do not allow to dry out. Serve hot with lemon wedge and dry white wine.

NOTE: Oysters may be served in their own shells using same basic recipe.

A little Parmesan cheese blended with the Gouda will prevent lumping.

Charles S. Hoster
Arlington, Virginia

🐚 🐚 🐚 🐚 🐚 🐚

Shad: Harbinger of Spring

Like the crocus, the shad heralds the spring in Virginia. Its annual run up the rivers to spawn in fresh water has always been a cause for celebration. George Washington ran a haul seine on the Potomac and kept himself well supplied with the ingredients for his favorite food, baked shad. In the early days the annual shad run provided an excuse for senators and representatives in Washington to hold weekly eating and drinking parties on the Potomac. Today Virginia politicians carry on the tradition at the annual shad planking in Wakefield, Virginia.

The colonists learned how to bake shad on a plank of wood over an open fire from the Indians who captured their shad in nets made of bushes stretched across a narrow part of the river.

The shad is one of Virginia's anadromous fish. Along with the striped bass, it spends its life in saltwater but returns each year to the rivers to spawn in fresh water.

Even though fish lovers say the sweet taste of shad can't be beat, its thousands of tiny little bones are a deterrent to many.* If the bones are too much to handle, there's always shad roe. When plentiful, the shad themselves are inexpensive, but the mild-flavored juicy roe remain a costly delicacy.

*For directions on boning a shad, see "Shad Secrets," page 242.

Oysters Casino Lofurno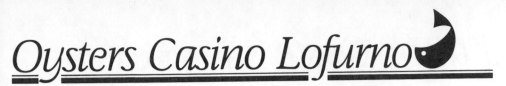

YIELD: 4 servings

2 slices lean bacon, diced
2 tablespoons butter
1 small onion, minced
1/2 green pepper, minced
1 stalk celery, minced
Salt and pepper to taste

1 pimento, chopped
1 teaspoon lemon juice
1/2 teaspoon Worcestershire sauce
Paprika to taste
4 slices toast or toasted French
   bread
2 dozen oysters, shucked

Place bacon in small skillet over low flame; fry slowly 3 minutes or until crisp. Melt butter in separate sauce pan over medium heat; add onion, green pepper, celery, salt, and pepper to taste; sauté 5 minutes or until vegetables are tender. Combine with bacon in skillet; add lemon juice, pimento, and Worcestershire sauce; mix well.

Arrange toast in shallow baking dish. Place 6 oysters on each slice; cover with bacon mixture; sprinkle with paprika. Place in preheated hot broiler 3 inches below flame. Broil 3 minutes. Serve piping hot on preheated individual plates. Garnish with watercress, if desired.

Carol L. Haggett
Norfolk, Virginia

Oven Oysters

YIELD: 6 to 8 servings

About 1 pint oysters, drained
1/2 cup (1 stick) butter
1/4 cup lemon juice
Freshly ground black pepper to
   taste

1/3 cup chopped green pepper
1/2 cup chopped green onion
1/2 cup chopped celery
1/2 cup minced fresh parsley
1/4 pound bacon, cut into 1-inch
   lengths

Preheat oven to 400°. Place oysters in individual baking dishes or flat bottomed casserole dish. Melt butter; add lemon juice and a bit of freshly ground black pepper to the melted butter. Add green pepper, celery, onions, and parsley to the butter mixture. Fry bacon until it is crisp; drain on paper towels. Evenly distribute the butter mixture over the oysters and top with bacon. Bake 10 minutes until oysters are cooked.

Ann K. Kahan
Stuart, Virginia

Patsy's Oysters Rockefeller

YIELD: 4 servings

16 to 20 raw oysters (about 1/2
    pint), drained
1 tablespoon dry sherry
Cayenne pepper to taste
Lemon juice as needed
2 tablespoons butter
1/4 cup finely chopped onions

1 tablespoon parsley flakes
1 7-1/4-ounce can spinach,
    chopped
1/4 teaspoon Worcestershire sauce
1 tablespoon Parmesan cheese
1/2 cup packaged stuffing, crushed
4 slices bacon, cooked and
    crumbled
1 tablespoon chopped pimento

Preheat oven to 450°. Grease 4 ramekin shells or individual baking dishes. Place 4 to 5 oysters in each ramekin and cut oysters in half. Brush oysters with sherry, sprinkle lightly with cayenne pepper, add a few drops of lemon juice, and set aside. Melt butter; add onions and sauté until tender. Remove from heat and stir in parsley flakes, spinach, Worcestershire, and Parmesan cheese. Top oysters in ramekins with equal parts of spinach mixture and sprinkle each with crushed stuffing. Garnish with crumbled bacon and chopped pimento. Bake for 15 minutes.

Patricia Q. Barker
Richmond, Virginia

Scalloped Corn and Oysters

YIELD: 12 servings

1 quart oysters, drained
2 1-pound 4-ounce cans cream-
    style corn
1/2 cup half and half cream

1-1/2 teaspoon salt
1/2 teaspoon pepper
1/2 teaspoon tabasco sauce
1 cup melted butter
4 cups coarsely rolled saltine
    cracker crumbs

Preheat oven to 375°. Drain oysters; pick over, remove shells, and chop coarsely. Mix the corn with half and half, salt, pepper, and tabasco sauce. Melt butter and add cracker crumbs. Toss lightly. Arrange in layers in 2-quart casserole: crumbs, corn, and oysters, having 3 layers of crumbs and two layers each of corn and oysters. Bake for 40 minutes, uncovered.

Chrarlene Stenger
Hampton, Virginia

Horray Scallops

YIELD: 4 servings

1 cup dry white wine
1/4 teaspoon salt
Dash pepper
1 cup water
1 pound fresh bay scallops
3/4 cup fresh mushrooms
4 tablespoons chopped onion

2 tablespoons butter or margarine
6 teaspoons flour
1/2 cup canned evaporated milk
2 ounces (1/2 cup) shredded Swiss
cheese
2 ounces canned sliced water
chestnuts
Parsley for garnish (optional)

In medium-sized, 1- to 1-1/2-quart sauce pan, combine wine, salt, pepper, and water; bring to full boil. Add scallops and mushrooms and return to boiling. Cover and simmer until scallops are tender, about 5 minutes. Remove scallops and mushrooms and set aside.

Preheat oven to 300°. Boil liquid uncovered until reduced to 3/4 cup, 10 to 15 minutes. In medium-sized, 1-1/2-quart sauce pan, cook onion in butter until tender and blend in flour. Add the 3/4 cup scallop liquid and milk. Cook and stir until thickened and bubbly. Stir in cheese until melted; add water chestnuts and season with more salt and pepper if needed. Remove from heat and stir in scallops and mushrooms. Turn into individual serving dishes and bake uncovered for 15 to 20 minutes.

Suzanne K. Davis
Petersburg, Virginia

Scallops Chesapeake

YIELD: 2 servings

6 to 8 ounces mushrooms
2 tablespoons butter
Freshly ground pepper

2 teaspoons chopped chives
1 pound scallops cut in 1/4-inch
rounds
1/2 cup heavy cream
1/4 cup brandy, warmed

Preheat oven to 350°. Slice mushroom caps thinly and sauté in butter for 2 minutes. Sprinkle with pepper and chopped chives. Add sliced scallops and cook about 2 to 3 minutes. Remove mushrooms and scallops from pan. Reduce pan juices by half by heavy boiling. Add cream and reduce again. Flame brandy and add to the sauce. Place mushroom-scallop mixture into scallop shells or individual ramekins. Spoon sauce evenly over scallops and bake for 5 minutes.

Carol L. Haggett
Norfolk, Virginia

"Scalloped" Potatoes

YIELD: 4 servings

4 large baking potatoes
7 tablespoons butter, divided
Salt and pepper to taste
1/2 cup chopped green onion
1/2 cup sour cream

1 pound scallops, cut into bite-
size pieces
2 tablespoons lemon juice
1/3 cup dry vermouth
1/4 cup chopped fresh parsley
1/2 cup mild cheese (Havarti, etc.)
shredded

Preheat oven to 400°. Scrub potatoes and pat dry. Slit potatoes down the center and cook at 375° for 1 hour or until done. Cut off the top and scoop out potatoes. Place shells on a baking sheet. Mix 4 tablespoons butter and salt and pepper into potato pulp. Add green onion and sour cream; beat well. Mixture will be very thick. Sauté cut scallops in 3 tablespoons butter, lemon juice, vermouth, and parsley until barely cooked, about 1 to 2 minutes. Remove from heat and drain, reserving pan juices. Add drained scallops and shredded cheese to potato mixture. Thin with pan juices until desired consistency is achieved. Mound scallop-potato mixture into reserved shells. Sprinkle with paprika and reheat for 8 to 10 minutes.

Elizabeth S. Courtney
Woolwine, Virginia

Blue Fish

YIELD: 2 to 4 servings

1 to 2 pound blue fish, fileted
Salt to taste

Lemon pepper to taste
Salad dressing or mayonnaise as
needed

Preheat oven to 350°. Place fish on greased cookie sheet. Salt and sprinkle with lemon pepper. Spoon enough salad dressing to cover each piece of fish. Place in oven till golden brown.

Marie Lane
Richmond, Virginia

Virginia
Dressed for Dinner

Main Dishes

Chesapeake Clam Casserole

YIELD: 4 to 6 servings

2 cups cracker crumbs
2 eggs, slightly beaten
1/2 cup (1 stick) melted butter

1 pint milk, warm
1 pound whole clams, steamed,
    shelled, and chopped
Salt and pepper to taste

Preheat oven to 350°. Mix crumbs with beaten eggs. Add remaining ingredients and mix well. Bake in 2-quart casserole for 45 minutes.

Betsy G. Skog
Alexandria, Virginia

Potomac Clam Pie

YIELD: 6 servings

3 pounds clams in shells, scrubbed
1-1/2 cups water
4 tablespoons butter or margarine
1/2 cup sliced mushrooms
2 tablespoons chopped onions
1/4 cup flour

1/4 teaspoon salt
1 cup half and half cream
1 tablespoon lemon juice
2 tablespoons chopped parsley
2 tablespoons chopped pimentos
1 9-inch deep dish pastry shell
Dough for 9-inch top crust
1 egg, beaten

Place clams in large pot with water. Bring to boil and simmer 8 to 10 minutes until shells open. Remove from shells, cut into quarters, and save 1 cup of juice. Preheat oven to 375°. Melt butter in skillet. Add mushrooms and onions; cook until tender. Stir in flour and salt. Gradually add clam juice and half and half. Heat, stirring occasionally until thick. Stir in lemon juice, parsley, pimento, and clams. Pour mixture into deep dish pie shell. Cut out pastry dough in 9-inch circle. Secure to rim of pan by crimping. Poke vent holes in crust with fork. Brush with beaten egg. Bake for 25 to 30 minutes or until browned.

Betsy G. Skog
Alexandria, Virginia

Baked Crab Imperial at its Best

YIELD: 4 servings

1/2 cup chopped green pepper
1 4-ounce jar chopped pimento, drained
2 tablespoons butter or margarine
2 teaspoons Old Bay seafood seasoning
1 tablespoon chopped parsley
1/2 teaspoon prepared mustard

1 egg, beaten
3 tablespoons mayonnaise
1 pound fresh crab meat, drained and flaked
4 frozen pastry shells, thawed
Mayonnaise as needed
Pimento strips (optional)
Sliced pimento-stuffed olives (optional)

Preheat oven to 375°. Sauté green pepper and pimento in butter or margarine in medium skillet until tender. Stir in seafood seasoning, parsley, and mustard. Combine egg and mayonnaise and stir into vegetable mixture. Genlty stir in crab meat. Spoon into thawed pastry shells. Top each with a small dollop of mayonnaise. Garnish each with pimento strips and 1 olive slice, if desired. Bake 15 minutes. Broil 5 inches from heat 3 to 4 minutes.

Shirley Jean Lewis
Charlottesville, Virginia

Baked Crab Meat Casserole

YIELD: 4 servings

1 medium carrot, diced
1 medium onion, diced
1 large green pepper, diced
2 large stalks celery, diced
1-1/2 pounds blue crab backfin meat

1/2 teaspoon salt
1/4 teaspoon white pepper
1 teaspoon Worcestershire sauce
1-1/4 cups mayonnaise
1 cup Italian bread crumbs
Butter as needed

Preheat oven to 350°. Combine all ingredients except bread crumbs and butter. Mix thoroughly and place into a well-greased casserole dish. Sprinkle bread crumbs on top and dot with butter. Bake for 30 minutes.

Wanda C. Sprinkle
Virginia Beach, Virginia

Blue Cheese and Crab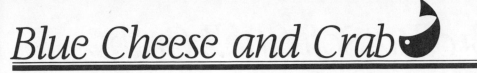

YIELD: 4 servings

2 tablespoons butter or margarine
2/3 cup finely chopped onion
1/2 cup chopped green pepper
1 cup diced celery
1 cup milk
1 cup light cream

2 3-ounce packages blue cheese, crumbled
1 cup sliced pitted ripe olives
1 1/2 pounds crab meat (backfin and regular)
1 teaspoon paprika
2 to 3 teaspoons chopped parsley

In hot butter in large skillet, sauté onion, green pepper, and celery, stirring over medium heat until vegetables are just tender. Remove from heat. In top of double broiler combine milk, cream, and blue cheese over hot water; heat until cheese is melted and mixture is smooth, stirring occasionally. Add cheese mixture to vegetables in skillet along with olives and crab meat. Combine well. Heat mixture slowly, stirring until hot, about 20 minutes. To serve, turn into chafing dish. Sprinkle with paprika, and circle edge with parsley. Serve on rice, noodles, puff pastry shells, or toast points.

Marilyn C. Fall
Virginia Beach, Virginia

Blue Crab-Filled French Toast

YIELD: 5 servings

3/4 pound crab meat
1/4 cup mayonnaise
1 tablespoon chile sauce

2 tablespoons pickle relish
5 slices Cheddar or Swiss cheese
2 eggs, beaten
1/4 cup of milk
Dash salt

Combine crab, mayonnaise, chile sauce, and pickle relish. Spread over five slices of bread. Top each with a slice of Cheddar or Swiss cheese. Close sandwich with another slice of bread. Blend together eggs, milk, and salt. Coat both sides of sandwich. Then brown in melted butter over low heat until the cheese melts. Serve hot.

Mrs. F. E. Blythe
Richmond, Virginia

Broiled Soft-Shell Crabs

YIELD: 3 servings

6 small to medium soft-shell
   crabs, cleaned
3 tablespoons flour
3-1/2 tablespoons olive oil

3 tablespoons butter
1 garlic clove, minced
Salt and pepper to taste
12 parsley sprigs, minced
Lemon wedges for garnish

Preheat broiler. Wash and dry crabs well. Dip into flour, shaking off any excess. Dip crabs in olive oil. Place crabs on broiler pan about 6-inches below source of heat. Broil on each side for 8 minutes. Warm butter; add garlic, salt, pepper, and parsley. Place crabs on warm serving dish and spoon butter mixture over the tops. Serve with lemon wedges.

Joan Gregory
Lively, Virginia

Cheesy Crab Casserole

YIELD: 6 servings

1 8-ounce package thin egg
   noodles
2 tablespoons butter
2 tablespoons sherry
2 to 3 tablespoons flour
1 cup milk

1/2 teaspoon paprika
Salt and pepper to taste
12 ounces mild Cheddar cheese,
   cubed
4 ounces Monterey Jack cheese,
   cubed
1 pound backfin crab meat

Preheat oven to 350°. Cook egg noodles according to package directions. Melt butter over low heat. Add sherry and mix with a wire whisk. Add flour, whisking constantly until well mixed. Slowly add milk, whisking constantly. Once sauce has started to thicken, add paprika, salt, and pepper. Taste and correct seasonings. Using a wooden spoon, stir in cheeses. Continue stirring until all cheese has completely melted. Drain noodles and toss with crab meat. Place in greased 3-quart casserole. Pour sauce over noodles and crab mixture and mix well. Bake for 20 minutes.

Diane M. Capone
Hampton, Virginia

Chesapeake Bay Crab Souffle

YIELD: 4 servings

2 tablespoons bread crumbs
8 ounces crab meat (or more, up
    to 16 ounces)
1/2 pound sliced mushrooms,
    sauteed
1/4 cup sliced green onions
8 slices white bread, crusts
    removed and cubed

2 1/2 cups milk
4 eggs
8 ounces Monterey Jack cheese,
    cubed
1/2 teaspoon salt
1/2 teaspoon dry mustard
Dash pepper
Dash curry powder (optional)

Grease a 2-guart souffle dish (or 6-by-10-inch baking disk), and dust with bread crumbs. Combine crab, mushrooms, and onions. Alternate layers of bread cubes and crab mixture, ending with bread cubes. Combine milk, eggs, cheese, and seasonings in blender; puree. Slowly pour mixture over bread cubes and crab. Refrigerate at least 4 hours. Preheat oven to 325°. Bake for 1-1/2 hours for souffle dish, 1 hours for 6-by-10-inch dish, or until golden brown and firm.

Carolyn B. Long
Norfolk, Virginia

Company Crab Casserole

YIELD: 6 servings

2 cups crab meat
2 cups cubed Monterey Jack
    cheese
1/4 cup toasted slivered almonds
1/4 cup chopped green pepper

1 cup sour cream
1/4 cup crumbled blue cheese
1/4 cup lemon juice
2 tablespoons minced onion
1 teaspoon salt
1/2 cup fine dry bread crumbs
2 tablespoons melted butter

Preheat oven to 350°. Combine crab, cubed cheese, almonds, and green pepper; set aside. Blend sour cream, blue cheese, lemon juice, onion, and salt. Combine crab and sour cream mixture and blend well. Divide among six well-greased ramekins or casseroles. Toss bread crumbs with melted butter and sprinkle over top of casseroles. Bake for 20 minutes.

Sharon Bayer
Bethesda, Maryland

Crab a la Tidewater

YIELD: 4 servings

1 medium onion, chopped
1/2 medium green pepper,
   chopped
3 tablespoons butter or margarine
3 tablespoons flour
1 teaspoon Dijon-type mustard

1/8 teaspoon cayenne pepper
1/4 teaspoon Worcestershire
   sauce
Salt to taste
1-1/2 cups light cream
2 tablespoons dry sherry
1 pound backfin crab meat

Preheat oven to 350°. Saute onion and green pepper in butter or margarine until tranluscent. Add flour and seasonings. Cook 5 minutes. Gradually add cream using a whisk to keep sauce smooth. Correct seasonings. Cook sauce until thick; if necessary it may be thinned with cream if too thick to fold in crab. Add sherry and cook 5 minutes more. Remove sauce from heat and fold in crab, keeping lumps intact. Put mixture into 4 large scallop shells or individual ramekins. Top with buttered bread crumbs. (Mixture may be made ahead to this point and refrigerated or frozen). Heat until bubbly about 15 to 20 minutes.

Elizabeth C. Holtzclaw
Arlington, Virginia

Crab and Cheese Sandwich

YIELD: 6 servings

6 individual Italian sub rolls
3 tablespoons butter
1 large garlic clove, minced

1 pound backfin crab meat
1/4 to 1/2 teaspoon tabasco sauce
1/8 teaspoon salt
12 ounces sharp Cheddar cheese,
   sliced in 6 equal portions

Preheat oven to 350°. Split rolls and heat. Melt butter and sauté garlic for 30 seconds. Add crab meat, tabasco, and salt. Heat through. Remove rolls from oven and turn oven to broil. Place equal portions of crab meat mixture on bottom half of rolls. Place cheese on top of crab mixture. Leave rolls open and run under broiler until cheese bubbles and top half of roll is brown. Remove and make into sandwiches, serving immediately.

    NOTE: Sandwiches may be spread with mayonnaise-type salad dressing or horseradish sauce.

Jean Roland-Pender
Richmond, Virginia

Crabby English Muffins

YIELD: 4 servings

1/2 pound Virginia crab meat
Juice of 1 lemon
1/4 cup mayonnaise
3 tablespoons heavy cream
6 ounces Havarti or other mild
    cheese, grated

1/4 teaspoon garlic powder
3 green onions, chopped, green
    part included
Dash Worcestershire sauce
Salt and pepper to taste
4 toasted English muffin halves
4 slices tomato
Paprika to taste

In a bowl marinate crab meat in lemon juice for 1/2 hour. Preheat broiler. Combine mayonnaise, cream, cheese, garlic powder, green onions, Worcestershire sauce, salt, and pepper to taste. Drain excess lemon juice from crab meat and add crab meat to mayonnaise mixture. Lay the 4 toasted muffin halves on a cookie sheet and place a slice of tomato on each half. Divide the crab mixture among the 4 toasted muffin halves, sprinkle with paprika, and put the sandwiches under broiler for about 3 minutes until tops are bubbling.

    NOTE: These are so delicious that most people will want to have 2 muffin halves; it is simple to double this recipe to serve 4 people.

Ann K. Kahan
Stuart, Virginia

Crab Cakes

This recipe featuring crab meat was furnished by Elsie Evans of The Surry House Restaurant in Surry, Virginia for the 1982 Governor's Tasting.

YIELD: 4 servings

1 pound backfin crab meat
1 egg

1 cup mayonnaise
1/3 cup cracker meal
1 lemon

Remove all shell from crab meat. Beat egg well and add the mayonnaise. Mix well. Add crab meat to mayonnaise and egg mixture and toss lightly. Add a little cracker meal and shape into cakes. Pat cakes in cracker meal. These can then be broiled or pan or deep fried. Serve with slice of lemon.

Chef Elsie Evans

Crab Cakes à la Tom's Cove

YIELD: 4 to 5 servings

1 pound backfin crab meat
2 slices stale bread
1 hard-boiled egg, finely chopped
1 small green pepper, finely chopped
1 tablespoon butter
1 tablespoon flour
1 cup milk, warmed
1 tablespoon mayonnaise
1 tablespoon mustard
Dash Worcestershire sauce
1/4 teaspoon salt
1/4 teaspoon coarsely ground black pepper
Cracker crumbs as needed
4 tablespoons vegetable oil

Mix crab meat, bread, egg and pepper. Melt butter, add flour and stir over medium heat for 2 minutes. Add milk and stir until thickened. Add mayonnaise, mustard, Worcestershire sauce, salt and pepper and blend well. Remove from heat and add to crab meat mixture. Shape mixture into 8 to 10 crab cakes and coat in cracker crumbs. Heat oil in skillet and fry cakes on both sides until golden.

Kathleen S. Johnston
Arlington, Virginia

Crab Cakes Supreme

YIELD: 5 servings

2 slices white bread
1 cup water
1 pound backfin crab meat
2 tablespoons prepared mustard
1 tablespoon mayonnaise
1 egg, well beaten
1 medium onion, minced
Paprika, salt, and pepper to taste

Soak bread in water. Drain off water and squeeze bread dry. Mix with crab meat. Add remaining ingredients. Make into oval shaped cakes, approximately 1/2-inch thick. Do not pack tight. Fry in vegetable oil, sprinkle with paprika, salt, and pepper while cooking. Drain on paper towels and serve hot.

Louise Suttle
Newport News, Virginia

Crab Casserole

YIELD: 6 servings

4 tablespoons butter
1 cup chopped celery
1/2 cup thinly sliced green onion
1/4 cup chopped green pepper
4 ounces fresh mushrooms, sliced
1/4 cup sliced water chestnuts
2 tablespoons chopped pimento
1/4 cup slivered blanched almonds

4 hard-boiled eggs, chopped
1 10-ounce can cream of shrimp
   soup
1/4 cup sherry
1/2 teaspoon salt
1 teaspoon Worcestershire sauce
1/4 teaspoon pepper
1-1/2 cups grated Swiss or
   Monterey Jack cheese
1 pound backfin crab meat

Preheat oven to 350°. Sauté celery, onion, green pepper, and mushrooms in butter until soft. Combine all ingredients except one-half of the cheese and the crab meat. Combine cooked vegetables with crab and the uncooked mixture. Pour into greased 2-quart casserole. Top with remainder of cheese. Bake for 30 to 40 minutes.

Marilyn C. Fall
Virginia Beach, Virginia

🐚🐚🐚🐚🐚

In 1706 the House of Burgesses passed the first legislation in America licensing the taking of oysters and fish. Directed at regulating the Indians' right to fish and harvest oysters, the legislation was not a very grateful response to the Indians' generosity. When the colonists first arrived, they were so intent upon making their fortunes that they came ill-equipped for mundane tasks such as fishing. The Indians taught them how to spear fish and how to trap schools of fish in "weirs" which were permanent nets made out of stakes and branches.

Crab Croquettes with Tangy Cheese Sauce

YIELD: 4 to 6 servings

CROQUETTES
1/2 pound claw or regular crab meat
1/2 pound backfin crab meat
1/2 cup finely chopped onions
1/2 cup finely chopped green pepper
1-1/2 cups fine bread crumbs
3 eggs
1 teaspoon tabasco
1/2 cup mayonnaise
3 tablespoons prepared mustard

1 tablespoon Old Bay seafood seasoning
Cracker crumbs as needed

TANGY CHEESE SAUCE
2 tablespoons butter or margarine
1 1/2 to 2 tablespoons flour
1/2 cup chicken broth
1/2 cup milk
1/2 teaspoon salt
1/2 teaspoon red pepper
1/2 teaspoon celery salt
Pinch garlic
3/4 cup grated Cheddar cheese

Mix croquette ingredients well. Chill in refrigerator for one hour. Shape into croquette and coat with cracker crumbs as needed. Fry in vegetable oil until brown. To make sauce, melt butter over low heat. Add flour and stir until blended. Slowly add chicken broth, milk, and seasonings. When sauce is smooth and hot, add cheese. Stir until melted and serve over croquettes.

Linda C. Poole
Richmond, Virginia

🐚🐚🐚🐚🐚🐚🐚

Flounder: Step Child of the Sea

The flounder begins life looking and swimming as any other fish would, but nature soon plays a dirty trick. By the time the flounder is one-inch long, it has metamorphosed into a bizarre, one-sided creature, flat as a pancake with both eyes on the left side and a distorted mouth. Adding insult to injury, nature has the flounder end up swimming on its side instead of swimming upright.

Nature did leave the flounder with one physically redeeming feature—the ability to camouflage itself. Resting on the bottom, it can partially cover itself with sand with a flip of the tail, its dark spotted back taking on the protecting coloring of the surroundings. When swimming, the flounder is protected from its enemies below because its white underside blends with the light filtering through the water from above, a fortunate turn of events since the flounder can look only up, not down!

With the availability of winter and summer species, consumers can enjoy local flounder year around. The firm, white delicate flesh adapts to any number of preparation methods. Flounder is always fileted unless it is dressed whole to be stuffed with crab meat and baked.

Crab Meat au Gratin

YIELD: 4 servings

6 tablespoons butter
4 tablespoons flour
1 teaspoon salt
1/8 teaspoon pepper
1-3/4 cup milk

1/2 cup light cream
1-1/2 cups grated sharp Cheddar
cheese
1 teaspoon Worcestershire sauce
1 tablespoon lemon juice
1 pound backfin crab meat
1 cup soft bread crumbs

Preheat oven to 425°. Melt 4 tablespoons of butter, stir in flour, salt, and pepper. Add milk and cream slowly, stirring constantly until sauce thickens. Stir in cheese. Stir in Worcestershire sauce, lemon juice, and crab meat very carefully, so as not to break up lumps of meat. Pour into greased 1-1/2 quart shallow baking dish, sprinkle with bread crumbs, and dot with the 2 tablespoons of butter. Bake about 15 minutes.

Eva G. Taylor
Mechanicsville, Virginia

A prehistoric-looking beast with a boney plate down its back, the Atlantic sturgeon closely resembles its ancestors of 100 million years ago. Less than 400 years ago, these creatures were so plentiful in Virginia waters that early colonists often remarked on the quality and quantity of the great sturgeon. Today, however, the fish is so rare that it is illegal to take any sturgeon in Virginia waters and the short-nosed sturgeon (which has been sighted only once in state waters) is on Virginia's endangered species list.

Crab Meat Crespelle (Thin Italian Pancakes)

YIELD: 6 servings

1 pound crab meat
1 small onion, minced
5 tablespoons butter, divided
2 tablespoons parsley
4 tablespoons Parmesan cheese
Dash cayenne pepper
3 tablespoons flour

1/2 teaspoon salt
1 cup milk

CRESPELLE
1 cup milk
3/4 cup flour
1/8 teaspoon salt
2 eggs
6 tablespoons butter
1 cup tomato sauce

Pick through crab meat to remove any shells. Sauté onion in 2 tablespoons butter and add crab meat, parsley, Parmesan cheese, and cayenne pepper. Heat just until warmed through. Over low heat, melt 3 tablespoons of butter. Add flour, salt and gradually blend in milk, stirring constantly over low heat until mixture thickens and turns a light yellow. Add half of the cream sauce mixture to the crab mixture. Heat until just warmed through.

To make 12 crespelle, blend milk with flour. Add salt and eggs; beat until batter is thoroughly blended. Melt 1/2 tablespoon butter over medium-low heat in an 8-inch round skillet, tilting pan until evenly coated. Pour 2 tablespoons of the batter into the center of skillet, tilting until thin layer of batter is spread evenly. Cook until one side of crespelle has set and is pale brown; turn with spatula and lightly brown other side. Transfer to platter. Place 1/2 tablespoon butter in skillet and repeat cooking process until all batter is used up and crespelle are made.

Preheat oven to 375°. Remove crab mixture from heat; portion and spoon filling mixture into the centers of 12 crespelle. Roll crespelle. Pour about 1/4 cup tomato sauce in the bottom of a shallow, greased baking dish large enough to hold crespelle. Place crespelle, seam side down, in dish. Spoon remaining cream sauce over crespelle and top with remaining tomato sauce. Sprinkle with additional Parmesan cheese if desired and bake for 20 minutes or until heated through.

Virginia Marine Products Commission

Photo - Crab Meat Crespelle (Thin Italian Pancakes)

This unusual dish of crabmeat in a creamy sauce rolled in thin Italian pancakes was created especially for the Virginia Marine Products Commission.

Crab Meat Delish

YIELD: 4 servings

3 cups buttered bread crumbs
1/2 pound crab meat
1/2 pound fresh mushrooms,
    sliced
1/4 cup diced green pepper
1 cup grated Cheddar cheese,
    divided

2 eggs, beaten
1/4 teaspoon dry mustard
1/2 teaspoon salt
1-1/3 cups milk
Paprika to taste
1/4 cup sliced olives

Preheat oven to 350°. Place half of the bread crumbs in bottom of a greased 8-inch square baking dish. Cover with crab meat, mushrooms, green pepper, and 1/2 cup cheese. Top with remaining bread and cheese. Combine eggs, mustard, salt, and milk. Pour over bread crumbs. Sprinkle with paprika. Garnish with olives. Bake for 45 minutes or until firm.

Charlotte M. Crews
Lynchburg, Virginia

Crab Meat Gruyère

YIELD: 4 to 6 servings

3 tablespoons butter or margarine
3 tablespoons flour
1/4 teaspoon salt
Dash white pepper

1 cup milk
1/4 pound grated gruyère cheese,
    divided
1/2 teaspoon marjoram
1 pound crab meat
1/2 cup bread crumbs

Preheat oven to 350°. Melt butter in small sauce pan; add flour, salt, and pepper to make roux. Slowly add milk; stir until thick and bubbly. Reserve 1/4 cup cheese. Add remaining cheese and marjoram to sauce and stir until cheese melts. Place crab meat in greased individual casseroles, top with cheese sauce. Mix bread crumbs with rest of cheese and sprinkle on top of sauce. Bake for 20 minutes.

Merrilyn S. Dodson
Newport News, Virginia

Crab Quiche

YIELD: 6 servings

2 eggs, beaten
1/2 cup milk
1/2 cup mayonnaise
2 tablespoons flour

8 ounces natural Swiss cheese, grated
1/3 cup grated onion
1 cup crab meat
1 9-inch pie shell

Preheat oven to 350°. Beat eggs. Mix in milk, mayonnaise, and flour. Add grated cheese and onion; mix. Add crab. Pour into pie shell. Bake for 40 to 45 minutes.

Nancy R. O'Brien
Richmond, Virginia

Crab Meat Perfection à la Phil

YIELD: 4 to 6 servings

1 medium onion, minced
1 medium green pepper, minced
1/2 cup sliced mushrooms
2 hard-boiled eggs, sliced
1 teaspoon Worcestershire sauce

1/2 teaspoon salt
1 pound crab meat
3 tablespoons butter
3 tablespoons flour
1 cup milk
1 cup grated Cheddar or Swiss cheese

Preheat oven to 325°. Mix onion, green pepper, mushrooms, eggs, Worcestershire sauce, salt, and crab meat. Melt butter and blend in flour with a whisk. Slowly add milk and cook and stir the sauce with the whisk until it is smooth and comes to a boil. Pour the sauce over the crab meat mixture. Mix and pour into a greased casserole. Top with grated cheese and bake for 15 minutes or until bubbly.

Virginia Huddleston
Covington, Virginia

Crab Meat Quiche

YIELD: about 8 servings

4 large eggs
1-1/2 cups milk
1/4 teaspoon salt
1/4 teaspoon white pepper
1/4 teaspoon nutmeg
1 tablespoon chopped fresh onion
1/4 package French onion soup mix
1/2 cup grated Cheddar cheese
1/2 cup grated Swiss cheese
1-1/2 to 2 pounds Virginia blue crab meat
2 tablespoons mayonnaise
1/4 cup slivered almonds

Preheat oven to 375°. Beat eggs with wire whisk; add milk, salt, pepper, nutmeg, chopped onion, and French onion soup mix. Stir well with whisk, and then add the Cheddar and Swiss cheese and stir lightly to mix these ingredients. Add mayonnaise and the Virginia blue crab meat, stirring lightly to avoid breaking up chunks of crab. Add almonds at this time, stirring lightly. Pour into a large greased quiche or pie plate and bake 45 minutes or until firm.

NOTE: This quiche is excellent with or without a crust and is delicious either way.

Betty K. Kirby
Chesterfield, Virginia

Crab Meat Rabbit

YIELD: 8 servings

3 tablespoons butter or margarine
1/2 cup flour
1/2 teaspoon salt
1/8 teaspoon prepared mustard
Dash cayenne pepper
3/8 teaspoon Worcestershire sauce
3 cups milk
2 cups grated natural mild Cheddar cheese
1 pound blue crab meat
Toasted pita points

In double boiler, over simmering water, melt butter. Gradually stir in flour, salt, mustard, cayenne, Worcestershire, and then milk. Cook, stirring, until mixture is thickened and smooth. Add cheese; cook, stirring occasionally until cheese is melted. Gently fold in crab meat; heat, stirring occasionally until crab meat is hot. Transfer to chafing dish to keep warm. Guests dip pita points into crab meat mixture.

PITA POINTS: Slice pita bread in half and then into triangles. Brush with garlic butter and toast.

Mrs. Samuel P. Reynolds
Lynchburg, Virginia

Crab Mushroom Casserole

YIELD: 4 to 6 servings

1 pound medium-sized mushrooms
1/2 cup (1 stick) butter or
    margarine
1/4 cup minced onions

1 pound crab meat
1-1/4 cups soft bread crumbs
1 tablespoon dried parsley flakes
1/4 teaspoon pepper
1 egg, beaten
6 ounces mozzarella cheese, sliced

Preheat oven to 425°. Either butter or spray with PAM a baking dish of 60 to 64 square inches; the shape of the dish does not matter. Wash the mushrooms and remove the stems. Chop the stems finely. Pat dry the mushrooms and arrange them in the baking dish as the bottom layer. Melt the stick of butter or margarine in a large skillet. Add to the melted butter the chopped mushroom stems and minced onions, stirring and cooking for 2 to 3 minutes. Stir in the pound of crab meat. Then immediately stir in bread crumbs and the dried parsley flakes. Remove the skillet from the heat and stir in the pepper and the beaten egg. Then pour the ingredients of the skillet evenly over the mushrooms in the baking dish. Bake for 20 minutes. Then turn off the oven and remove the baking dish from the oven. Place the slices of mozzarella cheese on top of the casserole. Place the baking dish back in the oven for 5 minutes or until the cheese has melted.

David C. Cover
Highland Springs, Virginia

Crab-on-Stove

YIELD: 4 servings

1 10-ounce can cream of
    mushroom soup, undiluted

1 pound crab meat
1 cup sour cream
Nutmeg to taste

Heat soup. Add crab and sour cream at last minute. Sprinkle with a drop of nutmeg. Serve on Chinese noodles, in patty shells, on toast, over wild rice, etc.

Bernice Honick
Norfolk, Virginia

Crab Quiche Surprise

YIELD: 9-inch pie

Crust for a 9-inch quiche pan
1/2 cup grated Swiss cheese
1/2 cup grated Cheddar cheese
1 tiny zucchini, peeled and sliced
1 tiny yellow squash, peeled and
  sliced

1 small onion, diced
1 tablespoon olive oil
3 ounces crab meat
2 eggs
1/2 cup sour cream
Salt and pepper to taste
1 teaspoon parsley

Preheat oven to 350°. Mix cheese together and sprinkle 3/4 cup in bottom of crust. Sauté zucchini, yellow squash, and onion in olive oil for 3 minutes (just to get them started). Spread crab meat, zucchini, squash, and onion on top of cheese. Mix together eggs, sour cream, remaining cheese, salt, and pepper to taste and spread on top of quiche. Sprinkle the parsley on top. Bake for 35 to 40 minutes until set.

Helen Pyrtle
Ft. Washington, Maryland

🐚 🐚 🐚 🐚 🐚 🐚

Monk Fish: Fisherman of the Sea

It takes an enlightened angler to feast upon a monk fish after it is caught. Perhaps the ugliest fish in the sea, the monk fish with a huge mouth almost as wide as its head and filled with sharp teeth is hardly appetizing. The smart fisherman, however, knows the monk fish is the poor man's lobster.

Long a gourmet item in Europe, monkfish are beginning to catch on in Virginia. They are often caught by fishermen harvesting sea scallops, flounder, and other species.

Other than being a bottom fish, the monk fish is not choosy about its habitat, living anywhere from the tide line to the continental slope and on bottoms consisting of sand, mud, or shell.

Quite a fisherman in its own right, the monk fish is one of a group of fish commonly called anglerfish. Its fishing apparatus is a little skin flap growing from the first dorsal spine. Long enough to dangle back and forth in front of the monk fish's head, the "fishing rod" attracts other fish within reach of its big ugly mouth.

A voracious eater, the monk fish may also be called the gourmand of the sea. In one sitting, it may eat as much as a third of its weight, feasting on anything from small sharks, to turtles, to sea birds. With eating habits such as these, the fish may grow as large as 45 pounds, however a 75-pound monk fish is the record.

Monk fish are cleaned and packed on ice at sea soon after being caught. Look for the white, lobster-firm meat as steaks and filets in the markets.

Crab Soufflé Roll

This delicate soufflé roll was the grand prize winner in the 1983 Virginia Seafood Month recipe contest.

YIELD: 8 servings

4 tablespoons butter or margarine
1/2 cup flour
2 cups milk
4 egg yolks
1/2 teaspoon salt
Dash ground red pepper
2 teaspoons snipped chives
4 egg whites
1/4 teaspoon cream of tartar
1/3 cup grated Parmesan cheese

CRAB MEAT FILLING
4 green onions, finely chopped
2 tablespoons butter or margarine
12 ounces crab meat, drained, flaked, and cartilage removed
1 3-ounce package cream cheese, at room temperature
1/3 cup half and half cream
2 tablespoons snipped parsley
Dash red pepper sauce
Salt and pepper to taste

Grease jelly roll pan (15 1/2-by-10 1/2-by-1-inch). Line bottom of pan with waxed paper; grease lightly and flour. Heat butter over medium heat until melted. Remove from heat; stir in flour. Cook over low heat, stirring constantly, until smooth and bubbly. Remove from heat; stir in milk. Heat to boiling, stirring constantly. Boil and stir one minute. Remove from heat. Beat in egg yolks, one at a time. Stir in salt, red pepper, and chives. Cool at room temperature, stirring occasionally. (Cover mixture to prevent formation of film.)

Heat oven to 350°. Beat egg whites and cram of tartar in large mixer bowl until stiff but not dry. Stir about 1/4 of the egg whites into egg yolk mixture. Gently fold egg yolk mixture and cheese into remaining egg whites. Pour into pan. Bake until puffed and golden brown, about 45 minutes. While soufflé is baking, cook and stir green onions in butter until tender. Stir in crab meat filling ingredients and heat. When soufflé is done, immediately loosen from edges of pan; invert on cloth covered cooling rack. Spread soufflé with Crab Meat Filling; roll up from the narrow end. Cut into 1-1/4-inch slices.

Betty L. Hamel
Onancock, Virginia

Crab Torte

YIELD: 2 servings

CRÊPES
1 egg
1/2 cup milk
1/3 cup flour
Dash salt

FILLING
2 tablespoons butter or margarine
1/4 cup minced shallots or onions

1/4 cup minced green pepper
1 cup sliced mushrooms
3 tablespoons flour
1-1/2 cups milk
6 ounces crab meat, drained
2 ounces ginger brandy or dry
    sherry
Dash salt and white pepper

1 tablespoon grated Parmesan
    cheese

To prepare crêpes, combine egg and milk, add flour and salt, and mix until smooth. Let batter stand 15 to 20 minutes. Heat small non-stick omelet pan or skillet; pour 1/4 of the batter into pan and move from side to side till batter covers pan bottom. Cook until underside is dry. Using spatula, turn crêpe over; cook other side briefly. Slide onto plate. Repeat process making 4 crepes.

To prepare filling, heat butter or margarine until bubbly; add shallots and pepper and saute until soft. Add mushrooms and cook, stirring occasionally, about 5 minutes. Sprinkle flour over vegetables stirring quickly to dissolve. Stirring constantly, add milk and cook over low heat until slightly thickened. Add remaining ingredients for filling and cook until thoroughly heated. Preheat oven to 350°. Place 1 crêpe in bottom of deep glass pie plate. Spread 1/3 of crab mixture over crêpe. Repeat layers, ending with crêpe. Sprinkle with grated cheese and bake for 20 mintues.

Richard B. Engard
Richmond, Virginia

❀ ❀ ❀ ❀

The menhaden fishery, one of the oldest and largest in North America, is an important commercial fishery in Virginia. Most people consider the little menhaden too oily too eat, however it is a source of industrial oil, fertilizer and protein for animal food. Centered around Reedville, the menhaden fishery here is said to have been started after the Civil War by a lone fisherman and his wife. He would catch the fish in a small seine and she would extract the oil from the fish in a kettle over an open fire. Now sophisticated boats and huge processing plants are the mark of Virginia's menhaden fishery which makes up the largest catch by volume in the state.

Creamed Crab Meat

YIELD: 4 servings

2 tablespoons butter
2 tablespoons flour
1 cup light cream
2 hard-boiled eggs, chopped

1/2 teaspoon salt
1/2 teaspoon paprika
Dash cayenne pepper
1 pound crab meat
1 teaspoon sherry
Toast or patty shells

Melt butter and stir in flour until smooth. Add the cream, eggs, and seasonings and cook until smooth and thickened. Add crab meat. Cook a minute or so, remove from the heat, and stir in the sherry. Serve over toast points or patty shells.

William A. Ross
Virginia Beach, Virginia

Deep Dish Crab Quiche

YIELD: 6 servings

1 cup shredded Swiss cheese
1/2 cup grated Parmesan cheese
3 tablespoons flour
1-1/2 cups half and half cram
5 eggs
1/4 teaspoon salt
1/8 teaspoon pepper

1/2 teaspoon nutmeg
1/2 pound crab meat
1 3-ounce can chopped
  mushrooms, drained
1 10-ounce package frozen
  chopped spinach, thawed and
  drained well
1 9-inch deep dish pie crust shell

Preheat oven and cookie sheet to 425°. Toss together cheese and flour. Combine half and half, eggs, salt, pepper, and nutmeg. Add crab, cheese mixture, mushrooms, and spinach to mixture. Pour into pie shell and bake on preheated cookie sheet for 15 minutes. Reduce temperature to 350° and bake an additional 30 to 35 minutes. After 15 minutes, cover crust with narrow strips of foil to keep from getting too brown. Insert a knife in center; when it comes out clean, quiche is done.

NOTE: If you use a regular size pie crust shell (instead of deep dish pie crust shell) divide filling between two shells. One may be frozen for later use.

Broccoli or kale may be substituted for the spinach.

Bernice Honick
Norfolk, Virginia

140

Deviled Crab

YIELD: 4 servings

4 tablespoons butter
1 small onion, minced
1 cup bread crumbs
1 pound crab meat
2 eggs, hard-boiled and finely
    chopped

1/2 cup mayonnaise
1 tablespoon mustard
1 tablespoon ketchup
1 tablespoon Worcestershire sauce
Dash red pepper
1 tablespoon lemon juice
Paprika to taste

Preheat oven to 350°. Melt butter in sauce pan. Add onion and brown slightly. Add crumbs and stir until lightly brown. Mix in crab meat; add all other ingredients and mix lightly with fork. Stuff into crab shells or ramekins; round off high. Sprinkle with paprika. Brown in oven about 15 minutes.

Betsi Radd
Norfolk, Virginia

Deviled Crab Casserole Brinkley

YIELD: 6 servings

1-1/2 cups milk
1-1/2 cups soft bread crumbs,
    crusts removed
6 hard-boiled eggs
1 pound crab meat

1/2 teaspoon salt
1/4 teaspoon dry mustard
1/8 teaspoon cayenne pepper
1/2 cup plus 1 tablespoon melted
    butter, divided
1/2 cup bread crumbs with crusts
1/2 teaspoon paprika

Preheat oven to 450°. Combine first two ingredients and set aside. Separate egg whites and yolks; finely chop egg whites and mash egg yolks. Gently stir crab meat, egg whites, and yolks into bread crumb mixture. Add salt, dry mustard, cayenne pepper, and 1/2 cup of butter. Mix well. Pour mixture into a greased casserole. Mix bread crumbs with 1 tablespoon butter and sprinkle on top of casserole. Season with paprika. Bake for 15 minutes or until dish is hot and golden brown.

Margaret Brinkley
Lynchburg, Virginia

Deviled Crab Casserole Killmon

YIELD: 8 servings

4 tablespoons butter or margarine
2 cups soft bread crumbs
1 pound Virginia blue crab meat
2 tablespoons finely chopped
    green pepper
1/2 cup chopped celery
2 tablespoons chopped parsley

2 tablespoons chives
2 hard-boiled eggs, chopped
1/2 teaspoon salt
Juice of 1 lemon, strained
1/2 cup mayonnaise
1 tablespoon prepared mustard
1/2 teaspoon Worcestershire sauce
1/2 teaspoon tabasco sauce
1 egg, beaten

Preheat oven to 375°. Melt butter or margarine and add 1 cup bread crumbs. Mix and set aside for topping. Mix remaining bread crumbs with rest of ingredients, adding beaten egg last. Turn into lightly greased casserole dish. Top with crumb mixture set aside earlier. Bake uncovered 30 minutes or until crab mixture is bubbly and crumbs browned.
    NOTE: Can also be baked in individual shells for shorter period.

Margaret G. Killmon
Annandale, Virginia

Deviled Crab Casserole Parks

YIELD: 8 servings

4 tablespoons butter
3 tablespoons flour
1 cup milk
2 pounds backfin blue crab meat,
    well picked

1 tablespoon mustard
1 tablespoon Worcestershire sauce
1 teaspoon Old Bay seafood
    seasoning
1/4 teaspoon salt
Dash pepper

Melt butter in small sauce pan and stir in flour. Add milk and stir until thick. Cool. Preheat oven to 400°. Mix crab, mustard, Worcestershire, seafood seasoning, salt, and pepper. Add to cooled sauce. Put in greased casserole dish and top with cracker crumbs and pats of butter. Brown in oven approximately 20 minutes.

Wanda Parks
Newport News, Virginia

Deviled Crab Imperial Cakes

YIELD: about 5 servings

1 pound Virginia crab meat
1 egg, beaten
1/4 cup mayonnaise
4 to 5 hard-boiled eggs, chopped
1 tablespoon chopped pimento
1 teaspoon Worcestershire sauce
1 teaspoon Old Bay seasoning
1 teaspoon dry mustard
Tabasco sauce to taste
1 cup chopped onion
1 tablespoon finely chopped
   celery
1 tablespoon dry parsley flakes
2 garlic cloves, finely-minced
Peanut oil for frying
Biscuit or roll crumbs for coating

Mix well all ingredients through garlic cloves. Shape into about ten crab cakes. Roll cakes in crumbs making sure crumbs are worked into entire surface of cakes. (If the cake is not sufficiently shaped and coated, it will break up in the oil and spatter.) Deep fry until golden brown on both sides.

NOTE: Cakes may be frozen after they are rolled in crumbs and later thawed and cooked.

Michael S. Forbes
Troy, Virginia

Deviled Style Crab Cakes

YIELD: 4 servings

1/2 cup fine bread crumbs
5 tablespoons mayonnaise
1 egg beaten
1 tablespoon finely chopped
   parsley
2 teaspoons Worcestershire sauce
1 teaspoon prepared mustard
1 teaspoon salt
1/4 teaspoon white pepper
1/4 cup finely chopped celery
1/4 cup finely chopped onions
1 teaspoon lemon juice
1 pound backfin crab meat

Mix crumbs, mayonnaise, egg, and parsley. Fold in Worcestershire sauce and mustard. Add salt, pepper, celery, onions, and lemon. Blend well all of above, add crab meat and stir well. Cook cakes in skillet with just enough fat to prevent sticking, until browned, about 5 minutes on each side.

James E. Marshall
Roanoke, Virginia

Devilishly Good Crab Cakes

YIELD: 3 to 4 servings

1 pound crab meat
1 egg, beaten
1 tablespoon prepared mustard
1/8 teaspoon red pepper
1 teaspoon Old Bay seafood
    seasoning

1 tablespoon Worcestershire sauce
1 teaspoon salt
1 tablespoon mayonnaise
1/2 cup cracker crumbs
1/2 cup bread crumbs
Finely crumbled cracker crumbs as
    needed
Paprika as needed

Mix all ingredients through bread crumbs together with a fork. Shape into cakes about 3/4-inch thick. Sprinkle with paprika. Dip into cracker crumbs so both sides are coated. Fry in heavy skillet, in oil, turning when browned.

Cecelia Robbins
Virginia Beach, Virginia

Divine Crab Quiche

YIELD: 6 servings

1/2 pound fresh mushrooms,
    sliced
2 tablespoons butter
4 eggs
1 cup sour cream
1 cup small curd cottage cheese

1/2 cup grated Parmesan cheese
1/4 cup flour
1 teaspoon onion powder
1/2 teaspoon Old Bay seasoning
1/4 teaspoon salt
2 cups shredded Monterey
    Jack cheese
1 cup crab meat

Preheat oven to 350°. In a medium skillet sauté mushrooms in butter until tender. Remove mushrooms with a slotted spoon and drain on paper towels. In a blender or food processor, blend eggs, sour cream, cottage cheese, Parmesan cheese, flour, onion powder, seafood seasoning, and salt. Fold in mushrooms, Monterey Jack cheese, and the crab meat. Pour into a 10-inch porcelain quiche dish or a 9-1/2-inch deep dish pie plate. Bake for 45 minutes or until knife inserted near center comes out clean. Quiche should be puffed and golden brown. Let stand five minutes before cutting into wedges.

Charlene Stenger
Hampton, Virginia

Easy Cheesy Crab Claw Casserole

YIELD: 4 to 6 servings

1 pound claw meat, shredded
1 cup sour cream
1 cup grated Swiss cheese, divided
1 cup dry bread crumbs

1 teaspoon lemon juice
1 tablespoon cooking sherry
1 teaspoon salt
4 tablespoons melted butter
   or margarine

Preheat oven to 350°. Mix all ingredients except 1/4 cup of cheese. Pour into greased 1-1/2-quart casserole. Sprinkle remaining cheese on top. Bake for 35 minutes or until top is lightly browned and casserole is bubbly.
    Note: Cheddar cheese may be substituted for Swiss.

Chris Frank
Newport News, Virginia

Elegant Crab Quiche

YIELD: 6 servings

1 cup grated Swiss cheese
1 9-inch unbaked pie shell
5 large eggs, beaten
1-1/4 cups milk or half and half
   cream

1/2 teaspoon salt
1/8 teaspoon black pepper
1/2 cup sliced mushrooms
1 cup Virginia blue crab meat

Preheat oven to 375°. Sprinkle cheese into pie shell. Mix eggs with milk, seasonings, and mushrooms; pour over cheese. Crumble crab meat over cheese mixture and bake 35 minutes or until firm and knife, when inserted in center, comes out clean.

Margaret G. Killmon
Annandale, Virginia

Fried Soft Shell Crabs

Clancy Lytle, head chef of The Tides Inn near Irvington, Virginia, gave us his own special method of frying soft shell crabs, along with his recipe for tartar sauce, both of which he offered at the 1982 Governor's Tasting.

YIELD: 4 servings

8 soft shell crabs, cleaned
   and dried
1 cup flour
salt to taste
White pepper to taste
Vegetable shortening for frying

TARTAR SAUCE
2 cups mayonnaise
2 ounces dill relish (strained,
   no liquid)
2 ounces sweet relish (strained,
   no liquid)
3 ounces chopped or ground
   onions
1 tablespoon drained capers
1 teaspoon Worcestershire sauce

Coat each crab with flour, adding a small amount of salt and white pepper. Heat approximately 1/4 inch of vegetable shortening in a heavy iron skillet until very hot. If the oil is not heated enough, the crabs have a tendency to soak up the oil. Place crabs in oil, back-side down and brown well. Then turn and brown on other side. Do not turn too soon. Make sure they are well browned. Then remove and drain long enough to remove any excess oil. Combine tartar sauce ingredients and blend well. Serve as accompaniment to crabs.

Chef Clancy Lytle

🐚 🐚 🐚 🐚 🐚 🐚

Catfish: Southern Soul Food

Catfish are high on the list of southern food fanciers. As freshwater bottom feeders, however, the catfish can take on the muddy flavor of the river bottom. Neophytes would do well to choose only the channel catfish which prefers clean moving water and gravel bottoms. Then its sweet taste can be discerned.

Gnocchi with Brandy Crab Sauce

YIELD: 6 servings

GNOCCHI
2 cups ricotta cheese
  (1 pound carton)
2 eggs, beaten
4 ounces mozzarella cheese,
  grated
2/3 cup flour
1/2 teaspoon salt
1/2 cup fresh grated Parmesan
  cheese

BRANDY CRAB SAUCE
4 tablespoons butter
4 tablespoons flour
2 cups light cream
Salt and pepper to taste
1 teaspoon curry powder
2 tablespoons brandy
1 pound crab meat
Butter as needed

To make gnocchi, mix all ingredients well and chill until firm and easily rolled, one to two hours. With floured hands, roll dough into balls, about 1 inch in diameter. Chill balls in refrigerator, making sure they don't touch each other, for 1 to 2 hours.

To make crab sauce, melt butter. Add flour and cook about one minute. Slowly add cream. Then add salt and pepper, curry powder, and brandy. Cook over medium-low heat stirring with wire whisk until thickened. Stir in crab meat and heat through.

Cook gnocchi, a few at a time, for about 10 minutes in boiling, salted water. Remove from pan with slotted spoon and drain well. Melt butter, beginning with 1 to 2 tablespoons in skillet. Brown cooked gnocchi in butter adding more butter as needed. Remove to warm platter. When all gnocchi are cooked, serve covered with brandy crab sauce.

Nancy Jo Leachman
Charlottesville, Virginia

Hampton Crab Cakes

YIELD: 4 servings

1-1/2 cups fine bread crumbs
1/2 teaspoon oregano
1/2 teaspoon basil
1/2 teaspoon salt

1 teaspoon dry mustard
1 teaspoon Worcestershire sauce
2 eggs
1/4 cup salad dressing
1 pound crab meat
4 tablespoons butter or margarine

Mix crumbs, oregano, and basil. Combine in bowl 1 cup of crumb mixture, salt, mustard, Worcestershire sauce, eggs, and salad dressing. Add crab meat to crumb mixture, gently stir together. Shape into 8 cakes. Roll cakes in remaining crumb mixture. Fry in butter until brown on both sides, about 6 minutes each side.

Note: Cakes may be frozen before frying. They keep well frozen and meat does not get stringy.

Louise Mancil
Hampton, Virginia

Hilda Crockett's  Crab Cakes

Betty Nohe of Hilda Crockett's Chesapeake House Restaurant provided this time-proven recipe for crab cakes, Tangier Island-style, both years at the Governors' Tasting. Tangier Island is a small island in the middle of the Chesapeake Bay.

YIELD: 4 to 5 servings

2 slices bread
Water as needed
1 pound crab meat
1 teaspoon Old Bay seasoning

1/4 teaspoon salt
1 tablespoon mayonnaise
1 tablespoon Worcestershire sauce
1 egg, beaten
1/2 teaspoon prepared mustard
Shortening as needed

Moisten bread slices with water until soft. Mix all ingredients together. Shape into cakes. Fry in shortening until golden. Do not deep fry.

Chef Betty Nohe

Jeanne's Crab Pie

YIELD: 4 servings

5 tablespoons butter, divided
1/4 cup sherry
1 cup well packed crab meat
1 tablespoon flour
3/4 cup light cream
2 egg yolks

TOPPING
1/4 cup cracker meal
1/4 teaspoon paprika
1 tablespoon finely crushed
   potato chips
1-1/2 tablespoons melted butter

Preheat oven to 300°. Melt 2 tablespoons butter; add sherry, cooking for 1 minute. Add crab meat and let stand. Melt 3 tablespoons butter; add flour and stir until it bubbles 1 minute. Remove from heat; slowly stir in cream and add wine drained from crab meat. Return to heat and cook, stirring constantly until sauce is smooth and thick. Remove from heat. Beat egg yolks, pour over crab meat. Add sauce, mix, and turn into greased deep pie plate. For topping, mix cracker meal, paprika, potato chips with butter and sprinkle over crab. Bake for 10 minutes.

Jeanne Y. Hester
Mechanicsville, Virginia

Martha Drummond Curry's Reedville Crab Cakes

Martha Drummond Curry, author of a seafood cookbook, named these crab cakes after the coastal Virginia town where she and her waterman husband Stalk, have lived for 26 years.

YIELD: 6 to 8 servings

1 pound crab meat
1/4 teaspoon vinegar
Dash liquid smoke
1 tablespoon prepared mustard

1/2 cup mayonnaise
1/4 cup pancake mix
1/2 teaspoon sugar
1 teaspoon parsley flakes
1/8 teaspoon hot sauce
1/4 cup bacon fat

Mix together crab meat, vinegar, liquid smoke, mustard, mayonnaise, pancake mix, sugar, parsley flakes, and hot sauce. Pat mixture into cakes and fry in bacon fat, turning once, until brown on both sides. Drain and serve.

Martha Drummond Curry
Martha's Cooking Seafood Cookbook

My Crab Meat Quiche

YIELD: 4 to 6 servings

1 9-inch pastry shell
1/2 pound crab meat, drained
2-1/2 to 3 cups skim milk
3/4 cup mayonnaise

3 to 4 eggs
1-1/2 cups stuffing mix
1 medium mild onion, chopped
Dash nutmeg
Paprika to taste

Preheat oven to 325°. Spray inside quiche dish with PAM. Pat pastry shell gently into bottom of dish. (It won't fill up dish or come up sides, but that isn't necessary.) Mix all ingredients together thoroughly with a spoon. (Do not use mixer or blender!) Pour into quiche dish. Sprinkle with paprika. Bake for 50 to 60 minutes, or until well set and slightly brown.

Note: This is good cold or reheated in a microwave. Cover lightly to store in refrigerator—if covered tightly while still warm, it will make the crust somewhat soggy.

Mrs. Orville C. Sigmon
Vinton, Virginia

Quick Crab Quiche

YIELD: 6 servings

1 tablespoon butter
1 cup flaked crab meat
1/2 cup sliced fresh mushrooms
1/4 cup sliced green onions,
    including green tops

1 cup grated Swiss cheese
1 cup biscuit mix
4 eggs
2 cups milk
1 teaspoon salt

Preheat oven to 400° and grease a 9-inch pie plate. Melt butter and sauté crab meat, mushrooms, and onions for two minutes. Pour into prepared pan and add Swiss cheese. Blend biscuit mix, eggs, milk, and salt thoroughly and pour over mixture in pan. Bake 30 to 40 minutes, or until knife comes out clean.

Priscilla B. Cady
Fairfax, Virginia

Savory Soft-Shell Crab Sandwiches

YIELD: 6 servings

1/2 cup (1 stick) melted butter
  or margarine
1/2 cup chopped green onion
2 teaspoons Worcestershire sauce
4 dashes tabasco

2 large garlic cloves, finely
  chopped
6 soft-shell crabs, cleaned
Lemon juice, salt, and pepper
  to taste
French or Italian bread

Preheat oven to 350°. Mix together melted butter, green onions, Worcestershire, tabasco, and garlic in a small bowl. Spread 1/2 of this mixture in an 8-inch baking pan. Place crabs in a single layer over this mixture. Season crabs with lemon juice, salt, and pepper. Spread remaining sauce over top of crabs. Bake 20 to 30 minutes or until golden brown and cooked through. Place each crab on a slice of bread. Pour on some pan juices and top with another slice of bread.

Sandra Carlin
Portsmouth, Virginia

Methods of catching oysters have not changed much over the centuries. Indians took oysters simply by raking them up with a forked stick. In the mid-1600's, the settlers began to use tongs and that is the method still used today by many oystermen. Tongs are hand-operated scissor-like iron rakes with baskets attached. Oyster dredges were introduced to the Chesapeake Bay in the early 1800's and still are used in deeper water. The dredge is a long steel rake to which a steel bag is attached. When dragged along the bottom, the rake picks up the oysters and they are collected in the bag which, when filled, is hauled onboard by hydraulically-operated winches.

Stuffed Soft Shell 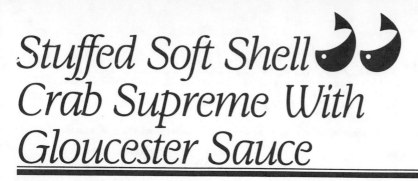 Crab Supreme With Gloucester Sauce

Bill Pearce of Pearce's Parties, Richmond, Virginia, offered this recipe for stuffed soft shell crabs at the 1983 Governor's Tasting. The Gloucester Sauce enhances the natural flavor of the fresh crab meat.

YIELD: 6 servings

6 hotel prime soft shell crabs
1 cup flour
1 teaspoon Old Bay seasoning
Clarified butter for frying

STUFFING
1 pound backfin crab
2 teaspoons sliced green pepper
1 teaspoon diced onion
2 teaspoons Dijon-type mustard
1/4 teaspoon garlic powder
1/2 teaspoon Old Bay seasoning
1 teaspoon lemon juice

1/2 teaspoon white pepper
1/2 teaspoon celery salt
3 tablespoons sour cream
8 crushed saltine crackers
4 teaspoons flour
4 egg whites

GLOUCESTER SAUCE
6 eggs, beaten
1/2 cup sour cream
1 teaspoon lemon juice
1 teaspoon Old Bay seasoning
1/4 teaspoon garlic powder
1 teaspoon paprika

Preheat oven to 325°. Clean soft shell crabs and remove top shell. Combine flour and Old Bay. Dip crabs in mixture. Pan fry soft shells in clarified butter until golden brown. Fill the top of each soft shell with stuffing mixture. Make stuffing mixture by picking crab meat to remove shell. Combine green pepper, onion, mustard, garlic, Old Bay, lemon juice, white pepper, celery salt, sour cream, crackers, and flour. Mix well. Beat egg whites until fluffy. Blend egg whites and green pepper-onion mixture together and fold in crab meat. Blend completely without breaking up large pieces of backfin. Fill top of each soft shell with stuffing mixture, place in baking dish, and cover with Gloucester Sauce. To make sauce, mix beaten eggs, sour cream, lemon juice, Old Bay, garlic, and paprika together. Pour over stuffed soft shells. Bake for 1/2 hour or until golden brown.

Chef Bill Pearce

Tidewater Crab Imperial

YIELD: 4 servings

2 tablespoons butter
2 tablespoons flour
1 cup milk
1 tablespoon minced green pepper
1 teaspoon minced onion

1/8 teaspoon dry mustard
1/4 teaspoon Worcestershire
   sauce
Salt and pepper to taste
1 egg, beaten
1 pound backfin crab meat
1/2 cup buttered bread crumbs

Preheat oven to 350°. Melt butter and add flour to make a roux. Add milk and stir well. Bring to boil and simmer to make cream sauce. Add minced green pepper, onion, and other seasonings. Remove from heat and add beaten egg. Gently fold crab meat into sauce. Divide mixture into 4 small casseroles or shell dishes. Top with buttered bread crumbs. Bake 20 minutes or until bubbling.

Note: These freeze well before baking.

Ellen Michel
Virginia Beach, Virginia

🐚🐚🐚🐚🐚🐚

Sea Trout: Chesapeake Bay Beauties

Many would say the gray trout and its cousin, the spotted sea trout, are the winners of the Chesapeake Bay beauty contest. The gray trout, a slim shapely fish, comes in many colors of the rainbow, its olive green back fading into shiny purple, lavender, green, blue, copper, and finally into a silvery-white underbelly. The equally pretty spotted sea trout has a lovely iridescent blue upper body flecked with black dots, giving rise to its nickname, "speck."

The gray trout's delicate mouth tissue is easily torn by hooks—hence the nickname "weakfish." Contrary to what one would expect of such a beauteous creature, the male gray trout not only lets forth with a raucous noise, just like that of the croaker, but it also has a voracious appetite feeding on the bottom and the surface devouring both shellfish and other little fish.

Local gray trout is usually available in the market except during the cold winter months while spotted sea trout is more often caught by the recreational fisherman. Both make delicious eating, fileted and prepared in any number of ways.

Virginia Cavalier Crab Meat

YIELD: 6 servings

6 tablespoons butter, divided
1 loaf French bread, sliced into
   1-inch thick rounds
1 tablespoon flour
1/2 cup dry white wine

1 cup half and half cream
Salt and pepper to taste
1 pound fresh asparagus, cut into
   2-to 3-inch lengths
Juice of 1 lemon
1 pound Virginia blue crab meat

Melt 4 tablespoons butter in a large skillet. Add French bread rounds and grill or sauté until browned on both sides. Remove bread slices from skillet and place in a 9-by-13-inch pyrex or oven proof dish and set in warmed oven while you prepare the crab and asparagus.

In the same skillet, melt remaining 2 tablespoons butter; add 1 tablespoon flour and cook stirring a few seconds. Add white wine; simmer, whisking in the four, and continue whisking until sauce is smooth. Add lemon juice to crab meat.

Drop asparagus into boiling water, cook 3 minutes, and drain. While asparagus is cooking, add crab meat to the cream sauce and heat just until crab is hot; do not boil. Thin crab mixture with a little extra cream or milk if necessary and taste to correct seasoning. Remove grilled bread slices from oven; spoon crab meat mixture over bread. Top with asparagus. Serve immediately.

Elizabeth S.Courtney
Woolwine, Virginia

🐚🐚🐚🐚🐚

Jonah Crab: Deep Water Denizen

Jonah crabs are large deep water crabs occasionally caught and sold commercially in Virginia. Reddish tan in color, the Jonah crab is larger and stockier-looking than its relative the blue crab.

Varying between a pound and a pound-and-a-half in size, Jonahs have two fat claws which alone hold more meat than all of the meat in a big blue crab.

Jonahs can be cooked and eaten in the same way as a blue crab but nutcrackers are necessary to crack the big claws. The claws must be strong enough to do battle with lobsters which find the Jonah crab as tasty a treat as humans do.

Virginia Crab Imperial

YIELD: 6 servings

2 tablespoons butter, divided
1 tablespoon flour
1/2 cup half and half cream
1 tablespoon finely chopped onion
1 tablespoon finely chopped
    green pepper
1 tablespoon Worcestershire sauce

2 slices of bread, cubed
1 tablespoon lemon juice
1/2 cup mayonnaise
1 teaspoon Old Bay seasoning
1/2 teaspoon coarse ground
    pepper
1 pound Virginia backfin
    crab meat
Paprika to taste

Preheat oven to 425°. In pan over medium low heat, melt 1 tablespoon butter and stir in flour. Slowly add cream, stirring constantly until thick. Mix in onion, green pepper, and Worcestershire. Add bread cubes; mix and cool. Mix lemon juice with mayonnaise and add to cooled mixture. Add Old Bay and pepper. In another pan melt 1 tablespoon butter until light golden brown, toss in crab meat, and combine with other mixture. Fill crab shells and sprinkle with paprika. Bake until hot and bubbly, about 20 minutes.

Sue Lunsford
Woodbridge, Virginia

Virginia Crab Meat With Scrambled Eggs

YIELD: 6 servings

6 eggs
1/2 cup heavy cream
Salt and pepper to taste
1/2 cup finely chopped green
    onions, including tops

2 teaspoons lemon juice
2 cups Virginia blue crab meat
3 tablespoons butter
Parsley sprigs for garnish
    (optional)

Beat together eggs, cream, salt, and pepper. Add onions to egg mixture. Sprinkle lemon juice over crab meat and add crab meat to egg mixture. Melt butter in a large skillet over medium-low heat. Add crab mixture and scramble slowly until cooked but still soft. Turn out onto platter. Garnish with parsley and serve.

    Note: The recipe can be easily halved or doubled depending on your need.

Ann K. Kahan
Stuart, Virginia

Alice Bell's Oyster Pie

YIELD: 8 servings

1 tablespoon vegetable shortening
3 cups flour plus two tablespoons,
    divided
1 teaspoon salt

Cool water
1 quart oysters with juice
4 medium large onions, sliced
4 tablespoons butter
Salt and freshly ground pepper
    to taste

Preheat oven to 350°. Cut the shortening into three cups of the flour. Add a few drops of cool water to the flour and work the dough into a ball, suitable for rolling. Put on floured board; roll thin and cut into strips. In a 2-quart casserole, layer oysters with liquid, onion, pats of butter, salt, and pepper. Sprinkle 1 tablespoon flour over the oyster mixture and put a layer of pastry strips in a criss-cross pattern over the flour. Repeat process for a second layer. Bake for about 1 hour and 15 minutes, or until pastry is brown on top. If the oyster mixture seems a little dry when it bubbles up, add a little hot water as it cooks so the liquid will be like gravy.

Note: This is also good cold the next day.

Jean A. Mulford
Portsmouth, Virginia

Chesapeake Shore Oyster Curry

YIELD: about 4 servings

1 pint oysters with liquid
4 tablespoons butter
1 small onion, chopped fine
1/2 medium apple, peeled, cored,
    and chopped fine

2 tablespoons mango chutney
1 tablespoon flour
1 tablespoon curry powder
1/2 teaspoon salt
1/2 cup milk

Drain oysters and save liquid. Melt shortening in large skillet. Stir in onion, apple, chutney, flour, curry powder, and salt. Cook about 5 minutes over medium to low heat, stirring constantly. Add enough water to oyster liquid to make a half cup. Add this and milk to skillet and simmer for 2 to 3 minutes. Add oysters and cook just until edges of oysters begin to curl. Serve over hot rice.

June E. Bowers
Sarasota, Florida

Dad's Baked Oysters on the Half Shell

YIELD: 4 servings

1/2 bushel Chincoteague oysters

Cracker crumbs as needed
Butter as needed

Preheat oven to 400°. Scrub and open oysters on deep shell; cut away from shell but do not remove, being careful to retain all juices. Place oysters on baking sheet. Add cracker crumbs to each oyster sufficient to absorb juices. Add 1/2 teaspoon butter to each oyster. Bake until golden brown.

Thomas G. Allen
Fairfax, Virginia

Deviled Oysters

YIELD: 6 servings

1 pint oysters
1 tablespoon butter
3 tablespoons minced chives
2 tablespoons flour
1/2 cup milk
1/4 cup light cream
1/2 teaspoon salt
1/8 teaspoon nutmeg

Dash cayenne
1/2 teaspoon mild mustard
1/2 tablespoon Worcestershire
   sauce
3 chopped mushrooms
1 egg yolk, beaten slightly
3 full stalks parsley, minced
1/2 teaspoon each salt and pepper
Buttered crumbs as needed

Preheat oven to 350°. Cook oysters, in their own juice, just until edges curl. Drain and cut into pieces. Melt butter; stir in the flour and add the milk and cream. Bring to a boil, stirring constantly to make a smooth sauce. Add all the seasonings, and cook about a minute. Remove from heat. Add mushrooms, chopped oysters, and egg yolk. Blend well. Place mixture in buttered shells or a casserole and cover with buttered crumbs. Bake until the mixture is hot and light brown.

Charlotte M. Crews
Lynchburg, Virginia

Divine Oysters

YIELD: 2 servings

3/4 cup dry bread crumbs
1/3 cup grated Parmesan cheese
1 teaspoon dried basil
1 teaspoon chopped parsley
1/2 teaspoon salt
1/2 teaspoon oregano
1/4 teaspoon pepper
1/4 teaspoon garlic powder
12 medium oysters
1 tablespoon olive oil
1 tablespoon white wine
1 teaspoon lemon juice

Preheat oven to 400°. Grease a baking dish large enough to hold the oysters in one layer. Combine crumbs, Parmesan cheese, and spices. Sprinkle one-third of the crumb mixture into the dish, top with the oysters, and then spread the rest of the crumbs over the top. Combine oil, wine, and lemon juice and sprinkle over the top. Bake uncovered for 30 minutes.

Joan Gregory
Lively, Virginia

Oyster Crisp

YIELD: 4 servings

1 pint shucked oysters, with
    their juices
1/4 teaspoon salt
1/8 teaspoon pepper
1/8 teaspoon ground nutmeg
6 strips bacon, cooked until crisp,
    then crumbled
1 cup shredded Swiss cheese
1 cup heavy cream
1/2 cup coarsely crushed
    saltine crackers
2 tablespoons butter

Preheat oven to 400°. Grease a shallow 1-1/2-quart baking dish. Arrange oysters evenly in dish, and pour their juice over them. Sprinkle salt, pepper, and nutmeg evenly over oysters. Scatter crumbled bacon over oysters; then top with cheese. Pour cream evenly over all; then cover evenly with cracker crumbs and dot with butter. Bake, uncovered, for 20 minutes.

Mrs. W.W. Simpson, Sr.
Hurt, Virginia

Oyster Loaf

YIELD: about 4 servings

1 round loaf French bread
1 garlic clove, split
1/2 to 3/4 cup melted butter, divided
Salt and pepper to taste
2 dashes tabasco sauce

1 teaspoon Worcestershire sauce
1 teaspoon sherry
2 eggs, beaten
1/2 cup flour
1 cup yellow cornmeal or bread crumbs
2 to 3 dozen oysters

Preheat oven to 400°. Cut the top off the bread to form a lid. Hollow out the inside, making a basket, leaving about 1/2-inch crust all the way around. Remove excess bread from the top crust or lid. Rub the inside of loaf with garlic and brush inside and out with 4 tablespoons melted butter. Toast in oven until crisp, 15 to 20 minutes. Remove and turn oven down to 300°. In a small bowl add salt, pepper, tabasco, Worcestershire, and sherry to beaten eggs. Place the flour and cornmeal or bread crumbs in separate small bowls. Dip oysters first in flour, then in egg mixture, and finally in cornmeal or bread crumbs. In a heavy skillet, fry the coated oysters until brown and crisp in the rest of the melted butter. Fill the loaf with hot fried oysters and put the lid on top. Heat in oven for 10 minutes or until ready to serve. Cut in slices and serve with ketchup and lemon wedges.

Note: The amount of oysters to buy varies according to the size of the oysters and the size of the loaf of bread. You want the "basket" of bread to be filled to the top with oysters.

Patricia S. Gibson
Chesterfield, Virginia

🐚🐚🐚🐚🐚🐚🐚

Eel: European Delight

Though the majority of eels caught in the state are shipped abroad, Virginians are beginning to recognize that this rich, fat fish can be delicious. Smoked eel also is considered a delicacy in the European market.

Several fish such as the shad and striped bass return from saltwater to freshwater to spawn, but the eel is the only species that does just the reverse. Spending most of its time in fresh or brackish water, the eel will migrate to open sea to spawn. Scientists think that both American eels and European eels return to the area near the Sargasso Sea each year to lay their eggs.

Oysters Newburg

YIELD: 4 servings

2 dozen oysters
4 tablespoons butter
1/2 pound mushrooms, sliced
1 teaspoon paprika
1-1/2 cups light cream

1/4 cup dry sherry
2 tablespoons brandy
6 egg yolks, beaten
1/4 teaspoon chives
Salt to taste
Pepper to taste
4 slices toast

Open oysters; drain their juice and set 1/2 cup aside. Melt butter in a heavy sauce pan over a very low flame; add oysters, sauté until oysters begin to curl at edges and remove from pan. Put mushrooms and paprika in pan and sauté until tender. Add oyster juice, cream, sherry, and brandy. Bring to a boil; reduce flame and simmer 2 minutes. Remove about 1/4 cup sauce from pan, mix with egg yolks, and then return slowly to pan, stirring constantly and cooking only until sauce shows first sign of thickening. Caution: Overcooking will curdle the mixture! Remove from heat; add oysters, chives, and salt and pepper. Serve over toast.

Andrew Ferraro
Cheriton, Virginia

Oysters Sarah Jane

YIELD: 2 servings

6 Ritz crackers
About 15 Virginia oysters,
    with juice
1/2 teaspoon Astor barbecue
    seasoning

Salt to taste
Freshly ground pepper to taste
Celery salt to taste
Paprika to taste
2 tablespoons butter
2 tablespoons half and half cream
1 teaspoon Worcestershire sauce

Preheat oven to 350°. Grease a 9-inch pie plate and coarsely crumble three crackers evenly over the bottom. Cover crumbled crackers with oysters so that oysters are barely touching. Do not overcrowd. Spoon one tablespoon oyster juice over this. Sprinkle oysters with barbecue seasoning, salt, pepper, celery salt, and paprika. Heat butter. Add half and half and Worcestershire sauce. Mix well. Spoon mixture over oysters until each is completely coated, allowing some to run off and down to the bottom of the pie plate. Crumble remaining three crackers over the top and bake until the center oysters bubble and bounce, about 20 minutes.

Note: Don't overcook. Too much cracker makes dish soggy.

James O. Moore
Lynchburg, Virginia

Scalloped Oysters Smith

YIELD: 6 to 8 servings

2 cups day-old bread crumbs,
    divided
2 dozen medium sized oysters,
    drained

Salt to taste
Pepper to taste
1/4 cup milk
2 tablespoons melted butter

Preheat oven to 400°. Grease baking dish and cover bottom with 1 cup bread crumbs. On these arrange 2 dozen oysters. Season with salt and pepper and cover with 1 cup bread crumbs; moisten with 1/4 cup milk. Add melted butter. Bake for 20 minutes.

Thomas L. Smith
South Hill, Virginia

Scalloped Oysters

YIELD: 6 to 8 servings

1 cup (2 sticks) butter, divided
1/2 pound mushrooms, sliced
1/4 cup chopped green pepper

1 teaspoon salt
1 pint oysters
3 cups crushed soda crackers
1/2 cup light or half and
    half cream

Preheat oven to 350°. In skillet, melt 1/4 cup butter, sauté mushrooms 5 to 10 minutes. Add green pepper and salt; cook gently for an additional 5 minutes. Drain oysters by placing a few oysters at a time in a sieve and removing any pieces of shell; reserve liquid. Sprinkle 1/3 of crackers over bottom of greased 9-inch square baking dish. Top with half of mushroom mixture and half of oysters. Dot with 1/4 cup butter. Repeat. Sprinkle last 1/3 of crackers on top and dot with last 1/4 cup butter. Add cream to reserved oyster liquid (about 3/4 cup) and pour over all. Bake for 30 to 35 minutes.

Maxine R. Harrison
Salem, Virginia

Sunny Side Up Oysters

Johnny Lockhart of Lockhart's Gourmet Seafood in Norfolk, Virginia, contributes this delicious recipe for an oyster brunch.

YIELD: 1 serving

1 pat butter
2 ounces light cream

8 large oysters
1 large egg
1/8 teaspoon ginger

Preheat oven to 350°. Melt butter in a small casserole dish. Add cream. Lay oysters side by side at one end of dish. Open egg and place sunny side up on other end. Sprinkle on ginger. Bake for about 5 minutes or until egg firms up. Garnish with parsley, watercress, lemon wedge and/or lime.

Johnny Lockhart
Norfolk, Virginia

🦪🦪🦪🦪🦪

Lobster: Virginia Resident

Though not many Virginians are aware of it, lobster is an offshore resident of the state. The one tidewater fisherman who traps lobster commercially even finds himself shipping Virginia lobsters to northern markets.

The only difference between the Maine lobster and the Virginia lobster is where it lives. Virginia lobsters must live 100 miles offshore in 600 to 1800 feet of water to find the cold conditions the Maine lobster can find right near shore. But when it comes to taste, both rank high on the seafood lover's scale.

Virginia Ham and Oyster Pie

YIELD: 6 servings

1 pint shucked oysters, drained
1/4 pound cooked Virginia ham,
    cubed
3 tablespoons butter or margarine
2 cups sliced fresh mushrooms
1/2 cup chopped onion
1/2 cup chopped green onion
1/4 cup flour
1/2 teaspoon salt

1/4 teaspoon cayenne pepper
1/4 cup chopped parsley
2 tablespoons lemon juice

BISCUIT TOPPING
1-1/2 cups flour
2-1/4 teaspoons baking powder
1/4 teaspoon salt
3 tablespoons margarine or butter
1/2 cup milk

Preheat oven to 400°. Dry oysters between absorbent paper. Fry diced ham in butter or margarine until heated through. Remove ham and drain. Add mushrooms, onions, and green onion to butter and ham drippings in the frying pan. Cover and simmer 5 minutes or until tender. Blend in flour, salt, and pepper. Stir in oysters, ham, parsley, and lemon juice. Grease a 9-inch pie plate. Turn oyster mixture into pie plate. To make biscuit topping, sift flour, baking powder, and salt together. Cut in butter until mixture is like coarse crumbs. Add milk all at once. Mix just to a soft dough. Turn onto lightly floured surface. Knead gently 5 to 6 strokes. Shape into a ball. Roll out to a 9-inch circle to fit on top of pie plate. Cover oysters with biscuit topping. Score biscuit topping. Bake for 20 to 25 minutes or until topping is lightly browned.

Virginia Marine Products Commission

Bay Scallops Italliene

YIELD: 4 servings

1 large onion, diced
1 green pepper, diced
1 garlic clove, finely chopped
1/4 cup olive oil
1 16-ounce can Italian tomatoes,
    drained, cut into bite-sized
    pieces

Black pepper to taste
1 tablespoon butter or margarine
1 pound bay scallops
1/2 cup dry white wine
1 tablespoon lemon juice
Italian bread crumbs to taste

Preheat oven to 375°. Sauté onions, green pepper, and garlic together in olive oil until onions are soft and translucent. Add the tomatoes and black pepper; simmer for 12 to 15 minutes. Pour into lightly greased baking dish and set aside. Sauté scallops in butter, stirring often. Add wine and lemon juice and simmer for 5 to 8 minutes. Combine scallops and reserved ingredients in the baking dish, mixing well. Sprinkle Italian bread crumbs on top of the mixture. Bake until bubbly. Serve over hot brown (or white) rice.

Kelson E. Slayman
Alexandria, Virginia

Cathy's Sea Scallops

YIELD: 6 to 8 servings

1/4 cup finely chopped green
    onions
1 cup sliced mushrooms
1 cup (2 sticks) butter
1/8 cup Worcestershire sauce

1/4 teaspoon Great Garlic (chopped
    garlic in soy bean oil)
1/4 cup cooking sherry
Salt and pepper to taste
1-1/2 to 2 pounds sea scallops

Preheat oven to 450°. Combine all ingredients except scallops in sauce pan and simmer over low heat until butter melts. Put scallops and juices into shallow dish. Pour mushroom mixture over scallops and bake for 20 minutes or until done.

Cathy Crider
Charlottesville, Virginia

Photo - Scallops

Scallops lend themselves to any number of preparations, but baking in individual casseroles or shells is one of the most popular. See pages 164-175 for a number of scrumptious dishes.

Coquille St. Jacques (Scallops)

YIELD: 4 servings

1 pound raw scallops
1/4 pound mushrooms, finely
   chopped
1 cup dry white wine
3/4 cup water
1 tablespoon lemon juice

1 bay leaf
1 tablespoon chopped parsley
3 shallots
6 tablespoons butter, divided
4 tablespoons flour
2 egg yolks
4 tablespoons heavy cream
Fresh bread crumbs

Preheat oven to 450°. Simmer scallops and mushrooms in mixture of white wine, water, lemon juice, bay leaf, parsley, and shallots for 5 minutes. Remove from heat and strain, reserving the liquid. In a separate pan, make a medium white sauce with 4 tablespoons of the butter, flour, and 1-3/4 cups of the reserved liquid. Cook sauce slowly over low heat, stirring constantly, for 5 minutes. Blend egg yolks into cream and add to the sauce; stir while cooking an additional 5 minutes. Season to taste. Place scallops in shells and spoon sauce over. Add mushrooms around edges. Sprinkle with bread crumbs, dot with remaining 2 tablespoons of butter, and heat until lightly browned. Serve at once.

Virginia Marine Products Commission

🐚 🐚 🐚 🐚 🐚 🐚

Sea Perch: Popular Panfish

In the 1800's, sea perch was considered "the panfish" among all small fish up and down the east coast. Today it is not found in the fish markets In as great a quantity as its panfish rivals, spot and croaker. Nevertheless its firm white flesh remains one of the best when pan fried.

Silvery in color, the sea perch is also called "white perch" or "silver bass." It is often caught up by the amateur angler because it frequents the tidal areas and also seems to be very comfortable in brackish water.

Lee's Scallop Supreme

YIELD: 4 to 6 servings

1 red onion, finely chopped
1 pound fresh mushrooms, sliced
4 tablespoons butter, divided
Juice of 1/2 lemon
2 tablespoons flour
1-1/4 cups chicken stock
1/2 cup dry white wine
2 cups boiling water
2 pounds scallops

1/2 teaspoon salt
1 tablespoon chopped fresh
  parsley
1/2 fresh garlic clove, minced
1/4 teaspoon tarragon
1/4 teaspoon Worcestershire
  sauce
1/4 teaspoon pepper
3 tablespoons grated Parmesan
  cheese
2 cups wild rice

Sauté onion and mushrooms with two tablespoons of butter and lemon juice, until tender. In another pan, melt remaining butter. Blend in flour, chicken stock, and wine. Stir until thickened. In a colander, pour boiling water over scallops and drain. Add scallops to combine sauces and season with salt, parsley, garlic, tarragon, Worcestershire, pepper, and cheese. Simmer for a few minutes. Spoon over rice and top with a sprinkle of Parmesan cheese.

Elizabeth Fulghum
Williamsburg, Virginia

Linguine with Scallops

YIELD: 4 servings

2 tablespoons olive oil
2 garlic cloves, minced
1 28-ounce can peeled tomatoes

2 teaspoons thyme
1 cup clam juice
1 pound linguine
1 pound bay scallops

Heat the oil in a sauce pan and sauté garlic until lightly browned. Add the tomatoes, crushing them well. Add thyme and simmer for 30 minutes. Add clam juice. Stir thoroughly and allow sauce to simmer for 45 minutes to 1 hour. Boil water for pasta. While cooking pasta, add scallops to the sauce. Scallops need to cook for about 12 minutes, just when the pasta should be ready.

Sharon Hwalek
Virginia Beach, Virginia

Scallops Benedict

YIELD: 4 servings

4 English muffins, split, toasted
   and buttered
3 tablespoons butter
1 pound scallops, cut into
   bite-sized pieces
3 tablespoons lemon juice
2 tablespoons minced parsley
4 green onions with tops, minced
8 eggs, poached

SAUCE
1/2 cup (1 stick) melted butter
4 egg yolks
3 tablespoons lemon juice
1/2 teaspoon salt
1/2 teaspoon dry mustard
Tabasco sauce to taste
2 tablespoons half and half cream
2 tablespoons minced parsley
1 cup grated Havarti or other
   mild cheese

Toast and butter English muffins. Set aside and keep warm in oven. Melt butter over low heat; when butter begins to foam, add sliced scallops, lemon juice, parsley, and green onions. Cook only for 2 to 3 minutes, stirring often. Remove from heat; cover to keep warm. To make sauce, in the top of a double boiler over *very low* heat add butter. Add egg yolks one at a time using a wire whisk or fork. Add lemon juice, salt, dry mustard, tabasco, and half and half. Heat sauce thoroughly but do not let water in double boiler come to a boil. On each toasted English muffin half, place 1 tablespoon grated cheese, followed by a helping of scallops with the pan juices. Place poached egg over scallops, followed by another tablespoon of cheese. Top with sauce and minced parsley.

Elizabeth S. Courtney
Woolwine, Virginia

Scallops Delight

YIELD: 3 to 4 servings

1 pound scallops
1/2 teaspoon Kitchen Bouquet
1/4 teaspoon salt
1/4 teaspoon celery salt
1/4 teaspoon paprika
1/4 teaspoon dry mustard
2 teaspoons vegetable oil
1 teaspoon lemon juice

Place scallops in mixing bowl. Combine remaining ingredients, pour over scallops and toss lightly with fork to coat evenly. Refrigerate for at least 3 hours. Broil and serve.

Joan Gregory
Lively, Virginia

Scallops en Casserole

YIELD: 4 servings

1/2 teaspoon salt
Dash pepper
Dash cayenne
1-1/2 cups herb-seasoned
    stuffing crumbs

2 eggs
4 tablespoons water
1-1/2 pounds large scallops
4 tablespoons melted butter

Preheat oven to 375°. Mix salt, pepper, cayenne, and bread crumbs together in bowl. Beat eggs and water with fork in another bowl. Dip scallops in egg, and then roll in crumbs to coat well. Place scallops in one layer in shallow casserole, close together, and refrigerate 30 minutes or until coating is firm. Pour melted butter over scallops. Bake 25 minutes until scallops are rich golden and crisp.

Marcelle Stephens
Richmond, Virginia

🐚 🐚 🐚 🐚

Squid: The Creature with Its Own Pen and Ink

Squid, known in the scientific community as a mollusk of the highest order, is more apt to be classified by the lay person as a shellfish with its shell on the inside. This internal shell is known as a "quill" or "pen," a remnant of a once more highly developed shell. Since squid is known for the ink it expels when frightened, the lay person also could classify it as a pen and ink fish!

The large, very human-like eyes of the squid are a striking feature as are its tentacles and arms which it uses for capturing food and for mating. Another unusual feature of the squid is its powerful, jet-propelled method of swimming which it accomplishes by pulling water through an opening around its head and forcing the water with muscular contractions through a smaller funnel-shaped tube. By directing the funnel properly, the squid can travel backwards or forward.

An important year-around coastal resource, Virginia's squid harvest, until recently, was shipped to the Mediterranean and the Far East where it is considered a gourmet item. There it is often served sauced in its own ink or fried as a quick snack. But because of the cavity remaining after the squid is cleaned and the internal shell removed,* it appears that God created the squid to be stuffed. Stuffings are often made of chopped tentacles and arms, mixed with vegetables, such as onions and tomatoes.

Virginians are beginning to appreciate this inexpensive, nutritious and tasty denizen of the deep. Today, it is generally available in local markets where it may be called "calamari," which means "squid" in Italian and Spanish.

*See "More Than One Way to Skin a Squid," page 242.

Scallops en Croute

Chef David Jordan from the Virginia Museum of Fine Arts furnished this recipe, featuring scallops in puff pastry covered with a cognac-flavored sauce, for the 1983 Governor's Tasting.

YIELD: 2 servings

1/2 cup diced onion
1/2 cup diced celery
1 pound bay scallops
1/2 pound (2 sticks) butter
6 tablespoons flour
2 cups milk, scalded
1/3 cup cognac

1/4 cup white wine
1/4 cup lemon juice
1 teaspoon coriander
1/4 cup fresh, grated Parmesan
   cheese
Dash pepper
3 sheets puff pastry
2 eggs, beaten
Fresh dill, to taste

Preheat oven to 300°. Sauté onion, celery and scallops in butter until done. Remove vegetables and scallops from pan with slotted spoon and return butter drippings to heat. Add flour stirring until well blended. Add milk, stirring until sauce thickens. Add cognac, white wine, lemon juice, coriander and cheese to make a sauce. Stir until cheese melts. Wrap scallops and vegetables in puff pastry to whatever size desired. Brush with beaten egg. Put on sheet pan lined with pastry paper and bake for 10 minutes until golden brown. Remove to serving dish; top with remelene sauce and garnish with fresh dill.

Chef David Jordan

Scallops in Lemon Sauce

YIELD: 6 servings

2 pounds mushrooms, sliced
2 garlic cloves, minced
2 green onions with tops, chopped
5 tablespoons unsalted butter,
    divided

1 tablespoon flour
1/2 cup vermouth
1 pound scallops
2 egg yolks
2 tablespoons lemon juice
Pepper to taste

Sauté mushrooms, garlic, and green onions in 4 tablespoons butter until liquid is absorbed. Sprinkle mushrooms with flour. Stir. Add wine and scallops. Cook 5 minutes until thickened. Mix egg yolks and lemon juice together. Remove skillet from heat and add egg yolks. Stir thoroughly with wooden spoon. Add chopped parsley and 1 tablespoon butter. Add pepper and mix.

Julia Williams
Richmond, Virginia

Scallops Piquante

YIELD: 4 servings

1 pound Virginia scallops
2 tablespoons butter
1/2 cup tarragon vinegar

1/2 cup heavy cream
1/4 teaspoon tarragon
Salt and pepper to taste
1 tablespoon Dijon-type mustard
1/4 cup chopped fresh parsley

Cut scallops in halves or thirds if large. Rinse and pat dry with paper towels. Sauté scallops in melted butter until just cooked, about 2 minutes. Remove from pan and keep warm. Add vinegar to skillet and cook to reduce vinegar to about 2 tablespoons. Add cream; cook over medium heat until sauce thickens slightly. Season with tarragon, salt, and pepper; add mustard and stir until well mixed. Return scallops to pan to coat with the sauce. Pour into serving dish and sprinkle with chopped parsley. Serve with rice.

Ann K. Kahan
Stuart, Virginia

Scallops Provencal

YIELD: 2 servings

8 ounces scallops, dredged in flour
1 tablespoon melted butter

1 cup crushed tomatoes
1 tablespoon garlic powder
2 tablespoons parsley flakes

Deep fry scallops until golden brown. Drain. In skillet heat butter, then add tomatoes, garlic powder, and parsley flakes. Simmer for 5 minutes. Add browned scallops and simmer for 5 minutes. Stir occasionally.

Scott Robertson
Newport News, Virginia

Simply Scrumptious  Virginia Bay Scallops in Wine Sauce

YIELD: 5 servings

3/4 cup bread crumbs
1/4 cup Parmesan cheese
4 tablespoons butter
2 tablespoons margarine
2 stalks celery, leaves
    removed, sliced

1-1/2 medium onions, chopped
6 tablespoons flour
1 cup milk
1/2 cup white wine
4 ounces medium sharp Cheddar,
    sliced
1 pound Virginia bay scallops

Preheat oven to 350°. Prepare topping by combining bread crumbs and Parmesan cheese in a small bowl. Melt butter and margarine in a medium (2-quart) saucepan. Sauté celery and onions in melted butter and margarine. Blend in flour to make a paste; cook one full minute over medium heat. Gradually add milk, stirring after each addition. Stir wine into sauce. Add cheese and let it melt into sauce, stirring frequently. Fold in scallops. Pour into a greased 2-quart casserole dish. Sprinkle on topping. Bake for 20 to 30 minutes until bubbly. Serve over noodles or rice.

Suzanne J. Engel
Vienna, Virginia

Scallops Smithereen

YIELD: 4 servings

1-1/2 cups (3 sticks) butter, divided
2 tablespoons chopped green onions or shallots
1 garlic clove, minced
2 tablespoons chopped parsley

1 tablespoon lemon juice
1/4 teaspoon crushed red peppers
Salt and pepper to taste
1-1/2 pounds scallops
Italian bread crumbs, crushed very fine
1/4 pound mushrooms

Preheat oven to broil. Make butter sauce by combining 1 cup butter, green onions or shallots, garlic, parsley, lemon juice, red peppers, salt and pepper. Roll scallops in butter sauce. Broil scallops in a single layer for 3 minutes. Sprinkle well with crumbs; toss and broil 3 more minutes. Meanwhile, sauté mushrooms in 1/2 cup of butter and gently add to cooked scallops. Sprinkle with salt, pepper, and lemon juice to taste.

Mary Smith
Suffolk, Virginia

Dolphin: Deep Sea Harvest

Fresh dolphin is generally available only to those who are the fortunate beneficiaries of some of the harvest from a deep sea fishing trip. These fish are not to be confused with the dolphin mammal which often is called a "porpoise." Dolphin fish are a beautiful iridescent blue gold or green gold and have no resemblance to the mammal at all.

Dolphin meat is sweetly delicious, however the lovely-colored skin is very tough and must be removed before cooking. After skinning, the meat adapts to almost any method of seafood cookery desired.

Virginia Scallop Fritters with Sweet and Sour Sauce

YIELD: 2 to 4 servings

Vegetable oil for frying
1 pound large scallops
1/2 teaspoon salt
1 tablespoon lemon juice

BATTER
1-1/2 cups flour
1/2 teaspoon baking powder
1/2 teaspoon dried sweet basil
1/4 teaspoon salt
1/8 teaspoon pepper

1 egg, slightly beaten
1 cup ice cold water

SAUCE
1/4 teaspoon salt
2/3 cup water
2 teaspoons soy sauce
4 tablespoons sugar
4 tablespoons vinegar
2 tablespoons cornstarch,
   dissolved in 1/3 cup water
1 teaspoon vegetable oil

Place oil in a deep fat fryer to a depth of 3 inches. Heat up to 375°. Meanwhile, clean and drain well the scallops. Slit them slightly in the center but do not cut deep. Sprinkle with salt and lemon juice. Set aside.

Make the batter: Sift flour, baking powder, sweet basil, salt, and pepper together. Combine slightly beaten egg with cold water. Gradually add to the flour mixture, stirring constantly to form a smooth paste.

Dip scallops in batter and deep fry a few pieces at a time 2 to 3 minutes or until golden brown. Drain on paper towels. Keep warm in a 250° oven while frying the rest. Serve with sweet and sour sauce.

To make sauce: Combine all ingredients except the cornstarch mixture and oil in a glass or porcelain saucepan. Bring to a boil. Stir in cornstarch. Cook until mixture becomes thick and transparent, about 2 to 3 minutes. Stir in the oil for gloss.

Mercedes Aurora B. Tira-Andrei
Falls Church, Virginia

Steamed Black Sea Bass

YIELD: 2 servings

1 1-to 1-1/2-pound sea bass,
   cleaned but whole with head on
4 slices ginger root, shredded

2 tablespoons black beans
1 teaspoon sherry or vodka
2 garlic cloves, smashed
1/4 cup peanut oil
Handful chopped green onions

Make slashes in the flesh of the fish with a knife, cutting to the bone. Mix the ginger slices, black beans, and sherry or vodka together in a small bowl, mashing the beans lightly with a spoon. Fill the cavities of the fish (they won't be filled by this amount, so really "place" some in the cavities), and on both sides of the exterior. Place fish on aluminum foil or on a platter and steam about 20 minutes. Remove from steamer, keep warm, and quickly brown the garlic in oil. Pour the flavored oil over the fish, sprinkle with garnish and serve.

The Virginia Institute of Marine Science
in cooperation with the Virginia Seafood Council

Golden Brown Blow Fish

YIELD: 4 servings

8 blow fish filets
1 teaspoon salt
1/2 teaspoon pepper
1/2 cup flour

1/2 cup finely ground white
   cornmeal
1 cup vegetable oil
Parsley sprigs for garnish
1 lemon, sliced

Pat the blow fish dry with a paper towel and season with salt and pepper. Blend the flour and cornmeal and roll the blow fish in the mixture until well coated. Heat the oil (do not let it smoke) and fry the blow fish for 2 minutes on each side or until golden brown. Serve garnished with parsley and lemon slices.

William A. Ross
Virginia Beach, Virginia

Baked Blue Fish Shonerd

YIELD: 4 to 6 servings

1/2 cup diced onion
1 cup diced celery
4 tablespoons butter or margarine
1 large blue fish filet
    (1 to 1-1/2 pounds)

Juice of 1 lemon
3 medium tomatoes, sliced thin
1 teaspoon sugar
1 teaspoon basil
1 teaspoon salt and pepper
2 slices white bread, broken
    into pieces

Preheat oven to 350°. Sauté onions and celery in butter for 10 minutes. Place blue fish in shallow, greased baking pan. Squeeze lemon juice over fish. Place tomatoes over fish and top with the sugar, basil, salt, and pepper. Place sautéed onions and celery over tomatoes. Place bread in sauté pan to absorb remaining butter and then place bread pieces over vegetables. Bake for 30 to 45 minutes or until fish flakes.

Kathi R. Shonerd
Chesapeake, Virginia

Baked Blue Fish Smith

YIELD: 4 to 6 servings

1 8-ounce bag poultry stuffing
1 large blue fish

Salt and pepper to taste
2 tablespoons flour
2 tablespoons melted butter
3 strips bacon

Preheat oven to 325°. Mix stuffing according to package directions. Stuff fish. Sew up cavity. Season with salt and pepper. Stir flour into butter and rub mixture on fish. Place 3 strips bacon on top of fish. Place in pan with a little water and butter. Bake 15 minutes to the pound basting frequently. Add a little flour or cornstarch to stock to thicken for gravy.

Thomas L. Smith
South Hill, Virginia

Baked Stuffed Blue Fish

YIELD: 6 servings

1 4-pound cleaned blue fish
1-1/2 teaspoons salt
1/4 cup finely chopped celery
1/4 cup chopped onions
2 tablespoons butter
2 cups bread cubes, moistened
    with milk

1 tablespoon chopped parsley
1 teaspoon salt
1/4 teaspoon pepper
2 tablespoons melted butter or
    margarine
4 thick slices bacon
4 thin slices salt pork

Preheat oven to 350°. Wash and dry bluefish. Sprinkle salt inside and out. Cook celery and onion in butter until tender. Combine cooked vegetables, bread cubes, and seasonings. Toss, mixing thoroughly. Fill cavity loosely with stuffing and close the opening with skewers. Make 4 gashes in fish crosswise and brush with melted butter. Wedge bacon strips in gashes. Place fish in a well-greased, shallow baking pan on top of salt pork slices. Bake for 40 to 50 minutes, basting occasionally with pan drippings or melted butter, until fish flakes easily when tested with a fork. Transfer to hot platter and remove skewers.

Virginia Marine Products Commission

Blue Fish Burgers

YIELD: 4 to 6 servings

1 quart water
1/4 cup white wine or 2
    tablespoons vinegar
1 bay leaf
1 stalk celery, chopped
1 onion, chopped
Salt and pepper to taste

2 pounds blue fish filet
2 slices firm white bread,
    crumbled
2 beaten eggs
1/2 teaspoon dry mustard
3/4 cup mayonnaise
1/4 cup chopped parsley
1 teaspoon Worcestershire sauce
1 teaspoon Old Bay seasoning

In deep skillet combine water, wine or vinegar, bay leaf, celery, and onion, salt and pepper to taste. Bring to boil covered. Add blue fish filets and simmer until filets are cooked, for 10 to 15 minutes. Drain fish and remove dark meat from filets. Flake white meat in bowl. Add white bread crumbs. Combine eggs, mustard, mayonnaise, parsley, Worcestershire sauce, and Old Bay seasoning in small bowl, mixing well. Add this mixture to fish and crumb mixture. Form into fish cakes 2 to 2-1/2 inches in diameter. Sauté in butter and oil.

Ellen Michel
Virginia Beach, Virginia

Blue Fish Cakes

YIELD: 3 to 4 servings

2-1/2 cups cooked blue fish,
    flaked
1 cup mashed potatoes
1/4 teaspoon onion powder

1/2 teaspoon parsley flakes
1/4 teaspoon dry mustard
1/4 teaspoon salt
Dash cayenne pepper
1 egg
Flour as needed

Mix all ingredients, except egg and flour, until blended. Add egg and mix well. Shape into 6 or 8 patties, roll in flour. Refrigerate 30 to 60 minutes. Fry in oil until golden; turn over and repeat. Serve with tartar sauce or ketchup.

Helen W. Chapman
Gaithersburg, Maryland

Blue Fish De-Lish

YIELD: 3 to 4 servings

1 12-ounce box Ritz crackers
1 cup grated Parmesan cheese

1/2 teaspoon garlic powder
Salt to taste
1/2 cup (1 stick) melted butter
1 pound blue fish filets

Preheat oven to 400°. Combine crackers, Parmesan cheese, and garlic powder in blender or food processor. Add salt to butter. Dip the fish fillets in the butter and then in the cracker mixture. Bake for 15 minutes. Broil for 1 to 2 minutes.

Note: Fish can be prepared ahead of time and then popped in the oven for 20 minutes before serving.

Elizabeth S. Courtney
Woolwine, Virginia

❀❀❀❀❀❀

Tuna: The Uncanned Variety

Fresh tuna and tuna in a can cannot be compared with one another. Fresh tuna, during the short deep sea fishing season, is occasionally available in fish markets. More often one needs a deep sea fishing friend to try this mild, meaty delicacy.

Many people prefer to soak tuna in a salt and water mixture the day before cooking since it is a very bloody fish. In addition, it is always advisable to remove the dark muscle meat before cooking as it can have a bitter flavor.

After soaking and removing the dark meat, poach the tuna in water until done. Add mayonnaise, lemon juice, a little diced celery and onion, some minced thyme and freshly ground black pepper for a salad that will leave you wondering what it was you used to fix from a can.

Blue Fish in 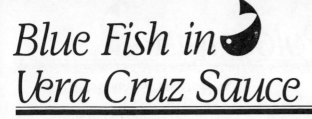 Vera Cruz Sauce

YIELD: 4 to 6 servings

2 pounds blue fish filets
Lemon juice as needed

SAUCE
3 tablespoons olive oil
6 garlic cloves, peeled and
    thinly sliced
1 medium onion, cut into
    thin rings
1 medium sweet red pepper,
    seeded and sliced into
    2-by-1/4-inch strips
3 large tomatoes, peeled and
    chopped

1 tablespoon oregano
3 bay leaves, crumbled
2 jalapeno peppers, cut into thin
    strips or 2 teaspoons hot
    jalapeno chili sauce
Freshly ground pepper to taste
12 to 15 pimento-stuffed olives,
    cut in rounds, in thirds

2 eggs
1/4 cup water
2 tablespoons butter
2 tablespoons corn oil

Squeeze lemon juice over fish and allow to stand at room temperature 30 minutes. To make sauce, heat olive oil in skillet and sauté garlic and onions until just tender. Do not brown. Add all other ingredients, mix well, and cook over low heat 15 to 20 minutes, or until thick. Set aside and keep warm.

Beat eggs with water until mixed. Heat butter and corn oil in skillet. Dredge fish in flour, egg mixture, and flour again. Place skin side down in hot butter/oil and fry until golden. Turn. Cook until golden. Arrange fish on a heated platter. Pour sauce over fish, and serve immediately.

Deborah E. Buchanan
Charlottesville, Virginia

Blue Fish Polonnaise

YIELD: 4 servings

1/2 medium onion, diced
1/2 cup chopped celery
4 tablespoons butter
1/8 teaspoon pepper
1/2 teaspoon salt
1 cup cooked rice, with
    1/2 teaspoon cinnamon

1 tablespoon sesame seeds,
    toasted
1 teaspoon chopped parsley
1 3-pound blue fish
1 pound can tomatoes
1/2 green pepper, sliced
1/2 medium-sized onion, sliced
1 teaspoon flour
1/2 cup croutons

Preheat oven to 350°. Sauté onion and celery in the butter; add seasonings, rice, sesame seeds, and parsley. Into the fish cavity, spoon the rice mixture; close cavity with skewers or sew closed. Place in a baking dish. Mix together the tomatoes, onion, and pepper; blend in the flour and then add the croutons. Pour this mixture over the fish. Bake for approximately 30 to 35 minutes, or until the fish flakes when tested.

Frances M. Biss
Washington, D.C.

Blue Fish Strips

YIELD: 4 to 6 servings

1-1/2 cup flour
2-1/4 teaspoons baking powder
3/4 teaspoon baking soda
1-1/2 teaspoon salt

1/2 teaspoon seafood seasoning
1-to 1-1/2-pound blue fish filets
    cut into 1/2-to 1-inch strips
1/3 cup lemon juice
2/3 cup beer

Mix flour, baking powder, baking solda, salt, and seafood seasoning. Coat fish with 1/2 cup of flour mixture. To remaining mixture add lemon juice and beer. Dip fish strips into this mixture and deep fry until golden brown.
    Note: Serve with tartar sauce or cocktail sauce for added flavor.

Doris Vick
Chesapeake, Virginia

Charcoal Broiled Blue Fish Oriental

YIELD: 4 servings

4 blue fish steaks
Juice of one lemon or lime
1/2 teaspoon fresh cracked
   pepper
1/2 teaspoon garlic salt

1/4 cup teriyaki sauce
1/4 cup vegetable oil
1/2 cup honey
2 ounces cooking sherry
1 piece fresh ginger root
   (1 to 2 ounces)
4 garlic cloves, finely chopped

Place filets in rectangular baking dish. Squeeze lemon juice evenly over both sides of fish. Sprinkle both sides with pepper and garlic salt. Cover and refrigerate for 10 minutes. Remove from refrigerator and pour teriyaki, oil, honey, and sherry over the filets. Grate ginger over filets and sprinkle with garlic. Spoon or baste fish thoroughly with mixture in dish. Cover. Let stand in refrigerator for 30 minutes, turning once.

While fish is marinating, prepare charcoal grill as for charcoaling steaks. Place filets in portable wire fish grill. Sear each side on grating for five minutes. Then cook each side for 10 to 15 minutes, basting liberally and frequently. (Fish should be flaky when pierced with a fork.) Serve at once.

F. Judson Hill
Virginia Beach, Virginia

Smoked Blue Fish

YIELD: 4 to 6 servings

Filets from one 6-pound blue fish
3 tablespoons melted butter
2 tablespoons lemon juice
2 tablespoons white wine
1/2 teaspoon tarragon
Pepper to taste
12 charcoal brickets
2 cups hickory chips, soaked
   and drained

Prepare charcoal fire on one side of grill. Place sheet of greased foil on grill rack on side opposite of fire. Place fish, skin side down, on foil. Cover grill, with open vent over fish side.

    Cook 1/2 hour. Sprinkle 1/3 of hickory chips on fire and recover. After 20 minutes, sprinkle fire with 1/3 more chips and baste fish with sauce of butter, lemon juice, wine, and seasonings. After 20 minutes repeat with remaining chips and sauce. Cook covered 20 additional minutes. Serve filets whole on platter.

    Note: Leftover fish may be flaked and made into a cold salad with mayonnaise, pickle relish, and chopped onion.

    Blue fish is one of the most commonly caught and inexpensive of Virginia's seafood. This recipe replaces blue fish's distinct oily taste with a delicious smoked flavor.

Janis Rietschel
Centreville, Virginia

🐚 🐚 🐚 🐚 🐚 🐚

Steamed Virginia Blue Fish Special

YIELD: 2 to 4 servings

2-1/2 to 3 pounds blue fish,
 cleaned
1-1/2 teaspoons salt
1/4 teaspoon white pepper
1 teaspoon fresh lemon juice
1 medium-sized onion, sliced
1 small carrot, coarsely chopped
1 teaspoon grated ginger

1 bay leaf
10 black peppercorns
1 teaspoon dried sweet basil
2 cups water
1 tablespoon sesame oil
1/2 cup mayonnaise
3 hard-boiled eggs, white and
 yolks chopped separately
1/4 cup mayonnaise
1/2 cup sweet pickle relish

Preheat oven to 350°. Clean and dry fish; rub with salt, white pepper, and lemon juice, inside and out. In an 11-inch baking pan, spread onion, carrot, and ginger evenly over the bottom. Lay the fish on the bed of onions, carrots, and ginger. Head of fish may be cut off if too long for the pan. Place the head inside the fish to cook. Add bay leaf, peppercorns, sweet basil, water, and oil. Bake covered for 30 minutes or until fish flakes easlly when tested with a fork. Transfer fish to an appropriate serving platter. Discard all other ingredients. Let cool. Attach head to body if cut off. Spread both sides of the fish with mayonnaise. Garnish body of fish with diagonal strips of the following: chopped egg whites moistened with 2 tablespoons mayonnaise, chopped egg yolks moistened with the rest of the mayonnaise, followed by a stripe of sweet pickle relish. Repeat until the whole fish is decorated. Serve right after garnishing. If prepared in advance, chill loosely covered with waxed paper and serve cold.

Mercedes Aurora B. Tira-Andrei
Falls Church, Virginia

Broiled Lemon Pepper Catfish

YIELD: 2 servings

2 whole catfish, about 1 pound
    each, cleaned without heads
1/4 pound (1 stick) melted butter
    or margarine

2 tablespoons lemon juice
1 teaspoon Worcestershire sauce
Lemon pepper to taste

Soak fish in salt water for 30 minutes. Drain well. Preheat broiler. Combine butter with lemon juice and Worcestershire sauce. Baste fish with butter mixture and sprinkle with lemon pepper. Place fish on greased broiler rack and line bottom of broiler pan with foil. Place broiler pan 6 inches from heat. Cook 5 minutes on one side, basting several times before turning. Cook 5 to 8 minutes on other side, basting several times; you may add lemon pepper during cooking. Cook until easily flaked with fork but moist. Do not over cook.

Note: This is an excellent way to clean catfish: Fill a large kettle about half full of water and cover tightly. Bring the water to a rolling boil. Place one fish at a time into the water, cover tightly and count to twenty. Remove fish from the water with tongs and clean immediately.

Place fish on a cutting board and with a sharp knife, cut around the head and the skin slips off very easily. Then remove head and insides.

Elizabeth Bates
Brookneal, Virginia

Deep Fried Croaker

YIELD: 6 servings

1 pound croaker filets
2 tablespoons lemon juice
1 teaspoon paprika

1 cup water
1 cup flour
1/2 teaspoon baking powder
1 teaspoon salt
2 cups vegetable oil

Cut fish into 2-inch squares. Sprinkle with lemon juice and paprika. Let set for 1 hour. Combine water, flour, baking powder, and salt in quart jar and shake until blended. Dip fish, one piece at a time, into batter. Fry in oil that has been preheated over medium heat. Cook until lightly browned; drain on paper towels. Serve hot.

Margaret G. Killmon
Annandale, Virginia

Photo - Croaker

Croaker is one of the best panfish in Virginia waters. For a variety of ways to pan-fry croaker, see Deep Fried Croaker on this page, and Gourmet Croaker and Spicy Pan-Fried Croaker, page 189.

Gourmet Croaker

YIELD: 2 servings

MARINADE
1/4 cup fresh lime juice
1/4 cup fresh lemon juice
1/4 cup white wine
1/4 cup cooking sherry
1/4 teaspoon dill
1/4 teaspoon nutmeg
1/8 teaspoon powdered ginger

1/4 teaspoon prepared
   horseradish (optional)
4 6- to 8-inch croaker with
   heads removed
Salt and pepper to taste
1 cup (2 sticks) clarified butter
2 tablespoons grated lemon peel
2 tablespoons snipped fresh
   parsley

Mix marinade ingredients. Score fish diagonally on both sides, three slits per side. Salt and pepper fish cavity and exterior. Place in a flat pan or casserole. Pour marinade over fish and marinate for at least one hour, turning the fish several times during the process to assure even distribution of the marinade. Remove fish from pan and reserve the marinade. Pat fish between paper towels to remove excess moisture, and brown fish in clarified butter, cooking until it flakes easily. Remove from pan and place on warm platter. Add the reserved marinade to the pan drippings and bring to a simmer. Add lemon peel and parsley. Pour over fish. Garnish with pimento, parsley, and lemon.

Sara T. Fisher
Hampton, Virginia

Spicy Pan-Fried Croaker

YIELD: 6 servings

3 pounds cleaned croaker
1 cup yellow cornmeal
1-1/2 teaspoons paprika
1 teaspoon salt
1/2 teaspoon celery salt

1/2 teaspoon pepper
1/4 teaspoon dry mustard
1/4 teaspoon onion powder
1 cup milk
Bacon fat for frying
Lemon wedges for garnish

Wash fish and pat dry. Combine cornmeal and seasonings. Dip fish in milk, and then roll in seasoned cornmeal. Place fish in a single layer in hot bacon fat in a 12-inch skillet. Fry at a moderate heat for 4 to 5 minutes or until brown. Turn carefully. Fry 4 to 5 minutes longer or until fish are brown and flake easily when tested with a fork. Drain on absorbent paper. Serve with lemon wedges.

Virginia Marine Products Commission

Atlantic Stuffed Flounder Supreme

YIELD: 4 servings

24 Ritz crackers
4 tablespoons butter
Tabasco sauce to taste
Garlic powder to taste
3 onions
1 bell pepper
6 mushrooms
1/2 cup water
2 tablespoons vegetable oil
1 8-ounce package cream cheese
8 slices toast
2 pounds flounder filets
1 lemon

Topping—Crumble the Ritz crackers by hand or with a food processor. Melt the butter and stir into the crackers. Season well with tabasco sauce and garlic powder, and stir.

Stuffing—Slice the onions, bell pepper, and mushrooms and place in a skillet. Add water and boil until most of the water is gone and the vegetables begin to stick to the surface of the pan. Reduce heat, add vegetable oil, and stir fry until the vegetables have browned. Turn off the heat, add the cream cheese, and stir until well mixed. Slice or tear the toast into pieces, add to the pan, and stir until well mixed.

Cooking instructions—Preheat oven to 425°. Grease an 8-by-12-inch pan and spread the stuffing evenly upon it. Layer the flounder filets over the stuffing. Sprinkle the topping evenly over the filets. Bake for 20 minutes or until the topping begins to brown. Putting the pan under the broiler very briefly will result in a nicely browned top. Serve with lemon wedges as an entrée or as a meal-in-itself. Other fish may be substituted for the flounder. Do not overcook!

Brian Phillippy
Falls Church, Virginia

Baked Flounder Filets in White Wine

YIELD: 6 servings

2 cups coarsely chopped celery
    leaves and stalks
1 onion, sliced
3 pounds flounder filets

Salt and pepper to taste
1/3 cup melted butter
1 teaspoon finely chopped onion
1 teaspoon lemon juice
Dash paprika
1 cup dry white wine

Preheat oven to 350°. Spread celery and onion in baking dish. Season fish with salt and pepper. Combine butter, chopped onion, paprika, and lemon juice. Dip fish into butter mixture; arrange on celery and onion. Pour leftover butter mixture and wine over top of fish. Bake uncovered for 25 to 30 minutes, or until easily flaked with fork but still moist. Lift fish to serving dish, keep warm. Discard celery and onion. Pour wine from fish into sauce pan; heat briskly to reduce to about 1/2 cup; pour over fish. Garnish with chopped parsley or watercress.

Note: Croaker or spot may also be used in this recipe.

Florence D. Reams
Lynchburg, Virginia

Baked Flounder in Yogurt Sauce

YIELD: 4 servings

1/2 cup chopped onion
1 cup thinly sliced celery
2 tablespoons diced green pepper
2 tablespoons butter or margarine

1 pound flounder filets
1 cup plain low-fat yogurt
1/2 teaspoon curry powder
1/4 teaspoon salt
1/4 teaspoon basil
1/8 teaspoon black pepper

Preheat oven to 350°. In skillet, sauté onion, celery, and green pepper in butter just until onion is tender. Place fish in greased baking dish, top with vegetable mixture. Mix together yogurt, curry, salt, basil, and pepper; pour over and around filets. Bake 30 minutes or until fish flakes easily with fork.

Margaret G. Killmon
Annandale, Virginia

Broiled Flounder Perfecto

YIELD: 1 serving

1 flounder filet about 1/2 pound
Italian salad dressing to taste

Pats of butter
Paprika to taste
Lemon slices as garnish

Rinse filet in cold water and allow to drain. Place filet skin down on individual fish or steak platter or pan lined with aluminum foil. Brush filet heavily with salad dressing. Dot with pats of butter and shake on paprika. Broil until slightly browned about 9 to 11 minutes or until fish flakes. Garnish with lemon slices.

Ernest C. Seiderman
Virginia Beach, Virginia

Crazy Fried Flounder

YIELD: 2 to 4 servings

1 tablespoon olive oil
1 package dry yeast
3 ounces beer
3 ounces chicken broth
1 cup flour
1/2 cup coconut, shredded

1 egg white, beaten
1 pound flounder
1/2 cup flour
1/4 teaspoon salt
Dash pepper
Oil (enough to fill heavy pan to a depth of at least 3 inches)

Combine first seven ingredients to make batter. Cut flounder into small pieces (about 2-by-2 inches). Season remaining flour with salt and pepper, then heat oil in heavy pan for deep frying. When oil is hot, dredge a piece of flounder in flour, dip in batter to coat completely, and then drop it into the oil. Deep fry, a few pieces at a time, for about 1 minute. Remove from oil with a slotted spoon and place on paper toweling to drain. Serve immediately or keep pieces warm in low (250°) oven until all pieces have been cooked.

Raymond J. Hanlein
Annandale, Virginia

Fabulous Flounder

YIELD: 4 servings

4 flounder filets
1 cup mayonnaise
Paprika to taste

Salt and pepper to taste
1/3 cup white wine
1/3 cup grated Parmesan cheese
1/3 cup slivered almonds

Preheat oven to 375°. Rinse flounder filets under cold water. Blot dry. Generously coat both sides of filets with mayonnaise. Place filets on a greased broiling tray and season with paprika, salt, and pepper. Bake for 20 minutes. Remove from oven. Sprinkle with wine, and then coat top lightly with Parmesan cheese and almond slivers. Return to oven and broil 6 to 8 minutes until cheese just begins to brown and almonds are toasted.

Arthur Upshaw
Midlothian, Virginia

Fancy Flounder

YIELD: 4 servings

2/3 cup butter
2 tablespoons dried chives
1/2 teaspoon garlic powder

1/8 teaspoon pepper
1-1/2 cups crushed thin
   bacon-flavored crackers
2 pounds flounder filets

Preheat oven to 350°. Melt butter over low heat. Add chives, garlic powder, and pepper; stir to blend. Dip flounder filets into melted butter and seasonings, then roll in crumbs to coat. Layer in baking dish. Add remaining crumbs to remaining butter, stir. Sprinkle over flounder. Bake for 25 to 30 minutes or until flounder flakes when touched lightly with fork.

Margaret G. Killmon
Annandale, Virginia

Filets of Flounder with Avocado and Cherry Tomato

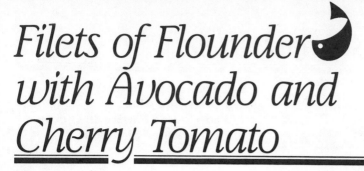

YIELD: 2 servings

1 tablespoon each butter and
  olive oil
Four 3-ounce filets of flounder
1 small avocado
6 similarly sized cherry tomatoes,
  rinsed, stemmed, and halved

1/2 cup dry white wine
1/2 cup heavy cream
1 garlic clove, peeled and halved
1/2 teaspoon crushed dried
  coriander leaves
Dash cayenne pepper
Salt and pepper to taste

In a skillet large enough to hold all of the filets without crowding, heat butter and olive oil over moderately high heat, shaking the skillet gently to swirl them together, until the butter foams. Add the flounder filets and sauté them, turning once, just until the flesh turns opaque most of the way through, about sixty seconds a side. With a slotted spatula, remove the filets to a heated serving dish, arranging them side by side, and keep them warm. The fish will continue to cook from its own internal heat. Remove the skillet temporarily from the burner and reduce the heat to moderately low.

Peel, halve, and pit the avocado. Return the skillet to the heat, adding more butter and olive oil in equal proportions if necessary. Cut each avocado half lengthwise into four equally sized crescents. Add the crescents to the skillet as you cut them, turning each slice to coat the cut surfaces with the butter and olive oil. Cook for about four minutes, turning once more, until the avocado is warmed through. With a slotted spatula, remove the avocado slices to a heated plate and keep them warm.

Increase the heat to moderately high. Add more butter and olive oil if necessary. Add the cherry tomato halves to the skillet, cut sides down, and sauté them for two to three minutes, shaking the pan gently, until they are warmed through. Remove them to the heated plate with the avocados.

Pour off the pan drippings and return the skillet to the heat. Add the white wine all at once, scraping up any browned bits from the bottom of the skillet with a spatula. The boiling wine will loosen them. Add the cream, coriander leaves, cayenne pepper and garlic; bring the mixture to a boil and cook, stirring frequently, until it is thickened and reduced slightly, about five minutes.

Filets of Flounder with Avocado and Cherry Tomato

Meanwhile, arrange two avocado slices on top of each filet, facing each other with concave edges in and ends touching. Arrange three cherry tomato halves, cut sides down, in a line between each pair of avocado slices.

Taste the sauce for seasoning, remove the garlic and add salt and pepper to taste. Pour sauce in a ribbon across the centers of the filets and serve at once.

Brie Combs
Virginia Beach, Virginia

Flounder Circles of Wheels

This unusual combination of fish and tomatoes was the grand prize winner in the 1982 recipe contest.

YIELD: 1 serving

1 6- to 8-ounce flounder filet, skinned
4 ounces lime juice
4 ounces Parmesan cheese

1 whole tomato (preferably Italian tomato)
Salt and pepper to taste
1 to 2 whole strips bacon, partially cooked

To make one "circle": cut filet into serving size strip, large enough to go around tomato. Dip filet in lime juice and sprinkle heavily with Parmesan cheese. Cap tomato. Sprinkle with cheese, salt, and pepper to taste. Wrap filet around tomato, resprinkle with cheese, and wrap bacon around filet Pin with toothpicks which have been soaked in water or a metal skewer and place in broiler pan. Broil 5 to 6 inches from source of heat about 10 minutes or until filet flakes easily.

Note: If filet tears, you may piece together with toothpicks.

Croaker, trout, blue fish, or spot can be used in this recipe. Each fish will have a different taste.

Valerie DiLorenzo Robinson
Lively, Virginia

Flounder, Creole-Style

YIELD: 6 servings

2 pounds flounder filets
1-1/2 cups chopped tomato
1/2 cup chopped green pepper
1/3 cup lemon juice

1 tablespoon vegetable oil
2 teaspoons salt
2 teaspoons instant minced onion
1 teaspoon basil
1/4 teaspoon pepper
4 drops tabasco sauce

Preheat oven to 375°. Place fish in a greased baking dish; combine all other ingredients and spoon on top of fish. Bake for 15 to 20 minutes, or until fish flakes with a fork. Garnish with tomato wedges and green pepper rings.

D.M. Grigel
Roanoke, Virginia

Flounder Filets à la Florentine

YIELD: 6 servings

1/2 cup herb-seasoned
    stuffing mix
6 tablespoons melted butter
2 flounder filets, 1-1/2 pounds
    each
4 pats of butter, 1 teaspoon each
1/4 teaspoon salt

1/4 teaspoon pepper
2 teaspoons lemon juice
1 teaspoon Worcestershire sauce
1/4 cup dry white wine
1 12-ounce box Stouffer's frozen
    spinach soufflé, thawed
1/2 cup grated Parmesan cheese
1 2-1/2-ounce jar sliced
    mushrooms, drained

Preheat oven to 375°. Toss herb stuffing mix with melted butter. Set aside. Pat filets dry and place in a greased shallow 9-by-12-inch baking dish. Dot filets with the pats of butter and sprinkle evenly with salt, pepper, lemon juice, Worcestershire sauce, and wine. Spread the thawed spinach soufflé evenly over the filets and top each with the Parmesan cheese, sliced mushrooms, and buttered herb stuffing mix. Bake uncovered about 25 minutes. Fish should flake when tested with a fork.

Mrs. Joseph H. Metzger, Jr.
Richmond, Virginia

Flounder Ooh La La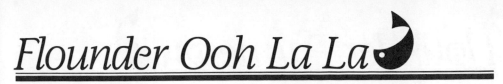

YIELD: 4 servings

1/3 cup chopped onion
1/3 cup chopped green or
   red pepper
1/3 cup chopped pecans
1 pound flounder filets, cubed

1 tablespoon lemon juice
1/4 teaspoon Worcestershire
   sauce
1/4 teaspoon tabasco sauce
1 cup mayonnaise
1 10-ounce can cream of celery
   soup, undiluted

Sauté onion, green pepper, and pecans until onions are clear. Add cubed fish and sauté 5 minutes longer. Sprinkle lemon juice, Worcestershire sauce, and tabasco sauce on fish. Add mayonnaise and soup. Heat gently—do not boil. Serve on toast points.

Kay Woodruff
Poquoson, Virginia

Crab: A delicacy by Any Name

The blue crab is perhaps Virginia's more famous seafood, having been popularized by William Warner in his Pulitzer Prize-winning book, *Beautiful Swimmer*. The book title is the English translation of the crab's Latin name, *Callinectus sapidus*.

Indeed a beautiful swimmer, the blue crab's swimming legs allow it to rapidly outdistance its other crab relatives which generally crawl along the bottom on their travels.

The blue crab gets its English nickname from the bright blue of the male's big pincer claws. The female crab's claws have some blue on them, but the tips are red. Those big male crabs are nicknamed "Jimmys" and the females are called "sooks."

A blue crab grows by shedding the entire outer covering of its body. Just before shedding, the new shell will begin to show through the old shell in the form of a red line most visible on the edges of the flat paddle fins. A crab in this stage is called a "peeler."

Once it has shed its skin, the crab becomes a soft-shell crab, a great delicacy to gourmets. Soft-shell crab processors must retrieve the crab from the water within an hour after it has shed in order to halt the hardening phase. Crabs whose shells have begun to harden again are known as "paper shells" or "buckrams."

Blue crabs mate when the female is in the soft stage. The Jimmy crab will carry a female peeler beneath him taking her to a safe place to shed. When she has finished shedding, the sook will again be carried by the Jimmy while they mate and until her shell hardens again.

By any name the blue crab is one of Virginia's favorite seafood delights. The soft-shell are available only in the summer months but crab meat is in the markets all year and the variety of ways to fix it is limited only by the imagination.

Flounder Parmesan

YIELD: 4 servings

4 flounder filets
Salt to taste
Pepper to taste
Flour as needed
2 eggs, beaten
Fine bread crumbs as needed
1/2 cup grated Parmesan cheese
Paprika to taste
Cayenne to taste
1 teaspoon chopped parsley
1/2 teaspoon oregano

3 to 4 tablespoons butter or
  vegetable oil

HOT TOMATO SAUCE
2 tablespoons butter
1 onion, thinly sliced
2 tablespoons flour
1-1/2 cups stewed tomatoes
Salt and pepper to taste
Dash sugar
Dash ginger
1 bay leaf

Wash and wipe filets. Season with salt and pepper. Dust with flour and dip in egg. Mix crumbs, cheese, and seasonings. Dip fish in crumbs and coat well. Let stand for 15 minutes (or refrigerate). Brown well in melted, frothy butter (or oil) on both sides. Sprinkle with chopped parsley and oregano and serve with Hot Tomato Sauce.

Melt butter and sauté onion until golden brown. Remove onion and add flour. Remove from heat. Blend well and brown ever so slightly. Add tomatoes, onion, seasoning, and heat to boiling. Simmer for 20 minutes. Serve as topping on flounder filets.

Note: This sauce can be used on other baked or broiled fish.

Charlotte M. Crews
Lynchburg, Virginia

Flounder Patrice

YIELD: 4 servings

6 tablespoons butter or
margarine, divided
2 slices whole wheat bread,
crumbled
1 4-ounce can mushrooms,
finely chopped
3 tablespoons very finely
chopped onion

Dash rubbed thyme
Dash garlic salt
1 pound Virginia flounder filets
3 tablespoons lemon juice
Salt and pepper to taste
Fresh parsley as garnish
Lemon slices as garnish

Preheat oven to 350°. Melt 4 tablespoons butter in skillet. Sauté bread crumbs, mushrooms, onion, thyme, and garlic salt 5 minutes. Set aside. Place filets in greased 9-by-13-inch glass baking dish. Sprinkle filets with lemon juice, dot with remaining butter, and sprinkle with salt and pepper. Spoon mixture from skillet onto filets. Bake for 25 minutes. Garnish with parsley and lemon slices just before serving.

Patricia W. Pope
Salem, Virginia

🐚🐚🐚🐚🐚🐚🐚

Flounder Pinwheels

YIELD: 6 servings

2 cups fresh basil, tightly
   packed (see note)
1/2 cup fresh grated Parmesan
   cheese
2 garlic cloves, chopped

1/2 to 3/4 cup olive oil
4 tablespoons butter
1 teaspoon salt
1/4 cup chopped walnuts
Melted butter as needed
6 8- to 10-ounce thin flounder
   filets per person

Wash and pick over basil leaves, removing stems. Pat dry. In blender, processor, or mortar and pestle chop basil leaves, and then add cheese, garlic, 1/2 cup olive oil, butter, and salt. Purée. Add more oil as needed if paste seems dry. Add walnuts last. Once walnuts have been added, be careful not to over mix. Some texture should remain.

Preheat oven to 450°. Place a little melted butter in ovenproof dish. Spread out each filet and spread each one with 2 tablespoons paste. Roll up jelly roll-style and place seam side down. Drizzle rolls with melted butter, and add on top a few lumps of paste. Bake 12 to 18 minutes, or until fish flakes easily.

Note: If fresh basil is not in season, substitute 1 cup parsley, 2 cups fresh spinach leaves, and 1 tablespoon dried basil. This works very well and can be used in the winter.

Fewer filets can be used and leftover paste will keep in refrigerator one week.

Nancy Jo Leachman
Charlottesville, Virginia

Flounder Reuben

YIELD: 2 servings

1 to 2 cups sliced mushrooms
1 large garlic clove, minced
2 or 3 shallots, chopped
4 tablespoons butter
Salt and pepper to taste
1/2 cup white wine
1 teaspoon oregano or Italian
    seasoning

1 pound flounder filet
2 tomatoes, sliced
1/2 cup chopped or sliced black
    olives
3 slices baked or boiled ham,
    cut into small pieces
1/2 cup grated Swiss cheese
Chopped parsley for garnish

Preheat oven to 350°. Sauté mushrooms, garlic, and shallots in 2 table-spoons butter until soft, about 5 minutes. Add the salt, pepper, wine, and oregano. Continue cooking butter mixture until somewhat reduced. Place half of the mixture in a baking dish; add the fish and cover with the rest of the mushroom mixture. Layer with the tomatoes, olives, and ham. Sprinkle with the cheese and rest of the butter. Bake for about 1/2 hour or until fish is done. Sprinkle with parsley.

Esther Blum
Baltimore, Maryland

Flounder Roulades

YIELD: 4 servings

4 flounder filets (about 2 pounds),
    split lengthwise
1 10-ounce package frozen
    chopped spinach or chopped
    broccoli

3/4 cup creamy Italian salad
    dressing
2 teaspoons cornstarch
1/2 cup grated Parmesan cheese
Paprika to taste

Preheat oven to 350°. Loosely roll founder. Secure with toothpick. Place upright in greased shallow baking dish. Cook and drain spinach or broccoli. Mix dressing, cornstarch, and Parmesan. Add to spinach or broccoli and mix thoroughly. Spoon into loosely rolled filets. Put remainder around edges. Sprinkle with paprika. Bake 20 to 25 minutes.

Marjorie A. Clark
Virginia Beach, Virginia

Flounder Scaloppini

YIELD: 6 to 8 servings

2 pounds flounder filets
2 tablespoons flour
1 teaspoon salt
1/4 teaspoon pepper
1 garlic clove

4 tablespoons butter, divided
2 tablespoons vegetable oil
1/2 pound mushrooms, thinly
   sliced
1/2 cup water
1 cup dry white wine

Preheat oven to 350°. Sprinkle flounder with mixture of flour, salt, and pepper. Brown garlic clove in 3 tablespoons of butter mixed with the oil. Remove garlic and add filets one or two at a time. Quickly brown on both sides and remove from oil to a shallow baking dish. Melt remaining butter in skillet. Add mushrooms and sauté until golden. Add water and wine. Scrape sides and bottom of pan. Bring to a boil and simmer 3 minutes to blend flavors. Pour sauce over fish. Cover and bake for 20 minutes, or until fish flakes with a fork.

Nancy Sparks Morrison
Roanoke, Virginia

Hidden Treasure Flounder  Bake

YIELD: 6 to 8 servings

4 tablespoons butter or margarine
6 to 8 flounder strips, serving-
   size portions
2 10-ounce packages frozen
   asparagus spears, thawed

2 tablespoons orange juice
   concentrate, undiluted
2 teaspoons grated orange peel
1 cup sour cream
1/2 cup grated Parmesan cheese,
   divided
1/4 cup crushed soda crackers

Preheat oven to 350°. Using 1 teaspoon butter, grease shallow glass baking dish. Wrap each flounder strip around 3 or 4 asparagus spears and place in baking dish. Combine sour cream, orange concentrate, 1/4 cup cheese, and grated orange peel. Spread over fish. Combine remaining cheese with cracker crumbs and sprinkle over fish. Combine remaining cheese with cracker crumbs and sprinkle over top of casserole. Dot with remaining butter and bake uncovered for about 30 minutes or until fish flakes easily. Serve immediately.

June E. Bowers
Sarasota, Florida

Lively Lemon Flounder Roll-ups

YIELD: 8 servings

1/3 cup butter or margarine
1/3 cup lemon juice
2 chicken-flavored bouillon cubes
1 teaspoon tabasco sauce
1 cup cooked rice

1 10-ounce package frozen
  chopped broccoli, thawed
1 cup shredded sharp Cheddar
  cheese
8 flounder filets (about 2 pounds)
Paprika as needed

Preheat oven to 375°. In a small sauce pan, melt butter. Add lemon juice, bouillon, and tabasco. Heat slowly until bouillon dissolves. Set aside. In medium bowl, combine rice, broccoli, cheese, and 1/4 cup lemon butter bouillon sauce. Mix well. Divide broccoli mixture equally among filets. Roll up and place seam side down in shallow baking dish. Pour remaining sauce over roll-ups. Bake 25 minutes, or until fish flakes with fork. Garnish with paprika.

Nancy Q. Hull
Hillsville, Virginia

Low Calorie Flounder Florentine

YIELD: 4 servings

1 egg, beaten
2 tablespoons lemon juice
8 ounces plain low-fat yogurt
1 10-ounce package frozen
    spinach, cooked and
    well-drained
3 tablespoons grated Parmesan
    cheese

1 8-ounce can water chestnuts,
    chopped
1 package Knorr's Vegetable
    Soup Mix
1 pound flounder filets
1 lemon, sliced
Paprika to taste

Preheat oven to 375°. Combine egg, lemon juice, and yogurt until well blended. Stir in spinach, cheese, water chestnuts, and soup mix. In a greased casserole, place 1/2 flounder. Top with spinach mixture, spreading evenly. Top with remaining flounder. Place lemon slices evenly over flounder and sprinkle with paprika. Bake 20 minutes or until fish flakes with a fork.

Shirley Jean Lewis
Charlottesville, Virginia

Quickie Cheesed Flounder

YIELD: 4 servings

1/2 cup flour
1/2 teaspoon salt
1/4 teaspoon pepper
4 flounder filets (about 2 pounds)
2 eggs beaten with 2 tablespoons
    water

3/4 cup fine bread crumbs
1/2 cup grated Parmesan cheese
Dash salt, pepper, and paprika
3 tablespoons butter and/or
    vegetable oil
1 tablespoon parsley
1/2 teaspoon oregano
2 cups tomato sauce, heated

Blend flour, salt, and pepper together and dip filets in this mixture. Dip filets in the beaten egg-water mixture. Combine crumbs, cheese, salt, pepper, and paprika. Dip filets in this mixture and coat well. Let stand approximately 15 minutes.

In skillet heat oil and butter, add the filets and brown well on both sides. Sprinkle with the parsley and oregano. Serve with hot tomato sauce.

Frances M. Biss
Washington, D.C.

Tempura Fried Flounder

YIELD: 4 servings

1/2 cup flour
1/2 cup cornstarch
2 teaspoons baking powder

1 tablespoon sugar
1/4 teaspoon salt
1/2 cup ice water
1 egg, beaten
1 pound flounder filets

Sift flour, cornstarch, baking powder, sugar, and salt together. Combine water and egg in a medium bowl. Carefully stir dry ingredients into egg mixture, leaving air bubbles. Heat about 2 inches of oil in skillet or electric skillet heated to 375°. Dip filets into the tempura batter and brown in oil on one side, turn and brown on other side. Drain filets on paper towels.

Nancy A. White
Falls Church, Virginia

Monk Fish Provencal

YIELD: 3 to 4 servings

1 1-pound monk fish filet
Salt and pepper, to taste
1 tablespoon vegetable oil
1 tablespoon butter or margarine
1 celery rib, thinly sliced
1 small onion, thinly sliced
2 garlic cloves, minced

1 16-ounce can whole tomatoes, drained and coarsely chopped
2 tablespoons chopped fresh parsley
1/2 teaspoon dried thyme leaves
2 teaspoons butter or margarine
2 teaspoons grated Parmesan cheese

Preheat oven to 400°. Cut fish into 1 and 1-1/2 inch chunks and arrange in a buttered 1-1/2-quart casserole. Sprinkle with salt and pepper. In skillet, heat oil and butter over moderate heat. Add the celery, onion, and garlic and cook about 5 minutes or until onion is translucent. Stir occasionally. Add tomatoes, parsley, thyme, salt, and pepper. Stir and cook 1 minute. Spoon over fish. Dot with 2 teaspoons butter and sprinkle with cheese. Bake 20 to 25 minutes.

Merrilyn S. Dodson
Newport News, Virginia

Monk Fish with Green Sauce

YIELD: 3 to 4 servings

1 cup packed fresh coriander
   leaves
Juice of 1/2 fresh lime
2 green onions, with tops, sliced

2 garlic cloves
Dash red pepper
1/2 cup brandy
1 pound monk fish filets, cut into
   1-inch size pieces
4 tablespoons butter, divided

Place coriander, lime juice, onions, garlic, red pepper, and brandy in blender and blend on high until thoroughly mixed. Sauté fish in 3 tablespoons butter over medium heat until firm and white. Remove fish to platter. Keep warm. Add contents of blender and 1 tablespoon of butter to remaining butter in pan. Reduce sauce over medium heat until most moisture is gone. Return fish to pan, mix well. Serve with rice or over fettucini.

Note: Rockfish, sea trout, or scallops may be used.

Susan B. Bostwick
Kensington, Maryland

Butter and Lime Fresh Perch Filets

YIELD: 6 servings

6 tablespoons butter
2 pounds fresh perch filets
1 teaspoon salt
1/4 teaspoon black pepper

1/3 cup fresh lime juice
1/2 teaspoon dill weed
1 fresh lime, thinly sliced
1/4 cup chopped fresh parsley
Tomato wedges for garnish

Preheat oven to 350°. Melt butter in 9-by-13-by-2 baking pan. Lay fish in pan over butter. Season fish with salt and pepper. Pour lime juice over fish. Bake for 20 minutes. Baste fish with pan juices. Sprinkle dill weed over fish. Place lime slices over fish. Continue to bake 5 more minutes or until fish flakes easily with fork. Scatter parsley over all. Garnish with tomato wedges.

Ruth Dykes
Beltsville, Maryland

Barbequed Sea Trout Harrell

YIELD: 4 servings

4 large trout (3/4 pound each),
    cleaned
4 tablespoons butter or margarine

1/4 cup lemon juice
1/4 cup soy sauce
3/4 teaspoon ground ginger
1/2 teaspoon pepper
Parsley for garnish

Cut 3 slashes on each side of fish. Mix other ingredients, except parsley, in small sauce pan and heat. Brush inside of fish generously with mixture. Place fish in flat wire basket or foil (with holes poked in). Cook on grill 5 minutes on each side or until fish flakes easily. Baste frequently. Garnish with parsley.

    Note: The grill, if gas, should be set on medium. Regular coals should be allowed to set about 30 to 40 minutes before using.

Sharon Harrell
Suffolk, Virginia

Barbequed Sea Trout Robertson

YIELD: 3 to 4 servings

1 trout filet (about 2-1/2 pounds)
1/2 tablespoon melted butter
1 teaspoon lemon juice

1 teaspoon Old Bay seafood
    seasoning
1 teaspoon fresh dill
Salt and pepper to taste
1/4 teaspoon garlic powder

Place filet on heavy aluminum foil. Mix remaining ingredients and pour over filet. Wrap foil around fish. Place foil pouch on hot barbeque grill. Poke small holes in top of foil. Cook over hot coals for 15 minutes.

Scott Robertson
Newport News, Virginia

Poached Sea Trout with Dill

YIELD: 4 servings

8 celery stalks
4 large carrots, cut in strips
2 zucchini, cut in wide strips
2 pounds filet of sea trout

1 cup white wine
1-1/2 teaspoons dried dill weed
1 tablespoon chopped fresh
   parsley
Fresh ground black pepper to taste
Lemon wedges (optional)

Place vegetables in large skillet. Lay trout on top. Pour wine over fish. Sprinkle dill weed, parsley, and pepper over fish. Cover and simmer 20 to 25 minutes or until fish flakes. Garnish with lemon wedges.

Karen Pearson
Norfolk, Virginia

Sea Trout in Sour Cream

YIELD: 3 to 4 servings

1 pound sea trout filets
Salt to taste
Pepper to taste
1/4 cup melted butter
2 tablespoons finely chopped
   dill pickle
2 tablespoons finely chopped
   onion

2 tablespoons finely chopped
   green pepper
1 tablespoon chopped parsley
1 tablespoon lemon juice
1/4 teaspoon dry mustard
1/4 teaspoon basil leaves
1 cup sour cream
Paprika to taste

Dry fish thoroughly with absorbent toweling; salt and pepper to taste. Place in shallow 1 quart baking dish; brush with melted butter; broil 8 to 10 minutes or until fish flakes when tested with a fork. Meanwhile in a bowl gently blend pickle, onion, green pepper, parsley, lemon juice, mustard, and basil into sour cream. Spoon sour cream sauce over fish and sprinkle with paprika; return to broiler 2 to 3 minutes to glaze sauce.

Maxine R. Harrison
Salem, Virginia

Flaked Sea Trout Company Dish

YIELD: 6 servings

3 cups flaked cooked sea trout
   (or flounder)
1 6-ounce package chicken-flavor
   stuffing mix
1/2 cup diced green pepper
2 teaspoons Worcestershire sauce
1 teaspoon salt
1 cup diced celery
1 8-1/2-ounce can sliced water
   chestnuts, drained
2 eggs, slightly beaten
2 cups shredded Cheddar cheese,
   divided
1 2-1/4-ounce package sliced
   almonds

Preheat oven to 350°. Prepare stuffing mix according to package directions; spread mixture in a 12-by-7-by-2-inch casserole dish. Combine remaining ingredients, except for 1 cup cheese and almonds. Spread fish mixture over stuffing mix. Combine cheese and almonds; place on top of casserole. Cover with foil and bake 30 to 45 minutes, or until heated through. Remove foil during last 10 minutes of baking.

Karen Anderson
Blacksburg, Virginia

❀❀❀❀❀❀

Virginia Shore Hash-Brown Sea Trout Filets

YIELD: 6 to 8 servings

1-1/2 to 2 pounds sea trout
    filets
1 teaspoon salt
1/2 teaspoon pepper
1 teaspoon baking powder

2 eggs, beaten
1 cup milk
2 cups flour, divided
1 cup instant mashed potato
    flakes
Parsley or spinach leaves and
    lemon slices for garnish

Cut filets into serving size portions, about 4-ounces. Dry fish completely. Mix salt, pepper, baking powder, eggs, milk and 1 cup of flour until smooth in a medium size bowl. Heat on medium heat about 1/8 inch of oil in a large skillet until hot, but not smoking. Dip fish in remaining cup of flour, then in egg batter, then in potato flakes. Fry on medium heat for 4 to 5 minutes until light brown on one side Then turn and fry 4 to 5 minutes longer until light brown on other side. Remove from pan and drain any excess oil on paper. Garnish with parsley or spinach leaves and lemon slices.

George W. Lerch
Beltsville, Maryland

Planked Shad Dinner

YIELD: 6 servings

2 pounds shad filets
1-1/2 teaspoons salt
4 tablespoons melted butter
    or margarine

3 cups seasoned mashed potatoes
6 cups seasoned cooked
    vegetables (beans, carrots,
    cauliflower, peas, onions, or
    tomatoes)

Preheat oven to 350°. Wash shad filets and dry. Sprinkle with salt. Place fish on a well-greased plank, oven glass, or metal platter, approximately 16-by-9 inches. Brush with margarine. Bake in a moderate oven for 25 to 30 minutes or until fish flakes easily when tested with a fork. Baste occasionally with remaining margarine. Remove from oven and arrange a border of hot mashed potatoes around fish. Place under broiler approximately 8 inches from source of heat. Broil for 3 to 4 minutes or until potatoes are slightly browned. Remove from broiler and arrange choice of hot vegetables around fish.

*Seafood Adventures from the
Gulf and South Atlantic*

Shad Roe Baked in Foil

YIELD: 1 serving

1 pair shad roe
4 tablespoons butter, at room
    temperature, divided
3 tablespoons finely chopped
    parsley

Salt and pepper to taste
2 tablespoons dry white wine
    or vermouth
Paprika to taste

Preheat oven to 350°. Cut a rectangle of aluminum foil large enough to encompass roe envelope fashion. Spread 3 tablespoons butter on center of foil. Sprinkle with parsley. Place roe on top, dot with 1 tablespoon butter, salt and pepper lightly. Pull foil up at sides, and then add wine. Close foil and seal so that liquids will not escape. Bake for 20 to 25 minutes. Fold back foil, sprinkle roe with paprika, and brown lightly under broiler. Remove from foil and serve roe and the juices poured over on hot plates.

Joan Gregory
Lively, Virginia

Shark Sauce Spaghetti

YIELD: 4 servings

1-1/2 pounds shark meat
1/4 cup peanut or vegetable oil
3 cups canned tomatoes
1/2 teaspoon garlic powder
1/8 teaspoon crushed red pepper
1/4 cup sauterne wine
1/4 pound hard salami, sliced
    and chopped

2 tablespoons capers, drained
1/4 cup parsley, chopped
1 teaspoon dill weed, crushed
1 tablespoon cornstarch mixed
    with 1/4 cup water
1/2 teaspoon monosodium
    glutamate
1 pound spaghetti, cooked

Cube shark meat into 3/4-inch pieces; set aside. In large sauce pan combine oil, tomatoes, garlic powder, red pepper, and sauterne. Cover and cook 12 minutes. Add salami, capers, parsley, dill weed, cornstarch, and monosodium glutamate. Continue cooking covered for 8 minutes. Add shark meat, stir, cover and continue cooking about 10 minutes, stirring occasionally. Remove from heat. Serve over hot spaghetti.

Lottie J. Pidgeon
Norfolk, Virginia

Mother's Spot Cakes

YIELD: 4 servings

1 diced carrot
2 stalks celery
1 whole onion, peeled
Salt and pepper, to taste
4 spot, cleaned

2 potatoes, peeled and cubed
1 egg, beaten
1 teaspoon prepared mustard
1 teaspoon finely chopped
   green pepper
1 tablespoon mayonnaise

Cover carrot, celery, and onion with water; add salt and pepper and bring to a boil. Add fish and potato. When the fish falls from the bone and potato is done, remove from heat and cool. Remove bones and discard. Remove fish and potatoes and mash the potatoes. Add fish, egg, mustard, a little of the cooked onion, mashed, green pepper, mayonnaise, salt and pepper and one tablespoon of fish stock to the potatoes. Form into cakes and fry.

Bernice Honick
Norfolk, Virginia

Casserole of Stuffed Baby Squid Provencal

YIELD: 4 servings

**3 pounds fresh Virginia baby
   squid, cleaned**
Salt to taste

STUFFING
2 teaspoons olive oil
2 garlic cloves, crushed
1 teaspoon fennel seed
2 cups long grain rice
4 cups water
1 teaspoon chopped parsley
Salt to taste

PROVENCAL SAUCE
1/2 cup olive oil
8 ounces finely chopped shallots
1 ounce garlic cloves, crushed
1 soup spoon herbs de provence
**2 pounds fresh ripe Italian
   tomatoes, chopped in 1/4-
   inch pieces**
2 bay leaves
8 ounces dry white wine
Salt and pepper to taste

Bring a large pot of water to a boil. Add a pinch of salt. Drop in squid and tentacles and simmer until nearly tender. Remove from stove and cool. To prepare stuffing heat olive oil and sauté garlic. Add fennel seed and rice. Add water and simmer until rice is well cooked. Cool. When mixture is cool, add parsley and salt. Chop tentacles finely and add to rice mixture. Mix until it forms a compact mixture. Fill the cavity of the squid with the stuffing mixture. Preheat oven to 350°.

To make provencal sauce, heat the olive oil and sauté shallots, garlic and herbes de provence. Add tomatoes, bay leaves, white wine, salt and pepper. Simmer for 15 minutes. Butter an earthenware casserole dish. Add a layer of provencal sauce. Place stuffed squid over sauce. Top with remaining sauce. Add a dash of white wine if desired. Cover and bake for 30 minutes.

Chef Peter Stogbuchner

Fried Squid

YIELD: 6 servings

3 pounds whole squid, cleaned
3 tablespoons lemon juice
1-1/2 teaspoons salt

1/8 teaspoon white pepper
2 eggs, beaten
3 tablespoons milk
1 1/2 cups flour
Lemon wedges for garnish

Cut mantle of squid crosswise into 1/2-inch rings. Cut tenacles into 1-inch pieces. Sprinkle lemon juice, salt, and pepper on squid. Combine egg and mlik. Dip squid in egg mixture and roll in flour. Place squid in a single layer in hot oil, in a 10-inch skillet. Fry at a moderate heat, 350° for 3 to 5 minutes. Turn carefully. Fry 3 to 5 minutes longer or until squid is lightly browned. Drain on absorbent paper. Serve with lemon wedges.

Seafood Adventures from the
Gulf and South Atlantic

Squid in Tomato Sauce

YIELD: 6 servings

2 pounds whole squid, cleaned
1 cup sliced onion
1 garlic clove, minced
2 tablespoons melted butter or
    margarine
1 can (1 pound) tomatoes,
    undrained

1/2 teaspoon basil leaves
1/4 cup water
1 tablespoon flour
1 teaspoon salt
Cooked hot rice, spaghetti or other
    pasta

Cut squid mantle and tentacles into 1-inch pieces. Cook onion and garlic in margarine until vegetables are tender. Add tomatoes and basil; simmer for 5 minutes. Add squid rings. Cover and return to a boil. Reduce heat and simmer for 3 to 5 minutes or until squid is tender. Blend water, flour and salt. Stir into squid mixture, stirring constantly, and continue to cook until thick. Serve with cooked rice, spaghetti or your choice of pasta.

Seafood Adventures from the
Gulf and South Atlantic

Striped Bass à la Vitale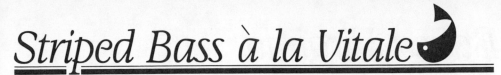

YIELD: 4 servings

1 striped bass (rock), 4 to 6
   pounds dressed weight
1 cup (2 sticks) butter, divided

2 lemons
1 teaspoon salt, divided
1/4 teaspoon pepper
2 teaspoons finely chopped white
   horseradish, divided

Preheat oven to 350°. Place the cleaned fish on a long strip of aluminum foil. Break 1 stick butter into chunks and place in, on, and around fish. Squeeze the juice of one lemon in, on, and around fish. Liberally salt and pepper fish inside and out. Wrap and seal in foil. Place fish in broiler pan to catch drippings should foil spring a leak. Bake for 1-1/2 hours. (Allow about 20 minutes per pound of fish.)

While the fish is baking, prepare the sauce. It should be reheated just before serving in a warmed sauce or gravy bowl to keep butter in a melted state. To a small sauce pan add remaining butter, 1 teaspoon of horseradish and 1/2 teaspoon salt and the juice of remaining lemon. Melt the butter slowly in the pan while stirring gently.

The whole baked fish should be placed on the table along with the bowl of sauce. The skin should be peeled from the fish and the white chunks of meat will lift easily from the bones with serving fork and knife. Sauce may be poured on top of the fish as desired OR the fish may be dipped into sauce served in individual bowls.

Note: The fish should be cleaned and scaled—head and tail may be removed before cooking if you desire, but the whole fish may be served on a large platter. The striped bass (rock) has a delicate unfishy flavor that resembles lobster when cooked and served in the described manner.

Herbert A. Vitale
Lynchburg, Virginia

Baked Virginia Seafood Casserole

YIELD: 5 to 6 servings

1 medium green pepper, finely
    chopped
1 medium onion, chopped
1 cup chopped celery
1/2 pound blue crab meat

1 pound scallops, quartered
1/2 teaspoon salt
1/8 teaspoon lemon-pepper
    seasoning
1 teaspoon Worcestershire sauce
1 cup mayonnaise
1 cup buttered bread crumbs

Preheat oven to 350°. Mix all ingredients, except crumbs. Spoon mixture into buttered, 8-by-10-inch casserole dish. Top with bread crumbs. Bake for 30 minutes. Serve on lettuce leaves if desired.

Rebecca Novak
Huddleston, Virginia

Casserole Supreme

YIELD: 10 servings

1 pound backfin crab meat
1 pound scallops
1/4 pound Smithfield ham, cubed
1 cup diced celery
3 chopped green onions with tops
1/2 small green pepper,
    chopped fine
1 tablespoon Worcestershire
    sauce

1 teaspoon chopped parsley
2 tablespoons lemon juice
1/2 pound fresh mushrooms,
    sliced (optional)
Salt and pepper to taste
1/2 pound mozzarella cheese
3 eggs, beaten
1 cup half and half cream

Preheat oven to 350°. Combine all ingredients except eggs and cream. Beat eggs with cream. Pour over other ingredients, mixing well. Pour into greased 4-quart casserole dish. Sprinkle with paprika. Bake for 45 minutes to an hour or until set.

    Note: Use salt sparingly, because of salt in ham.

Sally C. Condrey
Virginia Beach, Virginia

Crab Meat Stuffed Flounder

YIELD: 6 servings

2 tablespoons vegetable oil
1/3 cup minced onion
1/4 cup minced celery
1/4 cup minced green pepper
8 ounces backfin crab meat
3/4 cup stale white bread crumbs
1/2 teaspoon salt
1/4 teaspoon pepper

1/2 teaspoon Worcestershire
    sauce
1 egg, beaten
6 flounder filets (1-1/4 to 1-1/2
    pounds)
2 tablespoons white wine
2 tablespoons lemon juice
2 tablespoons melted butter or
    margarine

Preheat oven to 350°. Heat oil in large skillet over medium heat. Sauté onion, celery, and green pepper about 5 minutes. Combine crab meat and bread. Beat salt, pepper, and Worcestershire sauce into egg. Stir vegetables into crab meat, and then stir in egg mixture. Place about 1/6 of the stuffing on each filet. Roll filets around stuffing and place in 8-inch square baking pan. Combine wine and lemon juice. Pour over fish. Drizzle with melted butter Cover with foil and bake 15 minutes. Remove foil and bake 15 to 20 minutes longer or until fish flakes easily when tested with a fork.

Betty B. Maher
Richmond, Virginia

Crab-Stuffed Flounder with Seafood Sauce

YIELD: 4 servings

2 flounder filets (about 2 pounds)
1 teaspoon salt
1/4 teaspoon black pepper
2 green onions, minced
1/3 cup chopped fresh mushrooms
1/4 cup chopped green pepper
2 tablespoons butter or margarine
1/2 pound regular crabmeat,
  picked
1 tablespoon mayonnaise
1 teaspoon prepared mustard
1 teaspoon grated lemon peel
1/2 teaspoon tabasco sauce
1 tablespoon minced fresh parsley

SEAFOOD SAUCE
2 tablespoons butter or margarine
2 tablespoons flour
1/2 cup milk
1 cup clam juice
1/2 cup heavy cream
1/2 teaspoon salt
1/4 teaspoon lemon pepper
  seasoning
1/4 teaspoon thyme
1/4 teaspoon ground nutmeg
1 tablespoon dry sherry
1/4 teaspoon tabasco
1/4 pound crabmeat, picked
1/3 cup cooked, cleaned, and
  chopped shrimp

Preheat oven to 350°. Season flounder filets with salt and pepper. Make stuffing by sautéing onion, mushrooms, and green pepper in the butter. Add vegetables to the 1/2 pound crabmeat in a bowl. Add mayonnaise, mustard, lemon peel, tabasco sauce, and parsley. Mix until blended. Place stuffing on top of one filet. Place the remaining filet on top of the stuffing. Put stuffed flounder in a greased pan and bake for 25 minutes on until fish flakes easily with fork. Make sauce by melting butter in a skillet. Blend in flour and slowly add milk, clam juice, and cream, stirring constantly until thickened. Add salt, lemon-pepper seasoning, thyme, nutmeg, sherry, and tabasco. Stir until blended. Add crabmeat and shrimp and simmer until heated through. Pour over cooked filets. Garnish with lemon wedges, cherry tomatoes, and parsley sprigs, if desired.

Ruth Dykes
Beltsville, Maryland

Fish Cartoccio

This recipe for Fish Cartoccio (Fish in a Bag) was provided to the 1982 Governor's Tasting by Chef Andres Villena of the Il Porto Restaurant in Richmond, Virginia.

YIELD: 1 serving

1 8-ounce trout, cleaned and split
2 mussels (in shells), washed
2 "top neck"-size clams
3 ounces bay scallops (10 to 12)
1 cup tomato sauce
8 fresh basil leaves OR
    1 teaspoon dry basil

1 teaspoon oregano
1 pinch freshly ground black
    pepper
Salt to taste
2-1/2 teaspoons olive oil
1 garlic clove, diced
1 tablespoon minced parsley
1/4 cup dry white wine

Preheat oven to 375°. Place the fish lengthwise on a 16-by-16-inch sheet of aluminum foil. Bring up the edges of the foil, and top the fish with mussels, clams, and scallops. In a mixing bowl pour the tomato sauce and add the basil, oregano, salt, pepper, oil, garlic, and parsley. Slowly mix it all, thinning it out with wine until sauce is smooth. Pour the sauce over the fish. Completely enclose it, crimping the foil to seal the edges tightly. Place the foil-wrapped fish in a large baking pan and transfer to the oven. Bake until the fish flakes easily when tested with a fork, about 40 to 45 minutes. Serve hot from the foil.

Chef Andres Villena

Flounder and Scallops in Ginger-Lime Butter

YIELD: 4 servings

GINGER-LIME BUTTER
1/2 cup (1 stick) unsalted butter, at room temperature
1 tablespoon finely minced fresh ginger
1 tablespoon soy sauce
1 tablespoon sesame oil
Grated peel of one lime

2 tablespoons fresh lime juice
4 5- to 6-ounce Virginia flounder filets
16 Virginia scallops
1/4 pound fresh snow peas, julienned lengthwise into 1/4-inch slices
Salt and pepper to taste
Cherry tomato rosettes for garnish

Combine ginger-lime butter ingredients together in a small bowl, stirring until smooth and completely mixed.

Preheat oven to 400°. Spread one side of each filet with about 2 tablespoons each of the ginger-lime butter. Arrange filets butter side up in a single layer in a well-greased shallow baking pan. Place 4 scallops on each filet. Scatter snow peas over all. Sprinkle lightly with salt and pepper. Cover tightly with foil and bake for about 10 minutes or until fish flakes easily with a fork. Time varies with thickness of filets and size of scallops. Do not overcook.

To serve: Arrange filets topped with scallops and snow peas on a heated platter. Spoon some of the lime-butter juices over the fish. Garnish with a ring of cherry tomato rosettes around edge of platter. To make rosettes: Make two cuts at right angles to each other through center of blossom end of tomato—stop knife before cutting all the way through tomato. With fingers, gently spread the sections to form rosette "petals."

Dianna M. Winsor
Arlington, Virginia

Individual Seafood Casserole

YIELD: 6 to 8 servings

1/2 cup raw shrimp, cut into bite-sized pieces
1/2 cup crab meat, flaked
1/2 cup scallops, cut into bite-sized pieces
1/2 cup sliced fresh mushrooms
2 green onions thinly sliced with tops

7 tablespoons butter, divided
1/2 teaspoon salt
1/4 teaspoon pepper
2 tablespoons dry vermouth
3 tablespoons flour
1-1/2 cups milk
1/2 cup bread crumbs
1/4 cup grated Parmesan cheese

Preheat oven to 400°. Sauté seafood, mushrooms, and onion in 4 tablespoons butter. Season with salt, pepper, and vermouth. Prepare a cream sauce by melting three tablespoons of butter and stirring in flour until well blended. Add milk and stir over medium heat until thickened. Add seafood mixture to cream sauce and divide among individual ramekins or shells. Sprinkle tops with bread crumbs and Parmesan cheese. Bake 15 to 20 minutes or until brown and bubbly.

Priscilla Cady
Fairfax, Virginia

Liz's Seafood Imperial

YIELD: 6 servings

1 pound fresh mushrooms
1 red onion, chopped
1/2 cup chopped green pepper
1/2 cup chopped celery
1 tablespoon butter
1 garlic clove, minced
3/4 pound crab meat
3/4 pound shrimp, steamed
and cleaned
3/4 pound scallops
1 tablespoon chopped fresh
parsley
1/2 teaspoon salt
1/2 teaspoon pepper
1-1/2 tablespoons Worcestershire
sauce
1/2 cup Parmesan cheese
1 cup mayonnaise
5 slices bacon, cooked and
crumbled
Bread crumbs for topping

Preheat oven to 400°. Sauté mushrooms, onion, pepper, and celery in butter until lightly browned. Add garlic. Combine seafood, remaining seasonings, half the cheese, mayonnaise, and bacon. Pour into casserole dish, top with bread crumbs and remaining cheese. Bake 20 to 25 minutes.

Millard Radford
Richmond, Virginia

Neptune's Delight

YIELD: 8 servings

7 tablespoons butter, divided
1/4 cup flour
1-1/2 cups half and half cream
1/2 cup grated Parmesan cheese
1/2 cup heavy cream
1/2 teaspoon paprika
2 tablespoons sherry
1-1/2 cups crab meat
1 cup cooked shrimp, cleaned
1-1/2 cups onion garlic croutons
1/4 cup fresh parsley

Preheat oven to 350°. Melt 3 tablespoons butter in large sauce pan. Remove from heat and stir in flour to paste consistency. Slowly add half and half stirring vigorously. Return to heat. Add cheese and continue stirring until thick and creamy. Remove from heat again and add cream, paprika, sherry, and seafood. Mix. Spoon into eight shell-shaped baking shells. In food processor blend croutons and parsley. Spread over seafood mixture to edges and top with 4 tablespoons melted butter. Refrigerate until needed. Bake for 20 minutes or until bubbly.

Jacqueline E. Harkness
Virginia Beach, Virginia

Norfolk Flounder and Crab Casserole

YIELD: 6 servings

1 pound flounder filets
1 4-ounce can mushrooms,
    drained and chopped
1 medium onion, chopped
2/3 cup melted butter
1/2 pound crab meat, flaked
1 cup herb-seasoned stuffing
    mix, crushed

1 egg, beaten
2 tablespoons parsley
1/4 teaspoon salt
2 tablespoons lemon juice
1/4 teaspoon tabasco sauce

TOPPING
1/2 cup herb seasoned stuffing
    mix, crushed
2 tablespoons melted butter

Preheat oven to 350°. Place flounder filets in ungreased 8-inch square baking dish. Sauté mushrooms and onion in 2/3 cup butter and pour into large bowl containing crab meat, 1 cup of crushed stuffing mix, beaten egg, and seasonings. Mix well and spread over flounder. To make topping, combined 1/2 cup of stuffing mix and remaining butter. Sprinkle over crab mixture. Bake 30 to 35 minutes or until fish flakes easily.

Janice Young
Norfolk, Virginia

❀ ❀ ❀ ❀ ❀ ❀

Old Dominion Mariner's Quiche

YIELD: 2 9-inch pies

1 10-ounce package frozen
    spinach, thawed
1 large onion, chopped
2 tablespoons vegetable oil
1 3-ounce package cream cheese,
    at room temperature
1 cup creamed cottage cheese
1 teaspoon Italian herb seasoning
1 egg, beaten
Salt and pepper to taste
2 unbaked 9-inch deep-dish pie
    shells

1 10-ounce can cream of celery
    soup
8 ounces scallops
1 pound flounder filets, skinned
    and cubed
1/2 teaspoon horseradish
1 tablespoon chopped pimento
3-1/2 tablespoons grated
    Parmesan cheese
4 tablespoons fine bread crumbs
Butter as needed
3/4 cup shredded sharp Cheddar
    cheese

Preheat oven to 350° to 375°. Press spinach in strainer to remove all moisture. Cook onion in oil until softened. Blend spinach, cream cheese, cottage cheese, herb seasoning, egg, salt, and pepper. Divide mixture between pie shells. Combine soup, scallops, fish, horseradish, and pimento. Spread over cheese layers in each pie shell. Combine Parmesan cheese and bread crumbs. Sprinkle on pies. Bake for 40 to 45 minutes or until bubbly. Remove from oven and dot with butter and Cheddar cheese. Return to oven for 5 minutes to melt cheese. Let stand 20 minutes before cutting into wedges.

Note: One quiche may be frozen, if desired. If freezing do not add either cheese topping until quiche is removed from freezer.

Josie T. Bishop
Christiansburg, Virginia

224

Oysters Alex with Crab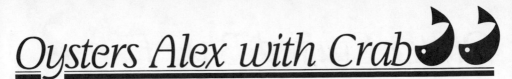

Coquille shells make for pretty presentation in this version of Bridget Meagher's celebrated Oyster's Alex, a favorite from Alexander's Restaurant in Roanoke, Virginia. It was served at the 1983 Governor's Tasting.

YIELD: 8 servings

8 coquille shells
1 pint select oysters
1/2 pound backfin crab
Buttered French bread crumbs

BEARNAISE SAUCE
1/2 tablespoon tarragon

1 1/2 tablespoons minced green onion tops
1/4 teaspoon minced garlic
1/4 cup dry white wine
1 cup red wine vinegar
1 cup (2 sticks) salted butter
4 large egg yolks
1/8 teaspoon cayenne pepper

Preheat oven to 350°. In each coquille shell, place 3 oysters and 1 ounce of crab meat. Sprinkle with bread crumbs. Bake for 10 minutes. To make bearnaise sauce, combine tarragon, green onion, garlic, wine, and vinegar in a sauce pan. Cook over medium heat until reduced to approximately 2 tablespoons. Remove from heat. Melt butter in separate pan. Remove from heat. Whip heat yolks over a double boiler until yolks begin to test warm with fingertips. Add yolks to reduced mixture and gradually pour in melted butter until thickened. Remove shells from oven and spread bearnaise sauce over each. Return to oven for 5 additional minutes.

Chef Bridget Meagher

Oyster Stuffed Blue Fish with Tangy Tomato Sauce

YIELD: 6 servings

STUFFING
1/2 pint oysters, drained
4 tablespoons butter or margarine,
    divided
1/4 cup chopped celery
1/4 cup chopped onion
1/4 cup chopped fresh mushrooms
2 cups chopped spinach
1/2 teaspoon ground nutmeg
1/2 teaspoon salt
1 cup cooked rice

1 3- to 4-pound blue fish, cleaned
1/2 teaspoon salt
Lemon slices and parsley sprigs
    for garnish

TANGY TOMATO SAUCE
1 15-ounce can tomato sauce
    with tomato bits
1/2 cup white wine
1/2 teaspoon sweet basil
1 small garlic clove, mashed
1/2 teaspoon sugar
1/2 teaspoon tabasco

Remove any shell from oysters. Chop oysters in half. Sauté oysters in 2 tablespoons butter Set oysters aside. In skillet, over medium heat, sauté celery, onion, and mushrooms in remaining butter until tender. Add spinach, nutmeg, salt, and rice. Add oysters. Mix gently until blended.

Preheat oven to 350°. Wash fish; dry with paper towels. Sprinkle salt inside fish cavity; then fill with stuffing mixture. Secure with wooden picks or small skewers. Place fish in a greased baking pan. Bake for 20 minutes. Place tomato sauce, wine, basil leaves, garlic, sugar, and tabasco in a small pan. Simmer 10 minutes, stirring constantly. Pour half of the sauce over fish and continue to bake 20 minutes or until fish flakes asily with fork. Pour remaining sauce over fish. Garnish with lemon slices and parsley sprigs.

Ruth Dykes
Beltsville, Maryland

Seafood Casserole

YIELD: 12 servings

3/4 cup (3 sticks) butter or
    margarine
1-1/2 pounds fresh mushrooms,
    sliced
3/4 cup flour
Dash garlic salt
2 cups chicken broth
1/2 cup cream
1-1/2 cups milk

1 teaspoon salt
2 tablespoons yellow mustard
Few drops tabasco sauce
1 tablespoon lemon juice˙
1 pound fresh crab meat
1-1/2 pound cooked scallops
2-1/2 pounds medium shrimp,
    cooked and shelled
1/4 cup dry sherry
1 cup grated Parmesan cheese

Preheat oven to 350°. Melt butter in a large sauce pan. Add mushrooms and sauté a few minutes. Stir in flour and garlic salt. Gradually add chicken broth, cream and milk. Stir until smooth and thickened. Add seasonings. Add crab meat, scallops, and shrimp and mix carefully. Stir in sherry. Put in large greased casserole. Put grated cheese on top. Bake for 20 to 30 minutes until hot and bubbly.

Virginia French
Virginia Beach, Virginia

🐚🐚🐚🐚🐚🐚

Seafood Extravaganza

YIELD: 6 servings

Lemon juice as needed
Salt and pepper to taste
2- or 3-pound sea trout, fileted
2 medium onions, diced
4 tablespoons butter
1 package herb-stuffing mix
2 eggs, slightly beaten

1 pound crab meat
1/2 pound steamed shrimp,
   shelled and coarsely chopped
1 ounce medium dry sherry
1/2 teaspoon oregano
1/2 teaspoon marjoram
1/2 teaspoon sage
1/2 teaspoon thyme
1/2 teaspoon ground pepper

Preheat oven to 450°. Lightly grease a 9-by-14-inch baking dish and
sprinkle with lemon juice, salt, and pepper. Place trout filets in dish, and
sprinkle with lemon juice, salt, and pepper. Bake uncovered for 10 to 12
minutes. Remove from oven and set aside. Reduce heat to 350°. Sauté
onions in butter until clear. Combine onions and all other ingredients in
large bowl. Mix well. (Mixture should be moist enough to mold—add
additional sherry if necessary.) Form a mound of seafood stuffing mixture
on trout to conform to shape of filets. Loosely cover baking dish with
aluminum foil. Bake for 1 hour. Garnish if desired with lemon slices, pimento
strips, halved black olives, and paprika.

F. Judson Hill
Virginia Beach, Virginia

Seafood Lasagna

YIELD: 8 to 10 servings

1/2 cup (1 stick) butter
   or margarine
1/2 cup flour
4 cups milk
1 tablespoon salt
1/2 teaspoon black pepper
1/2 pound Cheddar cheese, grated

1 cup fresh crab meat
1 pound scallops, cut in small
   pieces
1 16-ounce package lasagna
   noodles, cooked according to
   package directions
1 24-ounce carton cottage cheese
1/2 pound mozarella cheese
Bread crumbs as needed

Preheat oven to 375°. Make white sauce of butter, flour, milk, salt, and pepper. Blend in grated Cheddar cheese until melted. Blend in crab and scallops. Grease large baking dish and cover bottom with sauce. Add layer of noodles, layer of cottage cheese, and slices of mozarella. Continue layering until ingredients are used up. Sprinkle with bread crumbs. Cover dish with foil and bake for 20 minutes. Uncover and bake an additional 5 to 10 minutes or until bread crumbs are browned. Let stand a few minutes after removing from oven before slicing to serve.

Emilie Cantieri
Portsmouth, Virginia

Seafood Manicotti

YIELD: 6 to 8 servings

12 manicotti shells
1 tablespoon olive oil
Dash garlic powder

SAUCE
4 tablespoons butter or margarine
4 tablespoons flour
1/4 teaspoon salt
1/4 teaspoon monosodium
    glutamate (optional)
Few grains pepper
Milk as needed

2-6 1/2-ounce cans minced clams

FILLING
1 pound ricotta cheese
1 pound backfin crab meat
1/4 pound mozzarella cheese,
    finely diced
2/3 cup grated Parmesan cheese,
    divided
2 eggs, slightly beaten
1/4 cup bread crumbs
Salt, pepper, and fresh minced
    parsley to taste

Cook manicotti shells in six quarts of boiling, salted water with olive oil added and garlic powder for 8 to 10 minutes or "al dente," to taste. Drain. While cooking manicotti make the sauce. Melt butter in sauce pan over low heat. Blend in a mixture of the flour, salt, monosodium glutamate, and pepper. Heat until this mixture bubbles. Reserving juice, drain clams. Set clams aside. To clam juice add enough milk to make 2 cups. Remove from heat and gradually stir in the milk/clam juice mixture. Return to heat and bring rapidly to a boil, stirring constantly; cook a few minutes longer, until thickened. Add minced clams to this mixture, stirring well. There should be about two cups of sauce. Pour some of the sauce on the bottom of a 9-by-13-inch pan.

Preheat oven to 350°. Mix the filling ingredients thoroughly and stuff manicotti shells carefully. Lay manicotti side by side in a single layer. Pour the remaining sauce over manicotti and sprinkle with the remaining 1/3 cup Parmesan cheese. Cover with aluminum foil and bake for thirty minutes.

Note: This recipe may be assembled in advance and frozen, to be cooked when defrosted at a later date.

Mrs .William B. Byrd, Jr.
Hampton, Virginia

Seafood Newburg Casserole

YIELD: 4 servings

1 pound seafood (scallops, shrimp, crab, lobster, or any combination)
1 10-ounce can cream of shrimp soup

3 tablespoons sherry
3 tablespoons light cream
6 tablespoons melted butter
1 cup bread crumbs
1/2 cup grated sharp Cheddar cheese

Preheat oven to 350°. Combine seafood, soup, sherry, and cream and put in a 1-quart casserole or 4 greased ramekins. Mix butter, bread crumbs, and cheese and sprinkle on top of seafood mixture. Bake for 30 minutes.

Betty Ann DiMare
Virginia Beach, Virginia

Seafood-Stuffed Filets of Virginia Flounder

YIELD: 4 to 6 servings

2 tablespoons butter or margarine
1 cup mushrooms, minced
1 large onion, minced
2 tablespoons snipped parsley
1 cup blue crab meat or
   1 cup cooked shrimp
8 flounder filets (about
   3 pounds)

1/2 teaspoon salt
Pepper to taste
Paprika to taste
2-10 1/2-ounce cans condensed
   cream-of-mushroom soup,
   undiluted
1/4 cup water
1/3 cup sherry
1/2 cup greated mild Cheddar
   cheese

EARLY IN DAY: In hot butter, in skillet, sauté mushrooms, onion, and parsley until onion is soft. Add crab meat or shrimp and sauté just to mix the ingredients. Sprinkle both sides of each fish filet with salt, pepper, and paprika. Onto one end of each filet, spoon some of onion mixture; then roll up filet, securing with toothpick. Place filets in an attractive 12-by-8-by-2-inch baking dish. In medium bowl combine soup, water, and sherry; pour over filets; sprinkle with grated cheese; refrigerate.

ABOUT 40 MINUTES BEFORE SERVING: Preheat oven to 400°. Sprinkle filets and sauce with paprika. Bake filets 30 minutes or until easily flaked with fork but STILL MOIST. Serve right from baking dish with toast points or fluffy white rice.

Mrs. Samuel P. Reynolds
Lynchburg, Virginia

Surf 'n Seafood Casserole

YIELD: 4 servings

1 pound croaker or spot filets
Flour as needed
3 to 4 tablespoons olive oil
2 tablespoons brandy
1 medium onion, chopped
1 pimento, diced
2 garlic cloves, crushed

3 tablespoons ground almonds
1 cup canned tomatoes
1 teaspoon salt
1 pound shrimp, cooked
   and cleaned
1 dozen clams
1/2 cup white wine
Chopped parsley

Cut fish in chunks. Dredge in flour and brown in olive oil. Flame with brandy. Remove fish from pan. Sauté onion, pimento, garlic, and almonds in pan used for browning fish. Add more oil if needed. Add tomatoes and salt. Add shrimp, clams, and wine. Simmer until clams are open. Taste for seasonings and correct if necessary. Replace fish pieces and simmer 2 minutes longer. Garnish with chopped parsley.

Ellen Michel
Virginia Beach, Virginia

Susie's Dilly Seafood Supreme

YIELD: 4 servings

1/2 pound flounder
1/2 pound scallops
1 cup crab meat
1/4 cup chopped onion, sautéed
   until clear
1/8 teaspoon paprika

1/4 teaspoon salt
Dash pepper
1 tablespoon lemon juice
2 tablespoons butter
2 tablespoons flour
1 cup half and half cream
2 teaspoons dried dillweed
1/2 cup bread crumbs

Preheat oven to 350°. Cut flounder into 1-inch pieces. Place flounder, scallops, and crab meat in greased baking dish. Sprinkle with sautéed onions, followed with paprika, salt, pepper, and lemon juice. In small sauce pan, melt butter, blend in flour. Add cream, stirring until thick and bubbly. Remove from heat. Add dillweed. Pour sauce over seafood mixture. Sprinkle with bread crumbs and bake for 30 minutes.

Susan L. Morgan
Richmond, Virginia

Virginia Flounder en Papillote

YIELD: 4 servings

5 tablespoons butter, divided
3 tablespoons flour
1 cup half and half cream
3 tablespoons Madeira

1/2 teaspoon salt
1 tablespoon Hungarian paprika
4 flounder filets
1/2 pound cleaned cooked shrimp
1/4 pound backfin crab meat
1/4 cup sliced mushrooms

Preheat oven to 425°. Melt 3 tablespoons butter, add flour, and cook 1 minute. Stirring constantly, add half and half, Madeira, salt, and paprika. Cook until thickened and smooth. Use four 1-foot square pieces of aluminum foil. On each place one flounder filet and 1/4 of shrimp and crab meat. Sauté mushrooms in 2 tablespoons butter. Stir liquid from mushrooms into sauce and place 1/4 mushrooms on top of each fish. Pour sauce equally over fish, crimping along three edges. Place the 4 foil bags on cooking sheet in oven and bake for 25 minutes. Foil should be nicely puffed.

Lewis S. Pendleton, Jr.
Richmond, Virginia

Virginia Seafood Mornay

YIELD: 4 to 6 servings

6 tablespoons butter
4 tablespoons flour
3 cups milk
1/4 teaspoon salt
1/8 teaspoon pepper

2 teaspoons Worcestershire sauce
1/2 pound grated Swiss cheese
2 tablespoons dry sherry
1 pound fresh crab meat, flaked
1 pound shrimp, shelled and
   deveined

Melt butter and add flour mixing well. Add milk, salt, pepper, and Worcestershire sauce, stirring constantly until thick. Gradually add cheese and sherry while stirring. When cheese is melted, mix in crab meat and shrimp. Cook over low heat 5 minutes, stirring. Serve over rice.

Lois A. Gasparro
Charlottesville, Virginia

Virginia Surf-Arolle

YIELD: 8 servings

1/2 cup (1 stick) salted butter
1 cup bay scallops, in 1/2-inch
    cubes
1 cup shrimp, peeled
1 pound backfin crab meat
1 pint half and half cream

4 tablespoons flour
1-1/2 cups grated sharp Cheddar
    cheese
1 teaspoon dry mustard
1 teaspoon grated nutmeg
1 teaspoon Worcestershire sauce
1 cup dry sherry
1/2 teaspoon of salt (optional)

Preheat oven to 325°. In one half stick of butter, sauté the scallops and shrimp until they are no longer transparent. Set aside, along with the gently picked crab meat.

Make a roux of flour and the other half stick of butter, and stir until smooth. Add half and half to make a thick sauce. Add 1 cup cheese, stirring in mustard, nutmeg, and Worchestershire. Remove from heat when smooth.

Mix together seafood and sauce, add dry sherry, and pour into 2-quart casserole. Sprinkle top with rest of cheese, and bake until bubbly and spotted with brown. Serve over rice.

Katie Letcher Lyle
Lexington, Virginia

Fish Schooling

Advice on Buying, Cleaning and Cooking Seafood

How to dress a fish for dinner.

Dressed for stuffing.

1 Scale the fish, moving the scaler from the tail to the head. Be sure to remove the scales close to the fins. Scaling can be done with a fish scaler, a knife, or even a tablespoon.

2 Open the belly cavity by making a straight cut from the anal opening to the jaw. Scrape out the internal organs with your knife.

3 Be sure to remove any blood along the backbone of the fish. Cut out the gills with a knife or a pair of kitchen shears. Wash the fish thoroughly with cold running water. The fish is now ready to stuff.

How to dress a fish
for dinner (continued)

Fileting

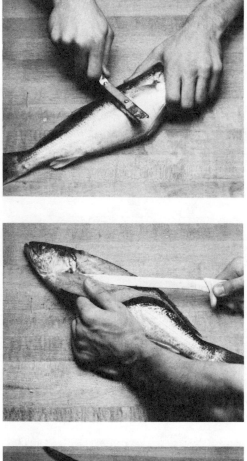

1 Scale the fish (unless you intend to skin the filet). Make a diagonal cut behind the pectoral fin toward the head. Cut down until you feel the backbone. It helps to have a fileting knife or other knife with a sharp, thin, blade.

2 Make a shallow cut from head to tail just above the dorsal fin. Carefully cut the fillet off by running the knife just on top of the backbone. To have a boneless fillet, avoid cutting into the belly cavity or, if you cut into the belly cavity, remove the rib bones by sliding your knife just underneath them and cutting them off diagonally.

3 The filet is now ready to be prepared in the way you like best.

How to dress a fish
for dinner *(continued)*

Steaking.

1 Steaking requires a large fish such as tuna, swordfish, bluefish, mackerel, or in this case a large trout. Cut off the head, remove the internal organs, and wash in cold water to remove any blood and remaining viscera.

2 Make a cut perpendicular to the backbone, about one inch from the head end. If you have trouble with this cut, tap the knife with a hammer.

3 Make perpendicular cuts at one inch intervals down the length of the fish. The "steaks" are now ready to grill, bake, or prepare in your favorite way.

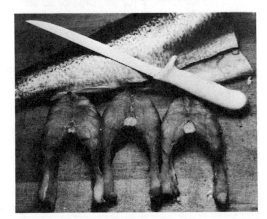

Shad Secrets

- With patience and a steady hand, it is possible to bone a shad. After scaling the shad, remove filets from either side. With the skin side down, feel for the three ridges of bones which run the length of the fish. With a sharp knife, slice through the flesh down to, but not through the skin, parallel to and on either side of each row of bones. Carefully tear each strip of flesh and bones away from the skin. This leaves a boneless filet with three wedges of flesh missing.

- It is possible to "cook away" the bones in a shad by steam-baking it at 300° for five hours. The backbone will be soft enough to eat while most of the small bones will have disappeared.

- Shad roe should be handled and cooked as carefully as possible to avoid disturbing the thin membrane holding the eggs. Also high heat can cause the tiny eggs to pop, resulting in painful burns to the cook and a less than perfect roe.

More Than One Way to Skin a Squid

- When purchasing squid, look for distinct, sharp spots on the mantle, bright, clear eyes and firm flesh. Since as much as 80 percent of the squid is edible, allow about three-fourths of a pound of whole squid per person.

- To clean a squid, cut through the arms near the eyes. With thumb and forefinger, squeeze out the inedible beak which will be located near the cut. Reserve tentacles. Feel inside mantle for chitinous pen. Firmly grasp pen and remove from mantle. Under cold running water, peel off speckled membrane that covers the mantle. Wash mantle thoroughly and drain. The squid is now ready for stuffing or for making rings by cutting across the mantle.

To cut strips and pieces of squid, lay the washed mantle flat and cut down the center from top to tail. Spread open and wash thoroughly. Cut mantle into size strips or pieces desired.

Tentacles can be chopped, minced or left whole.

The best way to catch fish in a store.

1 Check for Color and Sheen. The shiny iridescent luster and distinct coloration of freshly-caught fish fade gradually. Reject fish which appear dull, slimy or "washed-out."

2 Observe Eyes and Gills: Fresh fish have clear, bright, protruding eyes and reddish gills. A fish with clouded or sunken eyes, or slimy grey, greenish or brownish gills is not fresh.

3 Take a Sniff: The fresher the fish, the fresher it will smell. A "fishy" odor is a sign of aging. Choose fish with a mild, oceany scent. Reject any that have a disagreeably strong odor.

The Best Way
To Catch Fish
in a Store. (continued)

4 **Scratch and Press:** The scales of fresh fish will adhere tightly to the skin when scratched. The flesh is firm and springs back when touched. Flakey scales or spongey flesh indicate spoiling.

5 **Fresh in the Shell.** Shellfish must be alive to be fresh. Crabs should be active. Mussels, clams and oysters should feel heavy and be tightly closed, or close immediately when handled.

6 **Freshly Shucked.** Shucked oysters, clams and scallops must be completely covered in their own liquid, iced or refrigerated immediately and eaten soon after purchase. Clouded liquid indicates spoilage.

How to crack into a crab.

1 Remove the two large pincher claws by breaking them off at the body. Set the claws aside for cracking and removing the meat later.

2 Hold the crab in one hand and lift up on one point to remove the top shell.

3 Cut off the "face" of the crab where it joins the lower shell and remove the internal organs by scraping them out with a knife. It is not necessary to wash the crab at this point.

How to crack into a crab *(continued)*

4 Make a straight cut from the back to the front of the crab, just above the leg joints. This cut is important; be sure to make it deep enough. Repeat the procedure for the other side of the crab. Set aside the two pieces removed.

5 Cut off (do not pull off) the remaining legs where they join the body. It is advisable to keep the thumb pressed securely over the backfin meat when making these cuts. Note where the flat, paddle-shaped swim fin or backfin is attached to the body.

6 Locate the large chunk of white muscle on either side of the body of the crab (the "backfin" or "lump" meat) and remove it with the knife. (This muscle is located where the backfin was attached.)

How to crack
into a crab (continued)

7 The rest of the white meat in the body of the crab is located in the chambers separated by thin walls of cartilage. Remove the meat from the chambers by sliding the knife under and lifting it out. This meat is called the "flake" or regular meat.

8 Remove the meat from the two pieces cut off the top of the crab in step 4. There will be one chunk of white muscle (the top of the backfin muscle) that comes off easily, revealing a piece of cartilage. Make a diagonal cut just under this piece of cartilage and remove the rest of the meat from the chambers.

9 Tap the claw just below the pincher to make a straight, clean cut in the shell. Gently break the claw open and remove the meat with your knife. Repeat the procedure for the other claw.

How to Cope with a Soft-Shell Crab

- Purchase soft-shell crabs alive and have them cleaned at the market or buy them already cleaned but frozen. Soft-shell crabs should be used the day of purchase or frozen for later use.
- Prices vary according to how plentiful they are and what size they are. Sizes range from little 3-1/2 to 4-inch crabs known as "mediums," to "hotels," to "primes," to "jumbos" which are big 5 to 5-1/2-inch soft-shells.
- Cleaning a soft-shell crab is a fairly easy task because almost all of the crab is edible. Lift the large lateral spines of the shell top and scrape off the grayish white, feathery gills underneath each side. Remove the eyes and mouth parts by making one cut across the front of the crab just behind the eyes. Remove and drain the fluids from the stomach area by twisting the knife and pulling from the cut made to remove the eyes and mouth parts. At the base of the crab, remove the apron form the underside. Rinse well.

Crab Cues

- When purchasing live crabs, allow at least three crabs per person, more if they are small.
- To boil two dozen hard crabs, use six quarts of water, seasoned with one-third cup of salt or Old Bay seasoning to taste. Place live crabs in the boiling water. Cover and return to the boiling point; reduce heat and simmer for 12 to 15 minutes. Drain and rinse crabs in cold water.
- To steam crabs, place live crabs on a rack in a steamer over about two cups of water or beer. Steam for about 12 to 15 minutes.
- When purchasing crab meat, allow at least one pound for four persons.
- Crab meat is already cooked and comes in two forms: fresh or pasteurized. Fresh crab is generally packed in plastic containers and should be used in about three days or frozen. Pasteurized crab is most often packed in tins with cellophane lids and will keep for about two weeks but does not freeze well.
- Crab meat comes in three grades. Backfin, the most expensive, is in lump form and should be used in dishes which preserve the character of the meat. Special or flake crab meat is most often used in deviled crab or crabcakes. Claw meat, which has a sweeter flavor, is also used in crabcakes or left on the leg with the pincer removed and served as an hors d'oeuvre.

Nine ways to deal with a fresh fish.

1 Baking. Almost any fish, whole, or fileted, can be baked to perfection by allowing 10 minutes per-inch-thickness of fish in a very hot oven (425°-450°). Brush lightly with fat or oil to keep from drying.

2 Stews. From oyster stew or clam chowder, to bouillabaisse (right), fish stews, chowders and soups offer an endless variety of nourishing taste temptations.

3 Poaching. Low heat, plus the flavor of the poaching liquid (milk, bouillon, white wine, or water seasoned with spices and herbs) brings out the best in fish. Poached fish may be served hot, or chilled in salads.

Nine ways to deal with a fresh fish *(continued)*

4 **Kebob and Grilling.** For a "different" barbecue, skewer chunks of fish alternately with fresh vegetables or fruits, then grill about 4" from moderately hot coals, 8 to 10 minutes, basting frequently with lemon and butter, or vinaigrette.

5 **Broiling.** The simplest way to prepare whole fish, steaks, or filets. Just brush with butter or oil and lemon juice, place four inches from heat and turn once, allowing 6-8 minutes per side.

6 **Deep-Frying.** A crisp, tender treat. Dip fish filets in beaten egg, roll in seasoned flour, corn meal, or fine bread crumbs, then immerse in hot oil (375°) until golden. Serve with seafood sauce.

Nine ways to deal with a fresh fish *(continued)*

7 Steaming. This simple method of cooking fish on a rack in steam produced from a boiling liquid preserves natural juices and flavor. Liquids which may be used include plain water, water seasoned with herbs and spices, fish stock, or water flavored with wine.

8 Stir-Frying. The secret to this Oriental art is quick cooking over high heat. Tasty combinations of fish, shellfish, vegetables and spices are endless and equally tempting.

9 Microwave. Almost every variety of seafood is excellent for microwave cooking. Because fish has a high moisture content, it cooks quickly (in about 4 to 5 minutes per pound), and retains its natural flavor. Take care not to overcook. Fish is done when it turns opaque and will flake easily.

When's a Fish Too Fishy to Buy?

- Purchase about a pound of whole fish per person and a half pound or less of filet per person.
- When purchasing whole fish, look for fish with moist, shiny skin, bright, clear eyes, firm, elastic flesh and bright red or pink gills. Although the fish market may have a fishy order, really fresh fish will not.
- If purchasing filets or steaks, the same principles apply: shiny skin, firm elastic flesh and no odor.

More Bounce to the Ounce

- Seafood is full of excellent quality protein. A serving as small as four ounces will supply about half the total amount of protein required each day by an adult.
- Seafood is a good source of vitamins. Depending on the species, thiamine, riboflavin, niacin, vitamin B12, and vitamin C are among the important vitamins found in seafood.
- Seafood is low in calories. One hundred grams of a low-fat fish such as flounder contains about 80 calories while a high-fat fish such as blue fish has just 120 calories.
- What little fat there is in seafood is in a much greater proportion of polyunsaturated to saturated fat.
- Seafood is easily digestible.
- Though most seafood comes from salt water, the salt content is relatively low; therefore seafood can be used in low-sodium diets.

How to bisect
a bivalve.

Oysters

1 Make sure the shell of the oyster
is tightly closed, or closes quickly
when handled. Any that do not should
be discarded, since they are dead and
inedible.

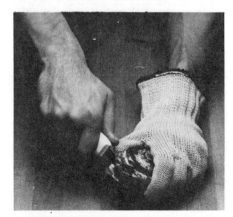

2 After cleaning by scrubbing the
shell with a stiff brush under cold,
running water, the oyster is ready to
be opened. Grip as shown, and force
shucking knife in side opposite the
hinge.

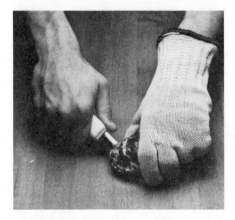

3 With a twist of the knife blade,
slowly force the oyster shell open.

How to bisect
a bivalve (continued)

4 In a quick side-to-side motion, slice through the large adductor muscle attached to the flat upper shell (note thumb position). Remove shell.

5 Cut the lower end of the same muscle, which is attached to the deep half of the shell. Remove any chips of shell that cling to the meat.

6 The most common way to serve is on the half shell with lemon. If not served immediately, place oysters in a container, cover with their own liquid, and refrigerate.

How to bisect
a bivalve *(continued)*

Clams

1 Like oysters, the shell should be tightly closed if the clam is edible. Hold the clam as shown and insert knife between halves of the shell.

2 Cut around the clam, using a twisting motion to loosen the shell and open it.

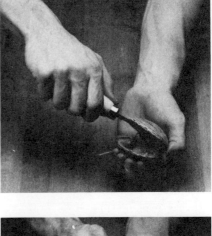

3 Serve on the half shell, taking care not to lose any of the delicious juice. Clams on the half shell must be served very cold.

Pearls of Oyster Wisdom

- Contrary to local lore, oysters are good year around. The myth about oysters being good only in the "r" months harkens back to the days of poor refrigeration.

- Oysters purchased in the shell should be alive. Their shells, when tapped, should close tightly. Unacceptable ones will be wide open and not respond to the touch. They should have a refrigerator life of about 8 days.

- Unwashed oysters are usually available where oysters are shucked on the premises or nearby. They should appear plump and creamy in their clear juices. They are usually packed by hand in cardboard cartons upon request of the consumer or they come from a nearby packer in clear glass jars. They should be eaten within a few days.

- Washed oysters are vacuum-packed in tins with cellophane lids. Though processing oysters this way results in a slight loss of flavor, they are more easily shipped and have a longer storage life.

- Shucked oysters are generally marked as to size. "Select" does not mean better; it means bigger. Selects are best for frying. "Standard" oysters are smaller and good in stews and casseroles and also can be fried. Every so often, the term "count" oyster is used. This refers to huge oysters preferred by those who love to eat raw oysters.

Quahog Qualities

- Clams purchased in the shell must be alive. All shells should be tightly closed or should "clam up" when tapped. Open shells that do not respond to the touch should be thrown out. Live clams should store well for 4 to 5 days in the refrigerator.
- Fresh shucked clams should appear plump and clean in an almost clear liquid with virtually no odor. They should be used within 2 to 3 days or frozen.
- Clam prices vary according to size, the smaller ones costing the most. "Littlenecks," measuring around 2 inches, are best for steaming or eating raw on the half shell. "Cherrystones," from 2-1/2 to 3-1/2 inches in size, are the clams generally used in clambakes. "Chowders," those over 3-1/2 inches, are generally chopped and used in fritters, stuffings and chowders.
- To prepare clams for steaming or shucking, cover them with 1/2 cup of salt to 1 gallon of water. Set aside for 15 to 20 minutes while the salt forces the clams to open up and cleanse themselves of sand. Then rinse several times to make sure the outer shells are free of sand and mud.
- To prepare clams in a way that makes chopping easy, clean them according to directions above and freeze them whole in the freezer. After they are frozen, the shells can be easily opened after holding them under warm running water. The meat and clam juices come out in one frozen piece which can be cleanly chopped.

Timetable for Cooking Fish

METHOD OF COOKING	MARKET FORM	AMOUNT FOR 6	COOKING TEMPERATURE	APPROXIMATE COOKING TIME (minutes)
Baking	Dressed	3 pounds	350°F	45 to 60
	Pan-dressed	3 pounds	350°F	25 to 30
	Filets or steaks	2 pounds	350°F	20 to 25
	Frozen fried fish portions	12 portions (2½ to 3 ounces each)	400°F	15 to 20
	Frozen fried fish sticks	24 sticks (¾ to 1¼ ounces each)	400°F	15 to 20
Broiling	Pan-dressed	3 pounds		10 to 16 (turning once)
	Filets or steaks	2 pounds		10 to 15
	Frozen fried fish portions	12 portions (2½ to 3 ounces each)		10 to 15
	Frozen fish fish sticks	24 sticks (¾ to 1¼ ounces each)		10 to 15
Charcoal Broiling	Pan-dressed	3 pounds	Moderate	10 to 16 (turning once)
	Filets or steaks	2 pounds	Moderate	10 to 16 (turning once)
	Frozen fried fish portions	12 portions (2½ to 3 ounces each)	Moderate	8 to 10 (turning once)
	Frozen fried fish sticks	24 sticks (¾ to 1¼ ounces each)	Moderate	8 to 10 (turning once)
Deep-Fat Frying	Pan-dressed	3 pounds	350°F	3 to 5
	Filets or steaks	2 pounds	350°F	3 to 5
	Frozen raw breaded fish portions	12 portions (2½ to 3 ounces each)	350°F	3 to 5
Oven-Frying	Pan-dressed	3 pounds	500°F	15 to 20
	Filets or steaks	2 pounds	500°F	10 to 15
Pan-Frying	Pan-dressed	3 pounds	Moderate	8 to 10 (turning once)
	Filets or steaks	2 pounds	Moderate	8 to 10 (turning once)
	Frozen raw breaded or frozen fried fish portions	12 portions (2½ to 3 ounces each)	Moderate	8 to 10 (turning once)
	Frozen fried fish sticks	24 sticks (¾ to 1¼ ounces each)		8 to 10 (turning once)
Poaching	Filets or steaks	2 pounds	Simmer	5 to 10
Steaming	Filets or steaks	1½ pounds	Boil	5 to 10

Sea Speak
A Glossary of Terms

Adductor Muscle: the muscle a bivalve uses to open and close its shell.

Backfin Crab Meat: highest quality meat taken from body next to the backfin; sometimes called "lump."

Bisque: a pureed soup made from shellfish and usually flavored with sherry and tomatoes.

Bivalved: having two valves, such as the two shells of a clam.

Bouillabaisse: a fish soup which originated in the Mediterranean and usually includes more than one type of fish and/or shellfish and is often flavored with saffron.

Calamari: Spanish and Italian for squid.

Ceviche: Spanish for dish made of fish and orange juice; in gourmet terms, a dish of raw scallops seasoned with citrus fruit.

Cherrystone Clams: medium-size clams, measuring 2.25 to 4 inches.

Chowder: from French "chaudiere," a fish or clam soup often made with salt pork, potatoes and milk.

Chowder Clams: clams measuring over 3.75 inches, good chopped in chowders.

Claw Crab Meat: meat taken from the large claws and other appendages.

Coquille: French for "shell."

Coquille St. Jacques: French for "scallops."

Devil: method of cooking where a highly-seasoned paste or breadcrumb mixture is applied to fish and shellfish.

Drawn Fish: fish with all entrails removed, a preparation which increases shelf life.

Dressed Fish: fish cleaned with head and tail removed.

Filets: the sides of a fish cut away lengthwise from the bones.

Fritter: batter, flavored in various ways with fish and shellfish and deep fried.

Jimmy: colloquial name for male blue crab.

Littleneck Clams: small clams measuring 1.5 to 2.25 inches, good for eating steamed and raw.

Mantle: In seafood, the external body wall which lines the shell of many invertebrates.

Molting: periodic shedding of outer covering, such as a shell, as part of growth process.

Peeler: blue crab about to shed its shell.

Planking: method of cooking fish on wooden board generally over an open fire.

Poach: method of cooking fish in liquid to cover.

Quahog: name for hard shelled clams which the settlers learned from the Indians.

Regular Crab Meat: the body meat of the crab minus the backfin; sometimes called "flake."

Roe: fish eggs before they are hatched; also name for female fish.

Select: the term used for large oysters.

Sharps: clams measuring 3 to 3.75 inches.

Soft Shell Crab: crab which has just shed its outer shell.

Sole: European flat fish much like American flounder.

Sook: name for female blue crab.

Standard: the term used for small oysters.

Steaks: cross-section cuts of large fish, ready for cooking.

Tailor Blue: small, pan-sized blue fish.

Truite: French for trout.

Index

Date: _____

Please send _____ copies of **The Great Taste of Virginia Seafood** at $10.95 each. I enclose a check in the amount of $ _____ , payable to The Donning Company/Publishers, 5659 Virginia Beach Blvd., Norfolk, VA 23502.

Name: _____

Address: _____

City and State: _____ Zip: _____

Date: _____

Please send _____ copies of **The Great Taste of Virginia Seafood** at $10.95 each. I enclose a check in the amount of $ _____ , payable to The Donning Company/Publishers, 5659 Virginia Beach Blvd., Norfolk, VA 23502.

Name: _____

Address: _____

City and State: _____ Zip: _____

Date: _____

Please send _____ copies of **The Great Taste of Virginia Seafood** at $10.95 each. I enclose a check in the amount of $ _____ , payable to The Donning Company/Publishers, 5659 Virginia Beach Blvd., Norfolk, VA 23502.

Name: _____

Address: _____

City and State: _____ Zip: _____

Date: _____

Please send _____ copies of **The Great Taste of Virginia Seafood** at $10.95 each. I enclose a check in the amount of $ _____ , payable to The Donning Company/Publishers, 5659 Virginia Beach Blvd., Norfolk, VA 23502.

Name: _____

Address: _____

City and State: _____ Zip: _____

- -

Date: _____

Please send _____ copies of **The Great Taste of Virginia Seafood** at $10.95 each. I enclose a check in the amount of $ _____ , payable to The Donning Company/Publishers, 5659 Virginia Beach Blvd., Norfolk, VA 23502.

Name: _____

Address: _____

City and State: _____ Zip: _____

- -

Date: _____

Please send _____ copies of **The Great Taste of Virginia Seafood** at $10.95 each. I enclose a check in the amount of $ _____ , payable to The Donning Company/Publishers, 5659 Virginia Beach Blvd., Norfolk, VA 23502.

Name: _____

Address: _____

City and State: _____ Zip: _____